INTRODUCTION TO MODERN BEHAVIORISM

THIRD EDITION

HOWARD RACHLIN

*State University of New York
at Stony Brook*

W. H. Freeman and Company
New York

Library of Congress Cataloging in Publication Data

Rachlin, Howard, 1935–
    Introduction to modern behaviorism / Howard Rachlin. —
3rd ed.
        p. cm.
    Includes bibliographical references.
    Includes index.
    ISBN 0-7167-2101-5 (hard) — ISBN 0-7167-2176-7 (pbk.)
    1. Conditioned response.   2. Behaviorism (Psychology)
I. Title.   II. Title: Modern behaviorism.
        [DNLM: 1. Behavior. 2. Conditioning (Psychology) BF 319
        R119i]
BF319.R33   1991
150.19′43 — dc20
DNLM/DLC
for Library of Congress   90-13951
                                                                  CIP

Printed in the United States of America

        1 2 3 4 5 6 7 8 9 0   VB   9 9 8 7 6 5 4 3 2 1

Contents

Preface

Introduction to Modern Behaviorism, Third Edition, is designed to serve as an introductory text in courses on learning and conditioning or as a supplement to standard textbooks in introductory psychology and cognitive psychology. Standard texts are notoriously weak in their discussions of the topics covered in this volume. Indeed, because of these deficiencies and the importance of the historical and philosophical background of behaviorism to the study of animal behavior and learning, this book may prove useful in more advanced courses as well. This edition may also be used together with my recent text, *Judgment, Decision, and Choice* (Freeman, 1988), in courses on the relationship of conditioning to more complex mental processes or in courses emphasizing philosophical and conceptual issues in modern psychology, especially the relationship of psychological research to contemporary views of the mind.

The central purpose of *Introduction to Modern Behaviorism* is to give students an accessible yet thorough grounding in the basic principles of learning and conditioning. In this Third Edition I have also attempted to illuminate the relationships between the findings of cognitive psychology and those of behavioral psychology.

Cognitive psychology and behavioral psychology represent two of the most important contemporary perspectives on understanding the human mind. Cognitive psychology asks *how* people behave as they do; behavioral psychology asks *why* people behave as they do. These two approaches are complementary rather than competitive. The sharpest picture of the workings of humans and other animals is achieved when we use *both* of these perspectives; the better we know how behavior occurs, the more we need to know why it occurs and vice-versa. This edition therefore retains the extensive historical and philosophical introduction found in earlier editions and, while still focusing on basic behavioral methods and theories, attempts to achieve a better balance between the two approaches with greatly expanded sections on language, consciousness, animal cognition, and self-control.

So far we humans have been much less successful understanding ourselves than we have been at understanding the world around us — witness the epidemics of drug and alcohol use, smoking, gambling, overeating, and overspending among us. That is why the discussion in this book builds up to the new, last chapter on self-control; there cognitive and behavioral approaches together illuminate a topic of vital interest to all of us. We begin with techniques for understanding the behavior of others, but we end with techniques for understanding ourselves — for predicting and controlling our own behavior.

If there are any ideas in this book that are new and worthwhile, they arose from conversations with Richard Herrnstein and with graduate students in the laboratories at Harvard University and at Stony Brook. I would also like to thank the following people who read and criticized parts of the manuscript in its various editions: William Baum, Jasper Brener, Robert Boakes, David Cross, Marvin Frankel, John Gibbon, Charles Gross, Peter Killeen, Roger Mellgren, John Schneider, Richard Solomon, and J. W. Whitlow, Jr.

Howard Rachlin
September 1990

INTRODUCTION TO MODERN BEHAVIORISM

1

Background

Animals try to influence the behavior of other animals by a variety of means and for a variety of purposes. Indeed, much of the interaction among humans and other living creatures consists of efforts to influence behavior. Consider a cow nudging its newborn calf or a victorious alley cat driving an intruder from its territory.*

Of course, not all interactions are so one-sided. Animals often simultaneously modify each other's behavior. Even when one animal is clearly dominant over another, as in the relation between ant and aphid or doctor and patient, there may still be an element of mutual influence. If we examine the teacher–student relationship, which, in formal terms at least, seems rather one-sided, we may find that a given student is trying to get a good grade as actively as his teacher is trying to impart information and stimulate thinking. Thus what the teacher sees as learning on the part of the student may be, from the student's

---

*At the cost of some awkwardness, this edition uses the more specific term *animal* rather than the more general *organism*, the term used in previous editions. Organisms include plants as well as animals, and the book is not generally about plant behavior! Readers of this edition may need to periodically remind themselves that the term *animal* includes the human species.

point of view, simply a means of influencing the teacher and obtaining a good grade.

Given a situation in which one animal is trying to influence the behavior of another animal, the purpose of the effort may not be readily apparent. A parent may spank a child to keep her from playing in the street. This punishment is intended "for the child's own good." On the other hand, if a parent spanks a child for not making his bed or cleaning his room, it may be the parent who hopes to benefit from the change in the child's behavior. Thus the motives behind the modification of behavior and the benefit to be derived from the modified behavior may critically determine the nature of a given interaction.

Another kind of relationship, a strange one to think about, exists between a person at the present time and that same person at a future time. Often we do try to control our own behavior at a later time, much as we try to control the behavior of other people, and, as is the case with other people, we often do not succeed with ourselves. As the mystery writer Rex Stout says, "The trouble with an alarm clock is that what seems sensible when you set it seems absurd when it goes off" (*The Rodeo Murders*). We will discuss this relationship regarding self-control in the last chapter.

One type of relationship between animals that will be discussed throughout this book is that of experimenter and subject. On the surface this relationship appears one-sided, with the experimenter observing, manipulating, and modifying the behavior of the subject. But in a deeper sense a truly reciprocal interaction occurs, for the subject helps determine the experimenter's behavior and causes him or her to modify old theories, to formulate new theories, and to design new experiments.

A look at the titles of articles by experimental psychologists yields clues to the objectives of their experiments. Here, for example, is a hypothetical set of titles corresponding to the experimental observations shown in Figure 1.1:

a. variables influencing the rate of motor learning,
b. the sense of time,
c. a study of appetite, and
d. anxiety as a determiner of performance.

Although authors almost always qualify such broad titles in subtitles or introductions, the titles do reveal the questions that the experimental reports are meant to elucidate.

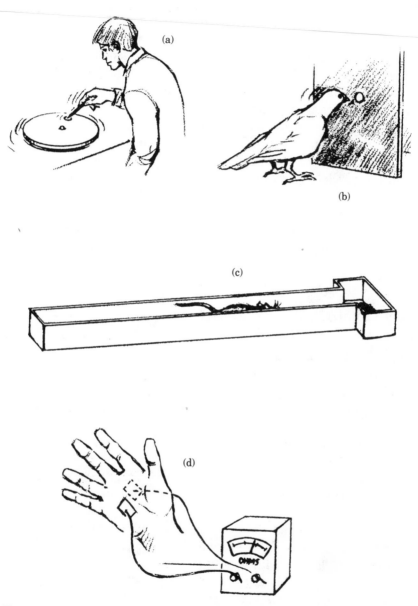

FIGURE 1.1 Four forms of behavior observed in the laboratory: (a) a man following a moving spot with a stylus; (b) a pigeon pecking at an illuminated disk on a wall; (c) a rat running down a straight alley with food at the end; (d) a change in electrical resistance due to sweat secreted on the palm of the hand.

Psychologists seem to expect to understand and explain all kinds of behavior. But looking at Figure 1.1, we see that they study narrowly defined bits of behavior in their laboratories. How, then, do they justify these grand expectations?

This chapter will be devoted to the theoretical and historical influences that have guided research in learning. Because the history of psychology is lengthy and complex, we shall concentrate primarily on one central problem: What kinds of events should a psychologist study? Through an understanding of some of the intellectual roots of modern psychology, we may come to understand behaviorists' purposes when they observe a human following a moving spot with a stylus, when they observe a pigeon pecking at an illuminated disk on the wall, when they observe a rat running down a straight alley to reach some food, or when they observe a person's sweating palm.

CARTESIAN DUALISM

In the Middle Ages, the theology of Western Christendom viewed reason as a handmaiden to faith. Faith had resolved the essential nature of humankind; reason's job was to support faith. Clearly, the intellectual climate was not hospitable to the scientific study of human behavior.

At the dawning of the modern age, science began to question many traditional beliefs. For example, in 1616 Galileo Galilei (1564–1642) earned harsh censure from established authority for denying the theological truth that the earth was fixed at the center of the universe. René Descartes (1596–1650) was about twenty years old when the Church first censured Galileo. When Descartes later undertook to study the nature of man, he found a way to compromise with tradition rather than clashing with it head-on.

Descartes was already a great mathematician and philosopher when he published his first essays concerning human and animal behavior. In these essays, he felt obliged to reconcile his findings with the fundamental precepts of theology. Descartes thus took the position—a position subsequently adopted by most philosophers*—

---

*The term *scientist* was not coined until 1840.

that there are two broad classes of human behavior: voluntary and involuntary. Descartes said that voluntary behavior is governed by the mind (a nonphysical entity) and that involuntary behavior has nothing to do with the mind but is instead purely mechanical. According to theology, nonhumans had no souls; all of their actions were involuntary. Descartes therefore considered them to be essentially like clockwork mechanisms. For this reason, their behavior could be studied directly.

Descartes may have gotten the idea that many human behaviors could also be mechanical from watching the movements of the mechanical statues constructed by ingenious seventeenth-century architects and hydraulic engineers. Many of these grotesque mechanical figures were activated by internal forces like the chimes of clocks, but some had a unique feature — they were triggered unknowingly by the observer of the mechanism. For instance, as the observer walked down a path, he stepped on a hidden treadle that activated a hydraulic mechanism that, in turn, caused a grinning Saracen automaton to emerge from the bushes brandishing a sword. (Similar mechanisms are still to be found at amusement parks like Disneyland.) To Descartes, this feature of the mechanisms, their response to a signal from the environment, was critically important. He reasoned that if human behavior could be simulated so well by these mechanical figures, then perhaps some of the principles on which the mechanisms operated also applied to the humans they were designed to imitate.

Figure 1.2 is a diagram by which Descartes showed the operation of an involuntary, purely mechanical act. The overall effect is that the fire (A) touching the foot (B) of the boy causes him to withdraw his foot. The mechanism acts through the nerve. The lower end of the nerve is set in motion by the fire, and this motion is transmitted upwards to the brain (parts d and e in the figure) "just as, by pulling one of the ends of a cord, you cause a bell attached to the other end to ring at the same time." At the brain, a substance (which Descartes called "animal spirits") is released from the cavity (F). The animal spirits travel back down the nerve, swell the muscle in the calf, and cause the foot to be pulled back. At the same time, animals spirits go to the eyes, head, and hand to direct them toward the fire. Although this primitive explanation is crude by today's standards, it was a great departure from earlier conceptions of the workings of the body in that it tried to explain the boy's action in physical terms — without recourse to his will, his mind, or his emotions.

FIGURE 1.2 This illustration from Descartes's *De Homine* was designed to show the response of an organism to a stimulus. [From F. Fearing, 1930.]

The dualism of Descartes's psychology is the feature that is essential to our understanding of the history of psychology. As we have noted, both mind and body were considered necessary to explain the totality of human behavior. Figure 1.3 illustrates human behavior as conceived by Descartes. In his view, objects in the physical world affect the sense organs, which send messages through the nerves to the brain. At the brain, two things happen. First, in a purely mechanical way, the brain causes action by sending animal spirits through the nerves to the muscles. (This mechanical chain of effects from the sense organs to the brain and back to the muscles by means of the nerves eventually became known as a "reflex arc.") At the same time, the body interacts with the mind at the pineal gland, near the center of the brain. This interaction, allows the mind to be aware of both kinds of the body's actions — reflex, involuntary actions, over which the mind has no control, and voluntary actions, over which the mind exercises complete control. All actions involve the same nerves and muscles, but voluntary actions originate in the mind, a nonphysical

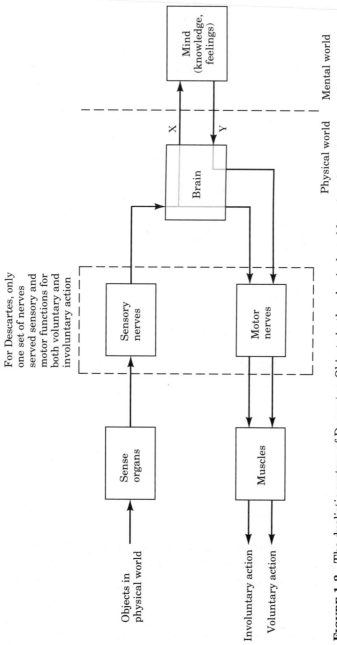

FIGURE 1.3 The dualistic system of Descartes. Objects in the physical world, acting through sense organs and nerves, send signals to the brain. Involuntary actions are caused by the direct transmission of signals through the brain to the motor nerves and muscles. The mind can sense input through arrow X. Voluntary actions are caused by the mind, which sends out signals at Y.

realm, and involuntary actions originate in objects in the physical world. Only humans possess the extra pathway that leads to voluntary action (Figure 1.3). According to Descartes, since much behavior (including all animal behavior) is as mindless as the behavior of a stone, it can be considered subject to the same physical laws that govern a stone's behavior. On the other hand, the actions of the mind are not subject to physical laws but are determined by other laws, unknown and perhaps unknowable.

The effect of Descartes's dualism was to divide the study of behavior: Involuntary behavior came to be studied by physiologists specializing in the study of the body, while voluntary behavior remained in the realm of philosophers. At first, these two branches of study had virtually nothing in common. They are of interest here because they gave rise to two distinct methods of collecting psychological data. We shall discuss first the mental branch of study and then the physical branch of study that grew out of Descartes's dualism.

THE MIND

Originally, psychology was that branch of knowledge that dealt with the human soul or mind. (Although *soul* and *mind* are not synonyms, the concepts are inextricably linked and the terms are often used interchangeably.) According to the dualism of Descartes, the mental world (which was identified with the soul) was the true realm of psychology, and the physical world — including the human body — was outside that realm.*

Introspection

In the age of Descartes, the concept of mind provided the very basis of philosophical speculation concerning human nature. How could the mind be studied? As we have noted, the study of mind through behav-

---

*Many modern psychologists turn these priorities around: For them, the object of psychology is to study behavior. They look for the explanation of all human and animal behavior wherever their quest takes them. Their ultimate objective is to explain behavior. If the concept of mind is useful in that respect, it must be part of the explanation. If it proves not to be useful, these psychologists are free to ignore it.

ior was held to be impossible because (1) involuntary behavior was not determined by the mind and (2) voluntary behavior, which was governed by the mind, was considered to be unpredictable, determined by human free will. Since philosophers could only observe the behavior of others (speech being included as a form of behavior), the minds of others were closed to them.

The most that one can do, these philosophers contended, is to study one's own mind by looking inward. Such a study was thought to be reliable because the information carried from the body to the mind (arrow X in Figure 1.3) was considered to be orderly and to affect the mind in orderly ways. To this day introspection remains a common technique for studying mental activity.

Innate Ideas

If we accept for the time being the notion that the mind can be examined by introspection and that the object of the examination is to determine the nature and origin of its contents, we can focus on one of the key questions that troubled Descartes and the philosophers who came after him: To what extent does the information entering the mind from the senses (arrow X in Figure 1.3) determine the contents of the mind? In other words, what is the effect of experience on ideas and emotions?

All philosophers agree that experience plays an important part in forming ideas. As we learn more about the world around us, our ideas change radically. A baby, for instance, sees a coin as a toy or as something to put in its mouth; an adult sees the coin quite differently. The question under debate was not whether experience modifies our ideas, but *to what extent* it does so. Descartes himself, while believing that experience played a role in forming some of our concepts of the world, held that our most basic ideas are innate. That is, they are common to all human beings simply because they are qualities of the soul, which all human beings possess. The idea of God, the idea of the self, the geometrical axioms (for example, that a straight line is the shortest distance between two points), the ideas of space, time, and motion are thus all said to be innate; experience is thus believed to fill in the details. (For example, experience can tell you what sort of objects move fast and what sort of objects move slowly or stay still, but the basic idea of motion in the world is present before experience.)

Those who hold that there are innate ideas or that innate ideas are more basic and important than what is learned from experience are called *nativists*. Those who deny the existence of innate ideas or hold that the idea of innate ideas is relatively unimportant are called *empiricists*. The controversy between nativists and empiricists is a theme that runs through philosophy and psychology to the present day. However, contemporary psychologists (who deemphasize mind as an explanatory concept) argue not about innate ideas but about innate *patterns of behavior*. Note that the nativism/empiricism dispute can apply to both halves of Descartes's bifurcated model of man. Although we have been discussing innate ideas, that is, inborn mental qualities, there are also innate physical qualities. Just as one can argue about the extent to which the idea of space is modified by experience, one can also argue about the extent to which the structure of the nervous system is modified by the environment. By and large, the beliefs of most contemporary psychologists fall somewhere between extreme nativism and extreme empiricism. Descartes, who is usually considered a nativist, played a role in the development of empiricism. For example, although he held that the idea of space was innate, he showed how experience might give rise to the ideas of size and distance.

The more extreme view, that all or almost all ideas are due to experience, was not formulated until after Descartes's death. The development of this more extreme form of empiricism took place in England, and its adherents came to be known as the "British associationists." This school of philosophy was a direct predecessor of experimental psychology, and we shall turn to it next (after a cautionary note).

WARNING

Because this chapter is about the historical background of behaviorism, we shall discuss a number of doctrines. So far we have mentioned mentalism, nativism, empiricism, and British associationism. Once we grasp the principles that underlie such doctrines, we are tempted to use "isms" as handy categories for grouping various philosophers and psychologists. This tendency should be resisted. Nativism and empiricism, for instance, should not be regarded as two discrete boxes. These two terms are better regarded as marking ends of a continuum that has an infinite number of gradations. Although, in our frame of reference, we see that philosophers X and Y are both relatively nativistic, X may have seen Y as an empiricist and may have spent most of his life arguing against Y's empiricism. The relativity of such perspectives is especially important when we discuss the British associationists. From our point of view two centuries later, it seems that they had so much in common that their thinking can be labeled with one "ism." We therefore ignore many of their differences. Nevertheless, we must be aware that there *were* differences that were sometimes important. Thus when we classify a given philosopher as a British associationist, we are not saying all there is to say about the characteristics of his or her individual philosophy.

Principles of Association

The British empiricists accepted Descartes's dualistic theory of human nature (Figure 1.3). They also accepted Descartes's belief that the seat of knowledge is in the mind; they generally agreed with him that the proper subject for psychological study is the mind of man; they accepted his idea that the mind could be known by "reflection upon itself" — in other words, by introspection. However, they did not accept Descartes's notion that man is born with a set of ideas. Their basic axiom was that all knowledge must come from the senses. Man may be born with the capacity to acquire knowledge, but everything we know, they held, comes from experience. If we lived different lives, if our experiences were different, if we had been transported to a foreign land in infancy, then our knowledge would be different, and we would essentially be different people. This assumption is clearly stated by John Locke, one of the early associationists, in 1690 in *An Essay Concerning Human Understanding*:

> Let us then suppose the Mind to be as we say, white Paper, void of all Characters, without any *Ideas*; How comes it to be furnished? Whence comes it by that vast store, which the busie and boundless Fancy of Man has painted on it, with an almost endless variety? Whence has it all the materials of Reason and Knowledge? To this I answer, in one word, From *Experience*: In that, all our Knowledge is founded; and from that it ultimately derives it self. Our observation employ'd either about *external, sensible Objects; or about the internal Operations of our Minds, perceived and reflected on by our selves, is that, which supplies our Understandings with all the materials of thinking.* These two are the Fountains of Knowledge, from whence all the *Ideas* we have, or can naturally have, do spring.

The empiricists held that all knowledge comes from the senses. But the senses by themselves (unaided by innate ideas) could provide only sensations: Eyes alone could detect a spot of color but could hardly provide the knowledge that the spot of color is a round, red ball.

The empiricists faced a dilemma. If we have no innate idea of a book, how do we know that a patch of light that is before us is an object that can be opened and read? That when we open it we can expect to find print on the pages? That the pages will be numbered consecutively? How do we know, in fact, that this object will not disappear after we have touched it? That it is capable of being lifted without falling apart? Or, for that matter, that it won't bite us or explode and destroy us? In other words, how is the mere sight of the object associated with sensations we do not feel but can *expect* to feel once we have lifted the object, opened it, and started to read it?

What the empiricists needed to find was some sort of "mental glue" to hold together all of the sensations capable of being experienced from a given object. "Association" — hardly a new idea — served this purpose. Aristotle (384 — 322 B.C.) formulated one of the first sets of associationist principles. He said that we remember things together (1) when they are similar, (2) when they contrast, and (3) when they are contiguous. This last principle, that of contiguity, is by far the most important, since all subsequent formulations of the principles of association contain it. It is perhaps worth stating formally:

> If two (or more) sensations are felt at the same time often enough, then one alone felt later can invoke the memory of the other (or others).

To summarize, then, the empiricists took as their basic axiom "All knowledge comes from the senses." Realizing that isolated sensations cannot convey the meanings or the connotations of objects, these philosophers adopted a further principle to explain how sensations are connected. This principle was the principle of association by contiguity: If sensations occur together often enough, one alone can cause the memory of the rest.

The task of the empiricists then became to explain how the principle of contiguity acts in particular instances to produce complex experiences from simple sensations.

Visual Distance

One kind of complex experience that concerned the associationists was the experience of distance. The world appears to us in three dimensions, yet the retina of the eye is a thin, fairly flat surface. How does the three-dimensionality of experience come from impressions on the retina? According to the associationist George Berkeley (1685–1753), one possibility was that our idea of visual distance comes from the sensation of moving the pupils of the eyes together.

Here is Berkeley's argument. For closer objects we have to move our eyes closer together to focus on the objects; for farther objects we must move our eyes apart. The sensations in the muscles of the eyes correspond to the distance of the objects. Other nonvisual sensations corresponding to distance are those involved in reaching for or walking to the object. These nonvisual sensations become attached to the sensations in the muscles of the eyes by contiguity. In other words, whenever we have to reach only a short distance to touch an object, our pupils have to move closer together to focus on the object. Whenever we have to reach far to touch an object, our pupils must move farther apart. Thus, the movement of our pupils and the movement of our hands become associated, and when we look at an object without touching it and only our pupils move, we remember the other sensation—that of our hands moving. This memory of our hands' greater or lesser movement is, according to Berkeley, what we mean when we say an object is far away or near.*

Meaning

Another problem faced by the associationists was that of meaning. How do we learn, for instance, the meaning of the word *chair*? The solution to this problem by the associationist James Mill (1773–1836) was essentially an extension of Berkeley's solution to the problem of perceived distance.

---

*Berkeley seems to have favored different explanations at different times. This account of his argument is based on proposition 45 in "An essay towards a new theory of vision," Dublin, 1709. Reprinted in Berkeley, *Works on Vision* (Indianapolis: Bobbs-Merrill, 1963, p. 39).

Here, in brief, is James Mill's reasoning. In our lifetime, we experience chairs by seeing them, touching them, sitting on them, and so forth. All these activities in relation to chairs produce their own sensations and contain many sensations in common. The "sittable-ness" of a chair is an association of the visual experience of chairs with the kinesthetic sensation of sitting. Also, the simultaneous seeing and hearing of the word *chair* produces sensations that become associated with each other and with the sensations resulting from the sight and feel of chairs. These all mix together in a huge bundle so that when we hear the word *chair*, the memories or ideas of all the other sensations come to our minds. These memories and ideas were conceived by Mill to be less vivid than the actual sensations but otherwise identical. The meaning of a word would thus be nothing but the bundle or total sum of associated ideas called to mind when the word is spoken or read. Figures 1.4 and 1.5 illustrates the process by which meaning is established.

Mental Chemistry

A more sophisticated concept of meaning was advanced by James Mill's son, John Stuart Mill (1806 – 1873), whose thinking was clearly influenced by the advancing science of chemistry. The younger Mill suggested that simple ideas might interact in a way analogous to a chemical process rather than by simply mixing together like salt and pepper. John Stuart Mill argued that just as the properties of water differ from those of its elements, hydrogen and oxygen, the properties of the meaning or connotation of a word could differ from the proper-ties of the sensations that went into forming it. He wrote:

> When many impressions or ideas are operating in the mind together, there sometimes takes place a process, of a similar kind to chemical combination. When impressions have been so often experienced in conjunction, that each of them calls up readily and instantaneously the ideas of the whole group, those ideas sometimes melt and coalesce into one another, and appear not several ideas but one. [Mill, 1843]

The idea that the operations of the mind could be studied in an experiment was a direct outgrowth of such speculations by British associationists. The groundwork for experimental psychology was laid when the apparent chaos of our thoughts, the infinitude of images and

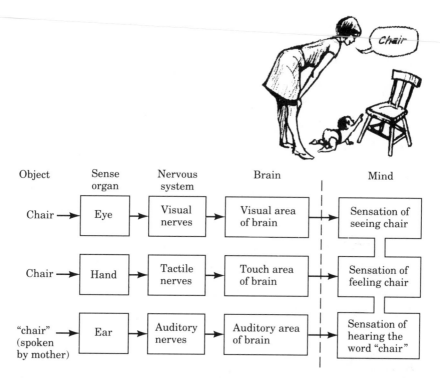

Object	Sense organ	Nervous system	Brain	Mind
Chair →	Eye	Visual nerves	Visual area of brain	Sensation of seeing chair
Chair →	Hand	Tactile nerves	Touch area of brain	Sensation of feeling chair
"chair" (spoken by mother) →	Ear	Auditory nerves	Auditory area of brain	Sensation of hearing the word "chair"

FIGURE 1.4 A common view of how meaning becomes established through association. The sketch shows a child touching a chair and hearing its mother say the word *chair*. The diagram shows the inputs to the various sensory systems of the child. The three sensations occur together, and the child associates them with one another.

ideas that seem to float so haphazardly through our minds, was seen to be a function of a restricted set of elements ("sensations") and of principles of association. The early experiments in mental experimental psychology took two forms: studies of sensations themselves and studies of their combination.

Studies of Sensation

The idea that a sensation as it occurs in the mind is not identical to a sensory process in the body had been present since ancient times, but the idea that sensation as a mental phenomenon could be studied and

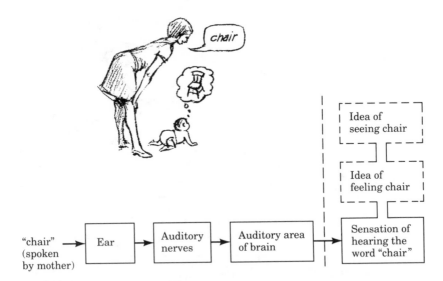

FIGURE 1.5 This sketch shows the child hearing the word *chair* later when no chair is present. This diagram shows that the word *chair* is now associated with past visual and tactile sensations depicted in Figure 1.4.

measured seems to have developed in German universities in the nineteenth century. It is to that time and place that most experimental psychologists today trace the origins of their science.

The first psychological experiments sought to explain how sensory impulses pass from the physical world to the mental world (arrow X in Figure 1.3). Two lines of investigation started separately and eventually fused. One line studied the intensity of sensations, and the other studied the quality of sensations. Let us discuss each of them in turn.

Intensity of Sensations

To some early investigators, the mental world, in contrast to the physical world, seemed discontinuous. Consider the following hypothetical experiment. Imagine a light controlled by a dial capable of producing a continuous range of intensity from complete darkness to blinding brightness (Figure 1.6). An experimenter turns the dial very slowly until a subject reports some light. The amount that the inten-

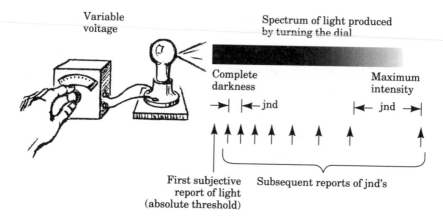

FIGURE 1.6 A light used to measure just-noticeable-differences (jnd's) of brightness. The arrows across the bottom of the brightness spectrum indicate points at which a subject reports a difference in brightness as the brightness is gradually increased. Note that the jnd's at the dark end of the spectrum are spaced more closely (that is, are smaller) than those at the bright end.

sity must increase from zero before light is reported is called the *absolute threshold* (or *absolute limen*). Then the dial is turned further until the subject reports that the light is noticeably brighter than it was before. Then the dial is turned further still until the subject again reports an increase in brightness. Each interval of brightness between reports is called a *just-noticeable-difference* (jnd). As the intensity of the light increases, the intensity of the sensation (brightness) seems to go up in discrete jumps, each jump corresponding to a jnd. Ernst Heinrich Weber (1795–1878) noticed that for many different stimuli there was an orderly relation of jnd's to the magnitude of the stimulus: The bigger the stimulus, the bigger the increase required to notice that the stimulus had increased.

This relationship is quite obvious in everyday life. If a goldfish grows two inches longer overnight, its owner is likely to notice it the next morning; however, if an elephant grows two inches longer, no one is likely to notice it—even if it takes place in front of his or her eyes. Weber's significant contribution was quantifying this observation. He stated that the increase in the stimulus for one jnd was exactly proportional to the intensity (or size) of the stimulus. The importance of this correlation was seen by Gustav Theodor Fechner (1801–1887).

He reasoned that since each jnd is the smallest increment possible to discern for the subject who is watching for a change, any jnd is equivalent to any other for that subject (in other words, Fechner reasoned that all jnd's are subjectively equal). But, whereas the jnd's may be *subjectively* equal, they are not *physically* equal. If the jnd's vary in the physical dimension, as Weber's theory states, and if all jnd's are subjectively equal, then the relation of subjective to physical size can be plotted (as in Figure 1.7).

According to Fechner, in this relationship "one has a general dependent relation between the size of the fundamental stimulus and the size of the corresponding sensation. . . . This permits the amount of sensation to be calculated from the relative amounts of the fundamental stimulus and thus we have a measurement of sensation" (Fechner, 1860). Fechner believed that the relation between stimulus and sensation bridged the gap between the mental (psychic) and physical worlds (arrow X in Figure 1.3). Accordingly, he chose the name *psychophysics* for this new science of the measurement of sensations, a name that persists today for the study of sensory magnitude.

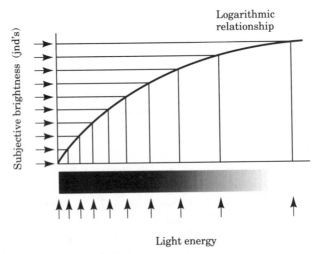

FIGURE 1.7 The relationship between the brightness of jnd's and the magnitude of the stimulus (measured by the voltage regulator). All jnd's are considered to be subjectively equal.

Quality of Sensations

The theory of the associationists was that complex mental phenomena could be constructed from a limited group of elements. What, then, are the elements? How can they be distinguished from complex mental phenomena?

Johannes Müller (1801–1858), another German scientist, made the argument that the thing that distinguishes one sensation from another is not the stimulus itself but the particular nerve stimulated. In other words, a sound seems different to us from a light not because sound energy is essentially different from light energy, but because sound and light activate different nerves.

Here are Müller's views. The mind decides whether a given stimulus is a light or a sound; if a light, what color; if a sound, what pitch. But the mind has no contact with the light or sound itself. The mind can only be sensitive to the nervous impulses leading from the receptors to the brain. The nerves alone tell the mind what sort of stimulation is impinging on the body. For instance, any one of a certain group of nerves can signal that a sound has occurred (the particular activated nerve corresponds to the pitch of the sound). The ear is constructed so that it allows sounds of only that particular pitch to stimulate that particular nerve. But, Müller argued, under certain circumstances the mind can be fooled. If the energy that usually goes to our ears and causes us to hear a sound can be made instead to stimulate the nerve that goes from our eyes to our brain, we would experience the sound as a light. In fact, any form of energy that succeeds in striking the nerve that corresponds to a given sensation would be capable of causing that sensation. He pointed out that electricity as well as sound energy could cause us to hear sounds if the electricity was applied to the nerves of the ears. Müller's contention that the nerve rather than the stimulus determines the quality of sensation became the doctrine of *specific nerve energies*. This principle led to more questions: How many specific nerve energies are there? In vision, for instance, is there one for each color? In hearing, is there one for each tone?

A great deal of subsequent experimentation was directed toward answering such questions. In vision, for instance, all the colors could be constructed by various combinations of three elementary colors, the primaries: red, green, and blue. These, then, could be the elementary sensations that reach the mind, and the vast array of colors that we see could be products of mental chemistry. Similar research was carried out for the other senses. Usually the method used was introspection and verbal report. Early experimental psychologists believed that people could be trained to analyze complex experience into its elements. For instance, an untrained observer experiences wetness as a unitary sensation, but observers experienced in introspection could analyze the experience of wetness into pressure and cold. As a check on this analysis, it was shown that a dry, cold, uniform pressure on the finger cannot be distinguished by a blindfolded observer from actual wetness.

Experiments in the analysis of sensations are still being carried on today, albeit in a more sophisticated way than those described here.

Secondary Laws of Association

Once it is accepted that simultaneously experienced sensations become associated in the mind, there is nothing more that the simple, unvarnished law of association has to say about them. How many times must sensations be experienced together before becoming associated? Which of several simultaneous sensations are more likely to become associated, or will they all become equally associated? Do sensations, once they become associated, remain so forever, or do they eventually separate again? These questions were not of great importance to the British associationists. However, the early experimental psychologists deemed them to be important because only by answering such questions would they be able to discover how the mind constructs the world out of elementary sensations.

It was the Scottish philosopher Thomas Brown (1778–1820) who first tried to answer these questions by formulating nine laws he called secondary laws of association (the three primary laws being those of Aristotle: similarity, contrast, and contiguity). The secondary laws were held to modify the primary laws and to enable one to predict which sensations out of a group of sensations were more likely to become associated. Because of their importance for psychology, it is worth listing Brown's secondary laws. They stated that association between sensations is modified by the following:

1. the duration of the original sensations,
2. the intensity of the original sensations,
3. the frequency of their pairing,
4. the recency of their pairing,
5. the number of other associations in which the sensations to be paired are involved,

6. the abilities, capacities, and dispositions of the person experiencing the sensations,

7. the emotional state of the person experiencing the sensations,

8. the bodily state of the person experiencing the sensations, and

9. the similarity of the association itself to other, previously acquired associations.

The nine secondary laws of association set forth by Brown, as he himself recognized, contained no new facts but were merely a new way to organize facts that separately were well known. However, new facts about association did come from Hermann Ebbinghaus (1850–1909), who was the first person to perform formal experiments in learning. His object was to study the quantitative relations implied by the nine secondary laws of association, particularly the third and fourth, which state that the mental association of two elements is modified by the frequency and recency of their pairing.

Ebbinghaus prepared lists of nonsense syllables to be memorized. These syllables were three-letter combinations like BIV, RUX, JIC, and KEL, with the first letter a consonant, the second a vowel, and the third another consonant. It is worth knowing the claims Ebbinghaus made for nonsense syllables, because similar claims have frequently been made by psychologists about the kinds of material they use in their experiments and about the kinds of behavior they choose to study. In fact, the apparently trivial observations depicted in Figure 1.1 are used in psychological experiments today for some of the same reasons that nonsense syllables were used in Ebbinghaus's classic studies. (Indeed, nonsense syllables are still used in many studies of learning.) The advantages claimed for such materials are the following:

1. *They are relatively simple.* It is important to understand the reason behind the search for simplicity in psychology. Many of the experiments that psychologists do otherwise seem incomprehensible. Essentially, psychologists hope that the underlying laws of behavior will prove to be simple and that the complexity we observe in everyday life will prove to be the result of the concatenation of simple, basic processes. The reason for this hope is that in other sciences a similar hope has frequently been fulfilled. For example, it is virtually im-

possible for a physicist to predict the everyday behavior of physical objects except in a most general way. When a piece of paper is dropped in a room, it is impossible to predict the path it will take as it flutters to the floor. However, it is relatively easy to predict the path the paper would follow if it were dropped in a vacuum, a simplified environment where several second-order phenomena—like friction and air resistance—are not present. The vacuum is artificial and so is the nonsense syllable. The intent of scientists, however, is the same in both cases: to find an area in which laws operate simply and directly and in which behavior can be easily predicted. Psychologists are continually seeking to devise a test condition that is the psychological equivalent of a physical vacuum, and many of their methods reflect this effort. Just as the vacuum eliminates friction and air resistance, the nonsense syllable, according to Ebbinghaus, eliminates meaning. For Ebbinghaus, as for the earlier associationists, meaning was equivalent to the accumulation of sensations attached to a given word. Because the syllables he devised were not words and thus not associated with any objects or any particular sensations, they had no meaning.

2. *They are relatively homogeneous.* This means simply that no one nonsense syllable stands out from the rest.

3. *They form an inexhaustible amount of new combinations, each of which can be compared with others.* In other words, a given list of ten nonsense syllables has no more meaning than any other list of ten nonsense syllables. Also, they may be compared in reverse. That is, CEV MEB has no more meaning than MEB CEV.

4. *They are capable of quantitative variations and may be divided at any point.* The only difference between a list of five nonsense syllables and a list of ten nonsense syllables, no matter how they are arranged, is that the latter is twice as long. On the other hand, consider the differences between these two lists:

TOM	BUT
MEN	SIX
SIX	MEN
BUT	SAW
HIS	TOM

```
GET
HIS
BIG
RED
CAR
```

The difference between them is not only that the second is twice as long, but that it is a meaningful sentence whereas the first is not. The second list, although twice as long as the first, is easier for most people to memorize because of its meaning.

The object of Ebbinghaus's experiments was to use nonsense syllables in a quantitative analysis of the development of associations. He was not satisfied to know merely that greater frequency of pairing leads to greater association. He wanted to know exactly how much pairing was necessary before an association would be formed.

In the course of his investigations, Ebbinghaus studied many different aspects of association. To better understand his method, let us consider one of his experiments. The purpose of this particular experiment was to test the concept that an association is formed in the mind of a subject between all members of a list of nonsense syllables and that the association is stronger for items on the list that are closer together and weaker for items that are further apart.

Consider the "original list" in Figure 1.8. According to Ebbinghaus, once the list is memorized, associations are formed between each item and all the other items. The association between neighboring items is strongest; the association between distant items is weak. This would imply, for instance, that ZEP LAN becomes strongly associated, ZEP NUR moderately associated, and ZEP ROL only weakly associated. In order to test this notion, Ebbinghaus invented what is called the *savings method*. He memorized several lists like those in the left-hand column of Figure 1.8; twenty-four hours later, he tried to relearn the same lists. The relearning of the lists, he found, took an average of 420 seconds less than the learning of the original list. The 420 seconds he saved he considered to be a measure of the strength of the associations 24 hours after they were formed. He reasoned that if he had forgotten the list completely, he would have shown no saving (learning and relearning times would have been equal), and if he had remembered the list completely, he would have had maximum saving (relearning time would have equaled zero). Thus, the amount of time saved became an index of how well he had remembered the list.

Strong association			Order of remoteness from original list			
Original list	0 Order	1st Order	2nd Order	3rd Order	7th Order
1 ZEP	ZEP	ZEP	ZEP	ZEP	ZEP
2 LAN	LAN	NUR	VEL	REG	ROL
3 NUR	NUR	REG	DEM	ROL	LAN
4 VEL	VEL	DEM	BUF	SID	BUF
5 REG	REG	ROL	SID	LAN	NUR
6 TAV	TAV	CES	FAC	TAV	CES
7 DEM	DEM	SID	LAN	BUF	VEL
8 MOC	MOC	GIZ	REG	QEB	VAM
9 ROL	ROL	LAN	MOC	NUR	REG
10 BUF	BUF	VEL	CES	DEM	SID
11 CES	CES	TAV	QEB	CES	TAV
12 VAM	VAM	MOC	NUR	GIZ	QEB
13 SID	SID	BUF	TAV	VEL	DEM
14 QEB	QEB	VAM	ROL	MOC	GIZ
15 GIZ	GIZ	QEB	VAM	VAM	MOC
16 FAC	FAC	FAC	GIZ	FAC	FAC

Strong associations   Mostly weak assocations

Weak association

FIGURE 1.8 Lists of nonsense syllables like those prepared by Ebbinghaus.

Then he constructed a series of derived lists from the original list. A derived list of zero order is simply the original list. A derived list of the first order contains the items of the original list so arranged that all but one of the adjacent items in the derived list were separated by one item in the original list. A derived list of the second order is arranged so that most of the adjacent items in the new list were originally separated by two items. Higher-order derived lists were constructed by the same principle. If, as Ebbinghaus theorized, the association on the original list was greatest for adjacent items, then a zero-order derived list, which retains the same adjacent items, should produce the most saving. A first-order derived list, which contains items from the original list spaced one item apart, should produce less saving. A second-order derived list, with items spaced two apart, should show still less, and so on. When the experiment was performed, this was exactly what Ebbinghaus found. A graph showing the decreasing amount of saving as the associations on the list became more remote is shown in Figure 1.9.

The experiments of Ebbinghaus were the first formal experiments in association, just as the experiments of Weber and Fechner were the first formal experiments in sensation. The goal of these experiments was to describe and measure scientifically the properties of the mind. The subjects were invariably human, and the data were collected in the form of verbal reports. The preferred method of obtaining these data was through introspection by the subject, although whether Ebbinghaus's experiments really relied on introspection is open to question. The introspective method in which the experimenter and subject are the same person was so influential, however, that even in his rather objective experiments, Ebbinghaus always served as his own subject.

For many years all scientists who called themselves psychologists were engaged in studying mental phenomena by methods like these. In the early part of the twentieth century, however, such methods were seriously challenged by physiologists who claimed that phenomena such as memory, emotion, and knowledge, hitherto seen as mental, were actually capable of being explained as bodily functions. Thus, they contended, the proper people to study such phenomena were not

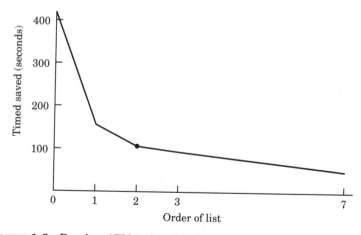

FIGURE 1.9 Results of Ebbinghaus's experiment. This graph shows that the amount of time saved in relearning lists decreases as a function of their remoteness from the original list (0). The time saved is the number of seconds required to learn the original list minus the number of seconds required to learn one of the derived lists 24 hours later.

psychologists trained in introspection, but physiologists trained in analyzing the discrete and delicate functions of the body and, in particular, the system of nerves that regulate bodily functions.

THE BODY

For a hundred years after Descartes, the methods of investigating the mind and the body could not have been more widely separated. On one hand, the British associationists and the German experimental psychologists studied the mind of man by means of introspection. On the other hand, physiologists studied the body by methods akin to those of physics. In general, the physiologists accepted Descartes's division: psychology, the study of the mind; physiology, the study of the body.

However, as their science gained precision, physiologists could account for much of the behavior previously thought to be controlled by the mind. For instance, in the seventeenth century, physiologists showed that after death (when, presumably, the soul had left the body) hearts could be kept beating. In fact, instances of hearts beating when entirely removed from the body were reported. Today we know that the heart operates like a muscle and that muscles can be activated by stimulating them appropriately even when they are detached from the body; however, in the seventeenth century most people believed that the soul gave life to the heart.

There are two possible resolutions to the problem posed by the observation that the heart, the muscles, and other organs are capable of functioning separately from the body. First of all, one could say that each of these organs has a soul — an animating force — of its own. This resolution was counter to the traditional belief that a human soul is in essence an *immortal entity*: Such an entity obviously could not be divided into several bits and pieces, some of which remained in human organs after death. The other solution to the problem was to deny that the soul has anything to do with the operation of the organs and to say that human organs work mechanically, like those of other animals. This was the position that most physiologists adopted and the notion that is generally accepted today. (Not many people object to heart transplant operations because they interfere with a patient's soul.)

With each new advance, the physiologists found mechanistic explanations for processes that were traditionally held to be controlled by the mind. Some people reasoned that physiology might continue to advance until it eventually captured the entire province of the mind. Might not all human behavior eventually be explained in mechanistic terms? By this reasoning, to say that a function was "controlled by the mind" was the same as saying that its causes were unknown, and that physiology had not yet advanced far enough to explain it. Perhaps Descartes's dualism was wrong, ran this mechanistic reasoning, and perhaps human behavior could eventually be explained without any reference to an animating force like the mind or the soul. Julien Offroy de la Mettrie (1709–1751), one of the first thinkers to espouse a completely mechanical explanation of behavior, said:

> To be a machine, to feel, to think, to know how to distinguish good from bad, as well as blue from yellow, in a word, to be born with an intelligence and a sure moral instinct, and to be but an animal, are therefore characters which are no more contradictory, than to be an ape or a parrot and to be able to give one's self pleasure. . . . I believe that thought is so little incompatible with organized matter, that it seems to be one of its properties on a par with electricity, the faculty of motion, impenetrability, extension, etc. [La Mettrie, 1748].

Most physiologists did not go so far as La Mettrie, preferring mechanical explanations for those functions of the body that they could analyze and mental explanations for those functions that they had not yet investigated. The subsequent physiological investigations that had the greatest effect on psychology were those that dealt with the reflex, that is, with the direct response of an organism to a stimulus in the environment. (We recall Descartes's example of the boy recoiling from the fire.)

As recently as the beginning of the twentieth century, there were still two principal areas of behavior that remained virtually unaffected by physiological research and almost wholly within the province of the mind:

1. Behavior seeming to arise from within the person, such as an apparently voluntary raising of the arm for which no cause or stimulus can be found in the environment, or complex behavior (singing an operatic aria in the shower, for instance) for which no correspondingly complex environmental stimulus can be found.
2. Learning. Most reflexes seem to be permanently fixed in the body. How can they explain learning to sing a song, for instance, or learning a whole repertoire of songs?

However, it was in the late nineteenth century and early twentieth century that the Russian physiologists Ivan Michailovich Sechenov (1829–1905) and Ivan Petrovich Pavlov (1849–1936) asserted that even these two areas of behavior could be understood in terms of reflexes.

In the next several sections, we shall trace the history of the physiological investigation of the reflex. We shall see how the concept of the reflex has become vital in psychology, especially in the study of learning. Let us begin by returning to the world of Descartes to look for the origins of the concept of reflex action in early discussions of nervous conduction.

Nervous Conduction

In general, early theories of nervous conduction held that the mind governs behavior through the transmission of some kind of vapor or substance to the muscles. Such theories reflected both traditional doctrine and the state of knowledge in the physical sciences. For Descartes, nervous conduction was based on a hydraulic model. As we recall, his opinion was that the soul interacts with the body in the pineal gland, near the middle of the brain. This gland, he thought, directs "animal spirits" through the nerves to activate the muscles mechanically. In 1662, he wrote that even though animal spirits must be "very mobile and subtle, they nevertheless have the force to swell and tighten the muscles within which they are enclosed, just as the air in a balloon hardens it and causes the skin containing it to stretch." (See Figure 1.10).

Descartes's views were highly influential. For a hundred years, controversy raged not about whether animal spirits existed but rather about what they consisted of. Some physiologists rejected Descartes's hydraulic model and adopted a pneumatic model; that is, they claimed that a gas rather than a liquid runs from the nerves to the muscles. Some (called iatrophysicists) claimed that there is a mechanical transmission of force, and others (called iatrochemists) claimed that the phenomenon is basically a chemical process. This speculation was generally nonexperimental.

Francis Glisson (1597–1677) made a clear experimental advance, however, when he showed in 1677 that whatever nervous conduction occurs when muscles contract, it does not consist of the transfer of a

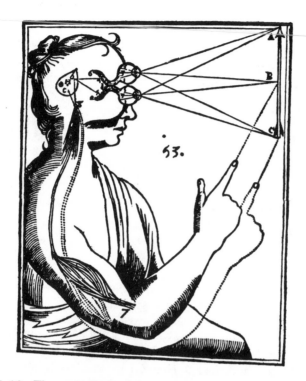

FIGURE 1.10 The central role of the pineal gland in Descartes's physiology is shown in this diagram from *L'Homme*. Images fall on the retinas (5, 3, 1) and are conveyed to the cerebral ventricles (6, 4, 2); these then form a single binocular image on the pineal gland (H), the site from which the soul controls the body. Stimulated by the image, the soul inclines the pineal gland, activating the "hydraulic system" of the nerves (8), causing a muscle to move (at 7). [Courtesy of the Curators of Bodlein Library, Oxford University.]

substance, either liquid or gas, from the nerves to the muscles. Glisson's experiment was simple. He had a subject put his hand in a tube full of water, as shown in Figure 1.11, and then contract and relax his muscles. When the muscles were contracted, Glisson found that the height of the water did not increase above the height for relaxed muscles, showing that no substance could be flowing into the muscles when they were contracted. From this evidence, it followed that muscles work by themselves once they receive proper stimulation. The question that remained was, What sort of stimulation do the nerves supply to the muscles?

Actually, a more sophisticated experiment had been done by Jan Swammerdam (1637–1680) prior to Glisson's work, but it had not

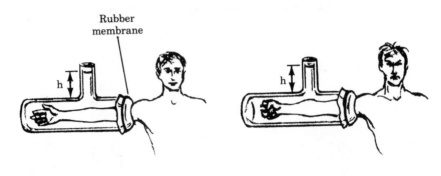

Muscles relaxed   Muscles under tension

FIGURE 1.11 Glisson's attempt to show that muscles do not gain in substance when they are contracted. The height of the water, h, is identical whether the subject's arm is tensed or relaxed.

become widely known. In 1660 Swammerdam had surgically isolated a nerve and muscle of a frog and had shown that mechanical stimulation of the nerve was sufficient to contract the muscle. In other words, no infusion of animal spirits or any other substance was necessary for the muscle to contract; simple irritation of the nerve was sufficient. Whether such a mechanical irritation is the actual process that takes place in the body when a muscle is contracted was another question. Figure 1.12 shows some of the illustrations of Swammerdam's experiments with nerves and muscles of frogs — experiments that have been repeated by countless students of elementary physiology.

In general, until late in the eighteenth century, some kind of mechanical conduction of energy was held to activate muscles, but the question of the exact nature of the energy was not resolved. For instance, according to David Hartley (1705–1757), to whose ideas we shall refer again later, the nervous impulse consisted of minute mechanical vibrations transmitted through the nerve like a wave. By the beginning of the nineteenth century, physiologists came to agree that however nerves might work, they were not adequately explained by references to animal spirits, mind, or soul.

Around 1800 there was great interest in electricity and much fruitful study of the subject. Some scientists speculated that nervous conduction might be electrical. As research progressed in the middle of the nineteenth century, it became increasingly clear that some form of

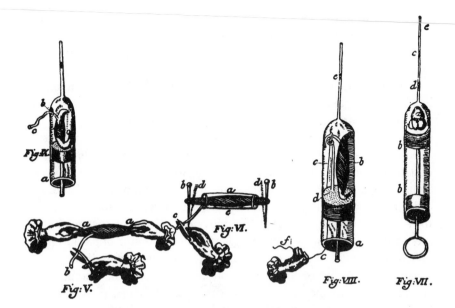

FIGURE 1.12   Early illustrations of Swammerdam's experiments. In Fig: VI, for instance, mechanical stimulation of the nerve contracts the muscle and draws the two pins together from b–b to d–d. The air tube apparatus in the other figures was used like Glisson's water tube to show that the muscle's volume remains constant when contracted.

electrical impulse was present in the nerve. Today, the nerve impulse is thought to be a combination of electrical and chemical events.

So we have, in the history of speculation about nervous conduction and research into its nature, a progression of theories — hydraulic to pneumatic to vibratory to electrical and chemical. These theories became more sophisticated and complex as the physical sciences offered successively better ways to understand how the human body functions.

The Reflex Arc

To those who have considered nonhuman behavior (and much of human behavior) to be machinelike, the basic element of such behavior has been the aforementioned reflex arc, the pathway leading from the sense organs through the nerves to the muscles. Descartes thought that sensory and motor signals travel through the same nerve. According to him, the sensory signal from the sense organ to the brain operated like a pull chain; the motor signal was hydraulic, consisting of the flow of animal spirits down through the nerve and into the muscle.

After Descartes's time, experimenters began to dissect animals to look for the organs necessary for various reflex functions. They found that certain parts of the nervous system (for instance, the cerebrum of the brain) could be entirely removed without destroying most reflexes; in contrast, severing some parts (notably, the spinal cord) immediately destroyed reflexes. This kind of investigation of the body may be compared to a mechanical investigation of an unknown machine. In order to discover whether a certain part of the machine is necessary for a certain function, you could remove or disconnect that part and see what functions were impaired. Does the carburetor of an automobile belong to its steering mechanism? One way to find out is to remove the carburetor and see if you can still steer the automobile. Because of experiments of this nature with animals, physiologists began to look upon the spinal cord and the base of the brain — but not the cerebrum — as necessary centers of reflex action.

However what happens in the spinal cord or base of the brain between the input and output was still a matter for speculation. According to George Prochaska (1749–1820), an early reflexologist, "This part, in which, as in a centre, the sensorial nerves, as well as the motor nerves, meet and communicate, and in which the impressions made on the sensorial nerves are reflected on the motor nerves, is designated by a term, now adopted by most physiologists, the *sensorium commune*" (Prochaska, 1784). But it was not clear in Prochaska's time, nor is it fully clear today, exactly what occurs in the sensorium commune, now called the central nervous system.

Although information on the central nervous system was scanty in the eighteenth century, physiologists were able to make lists of types of behavior that they thought were governed by reflexes. The following table shows one made in 1749 by Hatley, classified according to the sense organ stimulated.

In the early nineteenth century, physiologists develop a better picture of reflex mechanisms. In independent experiments with animals, François Magendie (1783–1855) and Charles Bell (1774–1842) discovered that when they cut the posterior branch of spinal nerves in an experimental animal, the animal could still move the denervated limb but did not react to a pinprick on the limb, whereas when they cut

SPECIAL SENSE	AUTOMATIC MOTION
1. "Feeling" — (touch, pain)	Crying, distortion of face, laughter following tickling, grasping, putting muscles into contraction following painful stimulation
2. Taste	Sucking, mastication, deglutition, distortion of mouth, peristaltic motion of stomach and bowels, vomiting, hiccough, expulsion of feces, spasms
3. Smell	Inspiration of air to "increase" odor, contraction of the fauces and gullet, sneezing.
4. Sight	Motions of globe of eye, motions of the eyelid, contractions of the lachrymal glands, contractions of the muscular rings of the iris, and the ciliar ligaments
5. Hearing	Contraction of small muscles of the auricle in adjusting to sound, contraction of muscles belonging to small bones of the ear

the anterior branch of nerves, the animal responded to a pinprick but was not able to move the limb. This discovery established a clear distinction between nerves with a sensory function and nerves with a motor function.

Meanwhile, lists of reflexes such as Hartley's were being expanded. Postural reflexes, such as those that allow a man to walk on a tilting ship or a cat to land on its feet when dropped upside down, and tendon reflexes, such as the knee jerk, were studied in detail. However, no matter how the list of automatic actions was extended, there still remained a host of actions, including most of the complex actions of everyday life, such as speaking, reading, and writing, that were unexplained by the physiologists and therefore classified as voluntary acts. We now turn to the attempt by the Russian physiologists Sechenov and Pavlov to explain such complex acts mechanistically.

Complex Behavior

Although the notion that all behaviors could be classified as either voluntary or involuntary (automatic) was a basic legacy of the dualism of Descartes, many observable behaviors simply could not fit into either classification. Sneezing and laughing seem involuntary enough, yet they can be suppressed; with much practice, some people have even learned to exert some control over the size of the pupils of their eyes. And what about breathing? We normally consider it to be quite automatic, but when a doctor puts a stethoscope to our chest, we breathe in and out on command; we can also hold our breath at will for short periods of time.

A different type of hard-to-classify behavior is represented by fast and accurate typing. Most skilled typists say that fast typing is automatic and that they do not concentrate on pressing each individual key. In fact, if they try to think of each key, they slow down considerably. Yet, clearly, when someone starts learning to type, he or she must concentrate on each key that is struck. This voluntary effort seems to become involuntary with practice. A similar shift from voluntary to automatic behavior can be seen in the acquisition of almost any skill. As an advertisement for a standard-shift Volkswagen once put it, "After a while, it becomes automatic."

Recognizing the tendency of many voluntary acts to develop into involuntary acts as well as the modifiability of many involuntary acts, nineteenth-century physiologists had to admit that they knew little or nothing about many forms of behavior. Nevertheless, they persisted in their hope that the idea of reflexes would eventually explain all behavior of animals.

It was Sechenov who attempted to show how complex, apparently voluntary acts can, in a broad frame of reference, be understood to be essentially involuntary. To demonstrate this, Sechenov addressed the problem of energy. One of the most basic laws of physics is that of the conservation of energy: Any energy that crosses the boundaries into a system must either remain in the system or come out in some other form. For instance, in an automobile engine, the energy contained in the gasoline that enters the engine eventually may leave it in the form of kinetic energy—the energy involved in the motion of the automobile—or in the form of heat lost to the environment, sound energy, or the chemical energy remaining in the exhaust gases. If you could keep a record of all the energy going into and coming out of the engine—or any other system—you would find that the two amounts are equal.

Many movements of organisms are caused by direct stimuli in the environment. A tap on a human knee, for instance, causes a reflex jerk in the leg. The energy input here is great enough so that it does not stretch the imagination to attribute the energy output of the knee jerk to the energy input of the blow on the knee. This view of the operation of this reflex is illustrated in Figure 1.13. Even though we now know it to be a gross oversimplification, it was nevertheless possible for early physiologists to think of the knee jerk as a mechanism that connected the stimulus to the response by various linkages within the body, with the stimulus providing the energy for the response, just as a blow on a key of a standard typewriter provides the energy for a typebar to strike the paper.

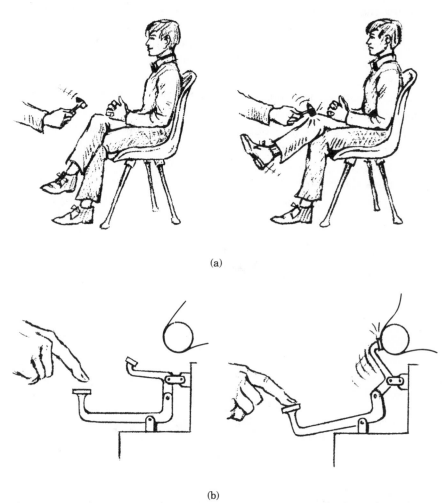

(a)

(b)

FIGURE 1.13 The reflex conceived of as a single mechanism: (a) a high-energy stimulus from the environment causes a high-energy response in the form of a knee jerk; (b) a high-energy blow on a typewriter key causes a typebar to strike the roller.

But consider another reflex: a baby's sneeze. Where is the stimulus that provides the tremendous energy exhibited in a good, satisfying sneeze? Could all that energy come from a mote of dust tickling the inside of the baby's nostril? It did not seem to Sechenov that it could. Instead, he proposed another kind of mechanism, one that we can compare to the electric switch that starts a fan. The energy that operates the fan is not supplied by the movement of the switch. The switch merely releases electrical energy to the fan, energy that is far greater than that required to turn the switch. While the switch is turned off, the pathway of electric current is blocked; turning on the switch removes the block. (In the nervous systems of organisms such blocking is called *inhibition*, and the stimulus that removes the inhibition is called a *releasing stimulus.*

Returning to the example of the baby's sneeze, we can think of the energy for the sneeze as being stored in the body of the baby, perhaps from milk drunk the previous day, ready to activate a sneeze at any moment but normally inhibited from doing so. When the baby's nose is tickled, the energy is released and the baby sneezes. Figure 1.14 illustrates the mechanism. For a long time, explanations of complex

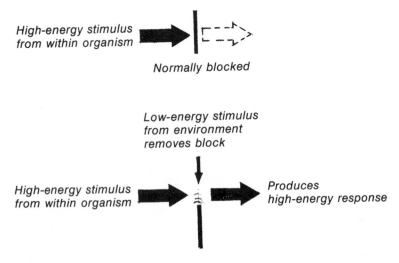

FIGURE 1.14 A low-energy stimulus can produce a high-energy response. This diagram suggests that the main source of energy lies within the animal but is normally blocked. A low-energy stimulus may temporarily remove the block and thus permit a high-energy response.

behaviors had relied on the idea of inhibitory and releasing mechanisms, but Sechenov was among the first to actually locate them in the body.

In one series of experiments, Sechenov measured the time taken by a frog to remove its foot reflexively when an acid stimulus was applied to its extended leg. Then he showed that this reflex could be modified by removing various portion's of the frog's brain. Sechenov essentially found that the stimulus–response reaction time decreased when he removed certain areas of the brain, a fact indicating that he had removed an inhibitory mechanism. When he put salt on parts of the frog's brain, the stimulus–response reaction time was increased, thus showing that he had excited an inhibitory mechanism. Figure 1.15 shows how Sechenov supposed this mechanism to work. In a series of experiments with humans, Sechenov showed that people's reflexes work more slowly when they are tickled than when they are not tickled; furthermore, the more tickling, the slower the reflexes. In other words, tickling serves to increase the inhibition of reflexes.

Sechenov reasoned that if stimuli, with little energy could trigger and control such relatively violent reactions, then perhaps all of those complex actions that appear to be voluntary (controlled from within the animal by the mind) are actually controlled from outside the animal by stimuli that have so little energy that the animal is not aware of them. Although the reactions to low-energy stimuli may be slight, they are present and are, according to Sechenov, purely mechanical. In other words, the small unnoticed external stimuli have two functions. First, they cause reactions within the brain, reactions we have come to call thoughts. Second, they activate or release inhibitions on gross motor reactions. Sechenov says of this sequence:

> It is generally accepted that if one act follows another, the two acts stand in causal relationship (post hoc — ergo propter hoc); *this is why thought is generally believed to be the cause of behaviour*; and when the external sensory stimulus remains unnoticed — which happens quite frequently — *thought is even accepted as the initial cause of behavior*. Add to this the extremely subjective character of thought, and you will understand how firmly man must believe in the voice of self-consciousness, when it tells him such things. In reality, however, this voice tells him the greatest of falsehoods: *the initial cause of all behavior always lies, not in thought, but in external sensory stimulation, without which no thought is possible.* [Sechenov, 1863]

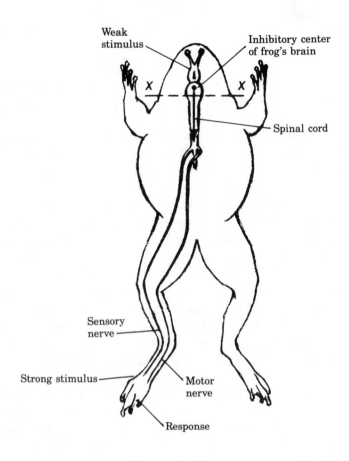

(a)

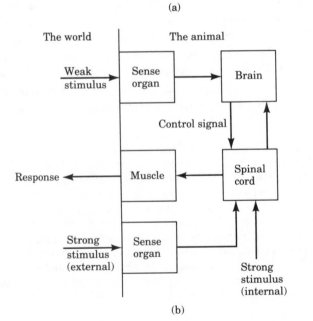

(b)

By this reasoning, Sechenov attempted to draw all the complexity of behavior within the realm of reflexology. No longer was a reflex seen to be a simple chain from stimulus to response; instead, it was seen as a complex machinelike process modified by unnoticed signals from the environment — much like the process by which a radio receives low-energy electromagnetic waves and uses them to modify the high energy from its battery or an electrical outlet so as to generate signals loud enough to be audible. But no matter how complex a radio may be, it is nevertheless fixed in its construction. If the signal to a radio is repeated, its response will be the same. In this respect, the behavior of an animal cannot be explained by Sechenov's theory. An animal does not always respond in the same way to a repeated stimulus. Its responses are modified, as we have seen, by experience; furthermore, how responses are modified depends on the nature of the experience. It was another Russian physiologist, Pavlov, who was to show how reflexes could be modified by experience.

Pavlov realized that inborn reflex mechanisms, no matter how precise and complex, were not enough to explain the various adjustments that animals make to their environments. In particular, such mechanisms could not explain the process that the psychologists who studied mental phenomena called *association*. For example, how could an inborn reflex explain the fact that people react strongly not only to heat on their skin but also to the sight of a fire, the smell of smoke, the word *fire* shouted in a loud voice, and the sound of fire engines in the street? Certainly it was too much to imagine that each of these stimuli is connected to an inborn reflex of its own; more likely, such groups of stimuli become associated through experience. But how? Pavlov's investigations were directed mainly towards this question.

The reflex that Pavlov and his students studied most closely was the salivary reflex in dogs. (We shall describe these experiments in more detail in Chapter 2.) In general, Pavlov found that dogs salivate when any stimulus is presented, such as a bell, a light, the experimenter, or a geometrical pattern, provided that the stimulus has been

---

FIGURE 1.15 (a) Sechenov's experiments on inhibition. Sechenov observed that (1) salt applied to an "inhibitory center" in the frog's brain slowed down the frog's withdrawal of its leg from an acid, while (2) severing the frog's nerves at X-X speeded up the withdrawal. (b) Sechenov's view of how the brain controls spinal reflexes.

presented together with food a sufficient number of times. There are parallels between Pavlov's work and Ebbinghaus's. Ebbinghaus presented two nonsense syllables together and observed association. Pavlov presented a neutral arbitrary stimulus (such as a bell) together with a stimulus (food) that was closely linked to a response. Like Ebbinghaus, Pavlov found that the more the paired stimuli were presented together, the greater was the strength of the association. Pavlov determined the strength of the association by measuring the amount of saliva secreted when the bell was sounded. As the amount secreted at the sound of the bell approached the amount secreted when food itself was present, the strength of the association was said to be increasing.

Pavlov decided that all animals must possess two sets of reflexes:

1. *A fixed, innate set of relatively simple reflexes.* (According to Pavlov, the path of these reflexes runs from the sensory nerves through the spinal cord to the motor nerves; these simple reflexes can be modified by innate inhibitory mechanisms, as Sechenov had shown, but essentially they are fixed.)
2. *A set of acquired reflexes.* (These reflexes, called *conditional* reflexes by Pavlov, are formed by pairing previously neutral stimuli with a stimulus that triggers an innate reflex; the path of these acquired reflexes goes through the upper parts of the brain, the cerebral hemispheres; when these parts of the brain are removed, the acquired reflexes disappear, leaving only the simple innate reflexes.)

It was Pavlov's view that

the basic physiological function of the cerebral hemispheres throughout the . . . individual's life consists in a constant addition of numberless signalling conditional stimuli to the limited number of the initial inborn unconditional stimuli, in other words, in constantly supplementing the unconditional reflexes by conditional ones. Thus, the objects of the instincts [our desires for food and the like] exert an influence on the organism in ever-widening regions of nature and by means of more and more diverse signs or signals, both simple and complex; consequently, the instincts are more and more fully and perfectly satisfied, i.e., the organism is more reliably preserved in the surrounding nature. [Pavlov, 1955, p. 273]*

Pavlov held that we (animals) steer ourselves through our environments by means of signals conditioned through experience to remove us from trouble and to lead us to the things we need. He contended that all complex learned behavior is brought about through the combination of several simple conditional reflexes, which are physiological processes. He believed that through objective investigations, physiologists would eventually be able to predict all of the behaviors of animals, including humans.

THE RELATION OF PHYSIOLOGICAL PSYCHOLOGY TO MENTAL PSYCHOLOGY

In the discussion of associationists, we pointed out that the basic outlook of parties to theoretical disputes are often seen as essentially similar from the perspective of time. To some extent, this observation applies to the reflexologists versus the associationists. The reflexologists, like Sechenov and Pavlov, thought that all complex behavior is mechanical; the associationists, like Ebbinghaus, thought that all complex behavior is influenced by the mind. Although these theorists differed in many obvious respects, they nevertheless shared several basic similarities.

Both the associationists and reflexologists believed that complex behavior is the result of the combination of simple elements. The associationists believed that the elements are simple sensations or ideas, that a complex idea is the combination of a group of simple ideas, and that the blending of simple ideas into complex ones takes place in the mind. The reflexologists believed that the elements are simple reflexes, that a complex action or behavior is the combination of a group of simple reflexes, and that the blending of simple reflexes into complex ones takes place in the brain.

---

*Early translations of Pavlov used the terms *conditioned* and *unconditioned* to modify *reflexes* and *stimuli*. More recent translations use the terms *conditional* and *unconditional*, as we do here.

The parallels between the basic concepts of these two outgrowths of Descartes's dualism, although often obscured, were not unnoticed at the time. Both the mentalists and Pavlov claimed that conditional reflexes might shed light on the concept of association. Even as early as the eighteenth century, the associationist philosopher Hartley, who was also a physician and a physiologist, attempted to explain all of human behavior in terms of both association and physiology. He believed that mental and physical processes were two ways of looking at the same thing and, that together they could account for all complex phenomena, each on its own terms, without interaction between them. In Hartley's book *Observations on Man* (1749) the chapters alternate, one explaining a given phenomenon physically and the next explaining it mentally. There is one chapter on the mental association of ideas and a tandem chapter—which anticipates Pavlov—on associative interactions within the brain.

An important point about both mental association and physiology as explanations of complex behavior is their common *structural* nature. Both systems have elements; the research pertinent to both systems has to do with the rules for the combination of these elements and the nature of the compound formed from the elements. In both systems the repeated pairing or grouping of stimuli attaches elements together in some way to build compounds. The general term for such systems is *structuralism*.

The next section is concerned with an alternative to and an attack on the structural method of analyzing behavior.

Molarism

So far what we have said about psychology can be understood in terms of Figure 1.3, Descartes's system for understanding man. We have looked at the work of both the associationist Ebbinghaus and the physiologist Pavlov. Since both of these experimentalists relied on the idea that elements become combined into complex entities, both are described as structuralists.

Structuralism is surely not the only doctrine by which man can be understood. For example, consider again how we might come to understand such a complex entity as an automobile. The engineer who built the automobile knows the relation between the temperature in the combustion chamber and the power output, and the diameter of each opening in the carburetor. The mechanic who regularly repairs the automobile knows that it needs a little extra oil in certain areas where it leaks, that the wheels are currently out of line, and that the exhaust system has another thousand miles to go. The driver knows that the car is hard to start, that the steering is rather loose, that the back seat is cramped, and that the windshield washers and the clock do not work.

If we offered $1000 to the person who knows the car best, who would be entitled to the prize—the engineer, the mechanic, or the driver? They all know the car quite well, and no one area of knowledge is really more basic than the others. The engineer may argue that his knowledge is the most basic because without him the car wouldn't exist. But the driver might claim that since the ultimate purpose of a car is to be driven, to know how to drive an automobile well is to know an automobile in its most basic sense. There is much room for heated —and unproductive—argument here. One must finally accept the fact that the ways in which the engineer, the mechanic, and the driver know the automobile are all valid ways of knowing automobiles and that, in fact, there are still other valid ways to know automobiles. Consider the traffic policeman, the road builder, the city planner, the traffic engineer, the automobile salesperson, and the pedestrian, to name a few.

Similarly, there are many ways in which the behavior of animals can be studied and known. The structural approach, whether mental or physiological, corresponds to an engineer's understanding of a car —the structuralist wishes to know the components and how they are put together. *Molarism* is another approach in psychology, one that attempts to know man as a whole. To return to our analogy, we might say that a driver has a molar view of a car's steering, acceleration, and braking characteristics. When psychologists say they are molarists, we can understand them to mean that they study large units of behavior rather than looking for discrete "building blocks." Molarists also differ from structuralists in how they go about their studies and especially in the kind of data they collect and the kind of observations they make.

The molarist observes a large psychological unit (like "personality") directly, without trying to break it into its elements, and just as there are structuralists on both the mental and physical sides of Descartes's dualism (for example, Ebbinghaus versus Pavlov), there are also molarists on both sides. A group of molarists who addressed themselves to mental phenomena were the Gestalt psychologists.

Gestalt Psychology

In Germany in the early twentieth century, the predominant approach in psychology was both mental and structural. The research was similar to that which had been done by Ebbinghaus, Weber, and Fechner and mainly consisted of trying to discover laws pertaining to the association of mental elements such as sensations and ideas.

Gestalt psychology arose in reaction to the structural aspect of German psychology. The emphasis of the Gestalt psychologists was on the study of whole mental entities rather than parts. The Gestalt psychologists were strongly influenced by the philosophy of Immanuel Kant (1724–1804). Their objections to structural psychology, which had largely been based on British empiricist philosophy, corresponded almost point for point to Kant's original objections to British empiricist philosophy itself. Kant had claimed that the fundamental contents of experience were not sensory elements — simple colors, sounds, smells, and so forth — but *whole* ideas and concepts. These ideas and concepts were neither mental nor physical in themselves, Kant claimed, but *phenomenological*. They arose, according to Kant, from the interaction of the physical world with a set of innate categories of the human mind: our conceptions of time and space and the fundamentals of logic, mathematics, and morality.

The job of philosophy, Kant claimed (and the job of psychology, the Gestalt psychologists claimed), is to analyze our phenomenal experience into its physical and mental parts. The picture of the human mind painted by psychologists would be, according to Kant, as much a theoretical construction as is the picture of the physical world painted by physicists. Neither is available to immediate introspection. What we see when we introspect — the interactions between the physical world and our innate categories — are whole phenomenal entities, not individual sensations as the structuralists had claimed.* The Gestalt

---

*Much of modern cognitive psychology may be viewed as an extension of Kant's search for innate categories. Cognitively oriented studies of language, for instance, frequently assume that common features found in the grammar of all known languages must be based on some particular innate feature of the human brain (see Chapter 6).

psychologists took up Kant's argument and applied it directly to human perception.

Let us consider a specific example of a phenomenon to which the Gestalt psychologists felt their argument was relevant: melody. The elements of a melody are tones. But, according to the Gestaltists, the essence of a melody is its organization. After all, a melody may be played in different keys (with different sets of tones), sung by different singers, played on different instruments, and rendered in different styles, yet it remains the same melody. If we try to break a melody down into discrete tones, we lose the very quality by which we can identify it — how it organizes tones. It is fruitless, according to Gestalt psychologists, to study a complex process like a melody by trying to list its elements. We must instead listen to the melody as a whole and concentrate on its organization.

Let us consider another example offered by the Gestaltists. When we recognize a friend, we recognize her all at once. We don't stop to compare her eyes with our memory of her eyes, her nose with our memory of her nose, her mouth with our memory of her mouth, and so forth. According to the Gestalt point of view, we recognize our friend by comparing the whole organization of elements before us with an equivalent organization in our memory; this recognition of our friend's identity is primary and basic and does not depend on the analysis of what we see into particular elements. If we do analyze our recognition into elements, said the Gestaltists, we do it after recognition occurs, not before.

The Gestalt psychologists realized that subjective judgments of qualities depend on relationships and patterns of organization. For instance, the headlights of an oncoming car seem very bright at night when the surroundings are dim, but they seem less bright in the daytime when the surroundings are bright. The important determinant of the brightness of the headlights as we experience it is not the constant intensity of the headlights themselves, as structuralism might lead us to believe, but rather the relationship of that intensity to the intensity of the surrounding light. In other words, we experience the total organization. Consider this experiment by the Gestalt psychologist Karl Duncker (1903–1940). In a dark room, the subject was shown only a spot of light located within a square frame. The frame was then moved while the spot was kept still, but the subject always thought that the spot moved within an immobile frame (Figure 1.16). Duncker called the apparent movement of the spot "induced move-

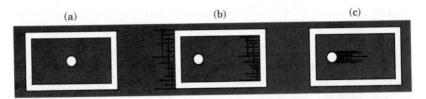

FIGURE 1.16 Duncker's experiments with "induced movement." (a) Spot of light within a frame in a dark room; (b) experimenter moves frame slowly to the right, but (c) subject reports seeing spot move slowly to the left.

ment." The Gestalt psychologists saw this experiment as proof that movement is seen subjectively in the relationships of an object (the spot) with its environment (the frame) and not in terms of isolated sensations.

The Gestaltists also objected to certain aspects of the dualism of the psychology of their time. They believed that there were not two separate sets of laws, one for the physical brain and another for the mind, but one set of laws, molar in character, that applied to both.

The Gestalt psychologists were mentalists, to be sure, but they broke with tradition on an important point. Although they were studying the mind and maintained that the mind could influence behavior (as indicated by arrow Y, Figure 1.3), they also maintained that there were no uniquely mental processes. Recall the structuralist view: The mind receives isolated sensations, then (on the right side of the dotted line in Figure 1.3), these sensations are combined by the process of association—a mental phenomenon—that takes place in the mind but not necessarily in the brain. The Gestaltists denied the existence of such unique mental processes. According to them, consciousness is isomorphic to (has the same form as) processes in the brain. But if we have no separate conscious processes, if everything we think of or are aware of has a physical counterpart in our brains, how can we explain those instances where our consciousness does not reflect the real world (as physics defines it)? For instance, how can we explain the misperception of movement in Duncker's experiment (Figure 1.16)? Previous mental psychologists would have said that the misperception occurs in the mind, but the Gestalt psychologists explicitly denied that anything could occur in the mind without a counterpart in the brain. If we see the spot of Duncker's experiment as moving, its representation in our brains must be a moving representation, and the representation of the frame must be standing still. When the perception of things differs from reality, the distortion occurs not only in our minds but in internal physical processes as well. The Gestalt psychologists went on to postulate certain innate physical characteristics of the brain that they believed might explain some of the phenomena they had discovered.

In the early twentieth century, physicists had begun to study electromagnetic fields. The Gestalt psychologist Wolfgang Köhler (1887–1967) thought that many of the processes of electromagnetic fields had parallels in human perception of form and motion. Therefore, he concluded, the brain contains magnetic fields and the (innate) physical properties of those fields determine perception.

Behavioral Molarism

The influence of the Gestalt psychologists was not limited to their attack on the structural doctrine of the mental psychologists. The Gestaltists' idea that the best way to study any process is to look at the organization of that process as a whole was extended to the behavior of the body as well as that of the mind.

Let us consider how reflexologists might try to explain the path taken by Mr. X, who walks to work every morning. From the time he kisses his wife goodbye to the time he greets his co-workers, X's behavior can be described as a series of movements — of steps, left turns, right turns, stops, and starts — that might well be interpreted as a series of reflexes learned by constant repetition.

Yet suppose one morning there is construction on the street X usually takes and that he must detour through a completely strange back alley. If he is a reasonably clever man, his detour will be successful and he will end up once more on the familiar street with the construction behind him. How could X have possibly made this detour if his behavior was running off mechanically as a series of reflexes, each triggered by a familiar stimulus? Some psychologists reasoned that such behavior could not be satisfactorily explained in terms of the kind of simple reflexes that the physiologists Sechenov and Pavlov studied. They claimed that X has, in fact, never acquired such reflexes, but rather that he has learned a *strategy*, an overall plan for getting to work, a sort of complex set of instructions to himself that takes into account the various possible environmental obstacles before they happen. What exactly the learning of such complex contingencies consists of remains a matter of dispute.

Some psychologists would say that the unifying theme of X's behavior is his purpose — getting to work — and that we must therefore study behavior in terms of purposes. They would contend that meaningful laws of behavior will never be expressed in terms of discrete reflexive actions but only in terms of aims and goals. X's ordinary path and his detour have one thing in common — their destination. Change his destination and you will change his behavior in a fundamental sense; keep his destination the same and all paths to the destination can be studied as a single kind of behavior.

Still other psychologists see X's detour as evidence that explanations of behavior in purely objective terms will never succeed — that we must study people in terms of their interior mental life. What X acquires when walking to work is a cognitive or mental map of the path to work, and his detour is made with reference to the map that he has learned and carries around in his mind. One need not talk about his purpose in walking to work, these psychologists argue, for he would have acquired this mental map even while strolling aimlessly around the neighborhood.

The Gestalt psychologists themselves would have claimed that X's successful detour was a product of *insight*. One characteristic of conditioned reflex behavior is that it is gradually acquired by repeated pairings. Yet, according to the Gestaltists, the man's solution to the problem of the detour on his way to work was sudden and immediate. Insight is not something that is gradually learned by repeated pairings but comes about by looking at a situation in a novel way, so as to grasp the structural and functional relationships of the problem.

Köhler, the Gestalt psychologist whose field theory of the brain we previously mentioned, was detained during World War I on Tenerife, an island that possessed a colony of apes for scientific study. Köhler performed a series of experiments with these apes in which he set problems for them and observed their solutions. Köhler almost invariably found that when the apes were given complicated problems, they would persist in an incorrect solution or merely do nothing until they suddenly performed the correct act without hesitation. Köhler ascribed this sudden change in the apes' behavior to insight — the seeing of a relationship between the elements of the problem. For instance, when a banana was hung out of reach of the chimpanzees in a room containing only an open box placed on the floor,

> all six apes vainly endeavoured to reach their objective by leaping up from the ground. Sultan [one of the apes] soon relinquished this attempt, paced restlessly up and down, suddenly stood still in front of the box, seized it, tipped it hastily straight toward the objective, but began to climb upon it at a horizontal distance of half a meter, and springing upwards with all his force, tore down the banana. About five minutes had elapsed since the fastening of the fruit; from the momentary pause before the box to the first bite into the banana, only a few seconds elapsed, a perfectly continuous action after the first hesitation. Up to that instant, none of the animals had taken any notice of the box; they were all far too intent on the objective; none of the other five took any part in carrying the box; Sultan performed the feat single-handed in a few seconds. [Köhler, 1925, p. 40]

In Figure 1.17, we observe an ape faced with a somewhat more difficult problem.

The Gestaltists' objections to the analysis of behavior into discrete elements convinced most contemporary psychologists that although it was useful and important to study reflexes as Sechenov and Pavlov had studied them, reflexes could not be regarded as the simple building blocks of all behavior (the behavior of Köhler's apes, for example). Something more than the conditional reflex was needed to account for truly complex behavior. It thus seemed necessary to radically modify the concept of the reflex or even to abandon it altogether as a basic mechanism of complex behavior.

The "Gestalt revolution" in psychology was only partially successful. Its negative purpose succeeded, for it demonstrated the inadequacy of a structural account of all behavior. However, its positive purpose failed, for it did not produce a completely molar account of behavior. Most psychologists see the value of both structural and molar analysis and are convinced that behavior can be understood on many different levels.

Functionalism

We have seen how Gestaltism, with its emphasis on the study of molar behavior, brought into question the premises of both physiological and mental structuralism. We now come to an even more influential doc-

FIGURE 1.17

trine, that of *functionalism*, which has flourished in the United States. The functional and molar revolutions in psychology overlapped considerably. Which came first is difficult to determine. Both made headway slowly, by fits and starts; the ultimate origins of both may be traced to historical arguments within philosophy and the physical sciences.

Functionalism stems from the theory of evolution put forward by the biologist Charles Darwin (1809–1882) over one hundred years ago. Darwin's theory, in capsule form, is that those organisms that are best able to survive in their environment tend to increase in number and those that are least able to survive tend to decrease in number. Because organisms within a species naturally vary in physical qualities and behavior patterns, those organisms that are better able to survive will reproduce more and their distinct adaptive qualities will tend to become dominant; by this process the whole species gradually changes so as to become better fitted to cope with its environment.

Let us consider one common illustration of the action of evolution: the origin of the extreme length of the giraffe's neck. All giraffes, no matter how long their necks, depend on foliage for food, and foliage is sometimes in short supply. In the course of natural variation, some early giraffes were born with longer-than-average necks — just as some humans are born very tall, in some instances even when they have parents of average height. Those giraffes with long necks were better able to eat leaves on the high trees in their environment and lived longer and produced more offspring. Those with short necks were unable to reach the leaves on the upper parts of the trees and tended to die earlier and to produce fewer offspring. Thus, as the generations went on, there were more and more offspring of long-necked giraffes, who tended on the average to be long-necked — just as the children of tall human parents tend on the average to be tall.*

Darwin saw natural selection as a process similar to the artificial selection used by animal breeders; for instance, a race of plump chickens or turkeys can be created by breeding plump fowl and not breeding lean or stringy birds. Figure 1.18 shows how the process of natural selection works in the case of giraffes. Note that this process is contrary to the notion that giraffes were constantly stretching their necks to reach the high leaves on trees, that this stretching made their necks longer, and that these giraffes passed this trait on to their young.

A profound implication of the theory of evolution is that all living creatures share a common biological inheritance. After Darwin, species were no longer regarded as immutable; there was no longer a sharp boundary separating "higher" animals from "lower" animals — or even humans from other animals. In regard to human life, evolution meant that the traits humans possess must have evolved from traits their ancestors once possessed.

---

*This is of course a great simplification. It ignores another advantage of having a long neck — the ability to spot lions far away on the African plain. It also ignores the great disadvantage of a long neck — the increased work the heart must do to pump blood to the brain. But most of all, it ignores the ecological balance of the giraffe in its environment — for instance, the effect of long-necked giraffes on the evolution of the trees on which they feed. If we were concerned here about the actual origins of the giraffe's long neck (and not just using it as an example), these factors and many others would have to be considered.

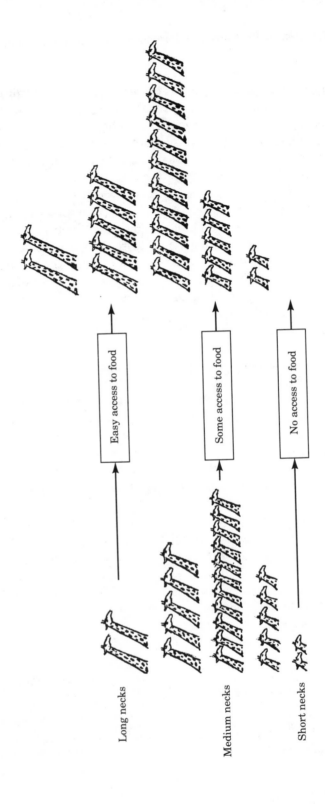

Long necks

Medium necks

Short necks

Easy access to food

Some access to food

No access to food

One of the first effects of this principle of *biological continuity* on psychology was the acceptance of the notion that because humans have minds and consciousness, then other animals also have minds and consciousness, although of a more rudimentary kind. This led psychologists who were studying the mentality of humans to become interested in the mentality of animals. The evidence for mentality in animals had long rested on anecdotes about the clever actions of pets and farm animals. However, a group of American psychologists (the functionalists) began to investigate animal behavior in laboratories, especially at the University of Chicago. One of the tools they devised to study the mental processes of animals was the maze, and some of the first animals to be studied in mazes were rats.

In 1901, in a paper entitled "Experimental study of the mental processes of the rat," Willard Stanton Small (1870–1943) introduced the rat in the maze to psychology. Small's maze was modeled on the Hampton Court Maze, a garden maze created for the amusement of the English nobility. (These mazes are shown in Figures 1.19 and 1.20.) The object of Small's maze experiments was to determine the conscious state of an animal by observing its behavior. In the following description of a rat's behavior, Small's observations and conclusions about the rat's conscious states are italicized. It might be instructive for readers to try to list those italicized words that seem to them to be direct observations of behavior and those that seem to express conclusions drawn by Small about the conscious state of the rat.

Analyses of Results

In appreciating the results of this series of experiments, . . . the [following] . . . facts come into view. . . . *The initial indefiniteness of movement* and the *fortuitousness of success*; the just *observable profit from the first experiences*; the gradually increasing *certainty of*

FIGURE 1.18 How natural selection altered the structure of the giraffe's neck. Leaves, the giraffe's favorite food, have been in relatively short supply during the long history between the earlier and the later populations shown; thus the long-necked giraffes, which were able to reach higher leaves, had a better chance of surviving and reproducing than the short-necked giraffes. Since the offspring of long-necked giraffes had, on the average, longer necks than the offspring of the general population, there was a gradual increase in the proportion of long-necked giraffes. Note also the disappearance of the short-necked giraffe.

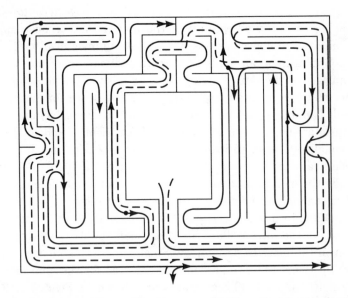

FIGURE 1.19 Floor plan of Small's maze. Small studied the "mental processes" of rats with this maze, which he based on the maze in the gardens at Hampton Court Palace in England.

knowledge indicated by *increase of speed and definiteness*, and the *recognition of critical points* indicated by *hesitation* and *indecision;* the lack of *imitation* and the improbability of *following by scent;* the outbreak of the instincts of *play* and *curiosity* after the edge of *appetite* is dulled. In addition are to be noted the further observations upon the contrast between the *slow and cautious entrance* into, and the *rapid exit* from the blind alleys, after the first few trials; the appearance of *disgust* on reaching the end of a blind alley; the clear indication of centrally excited *sensation* (images) of some kind; *memory* (as I have used the term); *the persistence of certain errors;* and the almost *automatic character of the movements* in the later experiments.

The historical importance for psychology of the notion of biological continuity is that it stimulated much research in comparative psychology — the comparison of the behavior of one species with that of another. At first the purpose of this research was to affirm or deny Darwin's theories by comparing the mental qualities of one species with those of another — for instance, to answer the question, Which

View from above

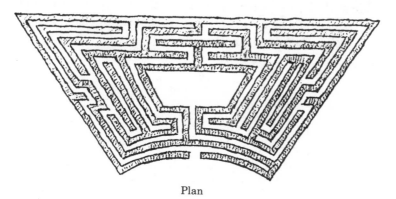

Plan

FIGURE 1.20   The Hampton Court maze.

animal has the higher developed mentality, the dog or the horse? —
and to thereby rank the various species by the properties of their
minds. Contemporary comparative research ignores the relative
"mental development" of species and concentrates more on the comparison of various complex behavior patterns.

The general principle that the process of natural selection embodies is critically important in modern psychology as well as in other
sciences; it is the principle of *feedback*. In a feedback system, a process
is regulated through testing the actual state of the process against a
selected potential state.

In Figure 1.21 the dotted lines represent a feedback loop whereby
information about the actual state of an ongoing process is compared
with information about a potential state of the process. In the case of
the natural selection of long-necked giraffes, a potential state was
signaled by the height of the leaves on the trees. Time after time, this
potential state was compared with the actual state of the length of the
giraffes' necks. The long-term result of this process was attainment of
a new actual state: a population of long-necked giraffes.

Feedback is a very common process in everyday experience. Consider a household thermostat. In this case, a potential state is represented by the setting on the thermostat, say 72° F. The actual state is
the current temperature of the house, say 65° F. The ongoing comparison of these two states controls a process — the burning of coal, gas, or
oil to warm the house. As soon as the difference disappears — that is,
as soon as the house becomes as warm as the setting on the thermostat
indicates it should be — the heater or furnace is turned off. Figure 1.22
shows such a thermostat mechanism.

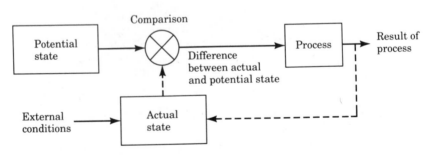

FIGURE 1.21 A simple feedback system.

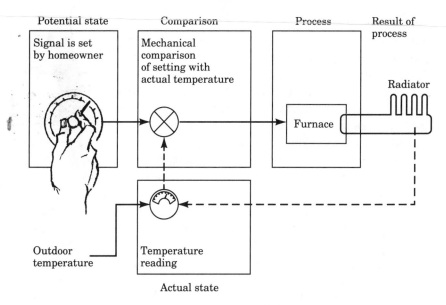

FIGURE 1.22   The operation of a household thermostat.

Such self-adjusting systems embody simple *negative* feedback (a term borrowed from engineering). The feedback is called negative because the ongoing comparison tends to decrease the difference between the actual state of the system and the selected potential state of the system. While external conditions remain constant, both the system of natural selection and the thermostat can eventually reach *equilibrium*. At equilibrium, the actual and signaled states are identical, and the process terminates.

However, it is possible to have other kinds of feedback. *Positive* feedback tends to amplify the difference between the actual state and the selected potential state, producing a runaway process. Suppose, for instance, that the thermostat we have been considering got connected by mistake to the air conditioner instead of the furnace. Then, the difference in temperature between the desired 72° F and the actual 65° F would activate the air conditioner, causing the actual temperature to drop further, increasing the difference. The thermostat feeds more power to the air conditioner, which in turn decreases the temperature still further, and so forth.

Positive feedback in everyday situations often causes havoc. A young man, for instance, thinks that a young woman is cool to him because he is not forward enough, whereas the reverse is actually true. He increases his forwardness and finds her cooler. He interprets this continued coolness as a sign that he is still not forward enough and so increases his advances in proportion to the degree of coolness his very advances are generating. Such miscalculations between persons can result in something unpleasant, like a slap on the face. In the case of an international arms race, they could lead to disaster.

The feedback principle, showing how a process could be controlled by a desired end or function, formed the basis for functional psychology. The functionalists, inspired by Darwin's theory, believed that mental processes had evolved to serve various useful functions for animals struggling to cope with their complex environments. According to the philosopher and psychologist William James,

> Mental facts cannot be properly studied apart from the physical environment of which they take cognizance. The great fault of the older rational psychology was to set up the soul as an absolute spiritual being with certain faculties of its own by which the several activities of remembering, imagining, reasoning, willing, etc., were explained, almost without reference to the peculiarities of the world with which these activities deal. But the richer insight of modern days perceives that our inner faculties are adapted in advance to the features of the world in which we dwell, adapted, I mean, so as to secure our safety and prosperity in its midst. Not only are our capacities for forming new habits, for remembering sequences, and for abstracting general properties from things and associating their usual consequences with them, exactly the faculties needed for steering us in this world of mixed variety and uniformity, but our emotions and instincts are adapted to very special features of that world. In the main, if a phenomenon is important for our welfare, it interests and excites us the first time we come into its presence. Dangerous things fill us with involuntary fear; poisonous things with distaste; indispensable things with appetite. Mind and world in short have been evolved together, and in consequence are something of a mutual fit. [James, 1893, p. 4]

Notice that the adaptation between our minds and environments is said to take place *in advance*. That is, our emotions and desires, which help us survive, are inborn, so that we are interested in an object that is important for our welfare "the first time we come into its presence." Furthermore, note that the locus of our sense that the object is important is said to be in the mind—considered a separate "organ" whose properties are as subject to the action of evolution as the length of the giraffe's neck, but which, like Descartes's concept, is still not to be found in the physical world (see Figure 1.3).

From the notion that the mind is subject to evolutionary changes and develops in response to the environment, it follows that complex behavior, which the mind controls, must also change with the generations of species so that individuals can cope better with their environments. This notion gave rise to research such as Small's, in which the complex behavior patterns of various animals were studied with a view towards determining their mental qualities.

To return briefly to the principle of biological continuity, recall that this principle implies that consciousness is not a purely human trait — that if it is possessed by humans, it must be possessed by other animals, at least to some degree. By 1912, some American psychologists had discovered the other side of the same coin. They observed that since both biologists and psychologists were studying animal behavior fruitfully without recourse to the notion of consciousness, then perhaps much of human behavior could also be explained without having to analyze or even refer to consciousness. The Russian reflexologists had previously abandoned the idea altogether as an explanatory concept. The important point for our discussion is not whether there really is such a thing as consciousness, but that when attention was no longer focused on consciousness, introspection lost its position as the prime method of psychological investigation.

John Broadus Watson (1878–1958) studied at the University of Chicago when the functionalist school of psychology flourished there. He was trained to perform animal experiments similar to Small's experiments with rats in a maze. Watson soon became convinced that he could separate his observations into those that could be verified by other psychologists and those that could not be so verified. In the former category, he placed observations of the overt behavior of animals — where and how they moved. Watson knew that such observations yielded general agreement. In the second category, he placed observations of the conscious states of animals. He knew that these observations consistently failed to yield much agreement. (In other words, Watson found it far more likely that three observers would agree on whether a rat turned left or right in a maze than on whether the rat was happy or sad while it was turning.)

Whereas some functionalists faulted each other's introspective training, Watson held that introspection itself was the source of the prevalent disagreement about animals' mental states. Watson de-

clared that introspection should be banished from psychology and that
psychological observations should be restricted, like other scientific
observations, to overt behavior.

Because Watson focused on observable behavior, he called himself a "behaviorist" and broke away from the other functionalists at
Chicago. As Watson's position gained adherents, behaviorism emerged
as a successor to functionalism. Both approaches share a common
attitude toward biological continuity, and both stress the adaptive
function of behavior, but whereas functionalism was devoted to examining the *mental life* of men and animals, behaviorism is devoted to
examining their *overt activities*.

Suggested Readings

The best way to get an idea of the history of psychology is to read the
original sources. A good place to start is R. J. Herrnstein and E. G.
Boring's *A Source Book in the History of Psychology* (Cambridge,
Mass.: Harvard University Press, 1965). The material that introduces
each section is particularly illuminating. Most of the quotations in the
present volume come from selections in Herrnstein and Boring. From
the sourcebook one can go to more comprehensive original sources.

There are two classic history books of experimental psychology by
E. G. Boring: *A History of Experimental Psychology* (New York: Ap-
pleton-Century-Crofts, 1950) and *Sensation and Perception in the
History of Experimental Psychology* (New York: Appleton-Century-
Crofts, 1942). The attitude toward the history of psychology in the
present volume is basically that of Boring's two history books; the
approach in these books is to follow the history of psychology from
Descartes through the British associationists to modern psychology.
For an approach centered on studies of behavior per se, see J. R.
Kantor's *The Scientific Evolution of Psychology* (Chicago: The Princi-
pia Press, 1963–1969, 2 vols.) For a history of studies on the reflex, see
F. Fearing's *Reflex Action* (New York: Hafner, 1930). An excellent
discussion of material covered in the latter part of this chapter is
Robert Boakes's *From Darwin to Behaviorism: Psychology and the
Minds of Animals* (New York: Cambridge University Press, 1984).

The material quoted in this chapter is from the following sources:

Descartes, René. *De Homine*. Leiden: 1662. Reprinted in Herrnstein and Boring, p. 269.
Fechner, G. T. *Elemente de Psychophysik*. Leipzig: 1860. Reprinted in Herrnstein and Boring, p. 75.
Hartley, David. *Observations on Man, His Frame, His Duty, and*

His Expectations. London and Bath: 1749. Reprinted in Fearing, p. 86.

James, W. *Psychology*. New York: Holt, 1893.

Köhler, W. *The Mentality of Apes*. Translated by E. Winter. New York: Harcourt Brace, 1925.

La Mettrie, J. O. de. *L'Homme machine*. Leiden: 1748. Reprinted in Herrnstein and Boring, p. 278.

Locke, John. *An Essay Concerning Human Understanding*. London: 1690. Reprinted in Herrnstein and Boring, p. 584.

Mill, J. S. *A System of Logic, Ratiocinative and Inductive, Being a Connected View of the Principles of Evidence, and the Methods of Scientific Investigation*. London: 1843. Reprinted in Herrnstein and Boring, p. 379.

Pavlov, I. P. *Pavlov: Selected Works*. Translated by S. Belsky. Moscow: Foreign Languages Publishing House, 1955.

Prochaska, George. *De functionibus systematis nervosi*. Prague: 1784. Reprinted in Herrnstein and Boring, p. 294.

Sechenov, I. M. *Refleksy golovnogo mozga*. St. Petersburg: 1863. Reprinted in Herrnstein and Boring, p. 321.

Small, W. S. Experimental study of the mental processes of the rat. *American Journal of Psychology*, 1901, **12**, 218–220. Reprinted in Herrnstein and Boring, pp. 552–553.

2

Basic Procedures
and Techniques

The emergence of behaviorism in the early twentieth century brought fresh approaches to the question, How do animals learn? There began a series of attempts to provide a systematic and thorough answer based on behaviorist principles. American behaviorists Edwin R. Guthrie (1886–1949), Clark L. Hull (1884–1952), Edward C. Tolman (1886–1959), and B. F. Skinner (b. 1904), among others, published influential works in which they tried to identify and fit together the pieces of this subtle and complex puzzle. We shall note in passing some of their experimental methods that have contributed to the study of behavior.

In general, contemporary behaviorists tend to set aside vast theoretical questions and ask instead how a particular animal acquires a particular behavior. In their work, they make free use of one of the many methods developed by various theorists and innovators. In other words, psychologists seem to have abandoned—at least temporarily—the effort to systematize and unify their field of study; they favor piecemeal attacks on specific areas of behavior for which they use whatever tools are convenient and effective.

The aim of this chapter is to give the reader an appreciation of the basic procedures and techniques that are the essential features of modern behaviorism. We shall first discuss *classical conditioning*, and then we shall take up *instrumental conditioning*.* Finally, we shall compare these two commonly followed procedures.

CLASSICAL CONDITIONING

Pavlov's Experiments

Nearly a century ago the Russian physiologist Pavlov was studying the salivation reflex in dogs when he discovered that systematic changes in the dogs' reflexes were clearly linked to his own pattern of behavior in the laboratory. Pavlov began to study this intriguing phenomenon and subsequently produced the first empirical reports on the conditional reflex.

Pavlov had initially set out to investigate the physiology of the secretion of various fluids within the mouth and stomach. By ingenious surgical techniques he was able to implant tubes leading from various points along the dogs' digestive tracts out through the skin. Some of the fluids secreted in the digestive tracts passed into the tubes and were collected, and the amount was measured. In effect, the questions that Pavlov asked were:

1. If I give the dog some food to eat, how soon will the food, acting as a stimulus, cause the mouth and the stomach to secrete their various digestive fluids?
2. What is the mechanism that links the insertion of food into the mouth and the secretion of saliva?
3. What is the relation between the amount of food and the amount of saliva secreted?

---

*Other names for classical conditioning include *Pavlovian conditioning* and *respondent conditioning*. Instrumental conditioning is also known as *instrumental learning* and *operant conditioning*. Some psychologists distinguish between instrumental conditioning, instrumental learning, and operant conditioning on the basis of the kind of response (locomotor versus nonlocomotor) or the procedure (trial-by-trial versus continuous observation of behavior). There is more similarity than difference among these techniques, however, and we will treat them alike here under the rubric of *instrumental conditioning*.

4. As the food reaches the stomach, how long does the stomach take to secrete the acids necessary to digest the food?

Such physiological questions seemed unrelated to psychology.

However, in the course of his research Pavlov began to be plagued by an annoying phenomenon: As dogs became familiar with the experimental situation, they would often begin to salivate and secrete stomach acids as soon as Pavlov walked into the room. Pavlov called these premature secretions "psychic" secretions because he believed at first that they resulted from the dogs' psychic (mental) activity. Later he realized that these "annoyances" bore certain similarities to the physiological reflexes he had been measuring, and he decided to study them.

One of the first of Pavlov's experiments on psychic secretions is particularly instructive. After a dog takes food into its mouth, the secretion of stomach acids increases and then decreases over the course of four hours, as shown in curve (a) of Figure 2.1. This curve represents (1) whatever was secreted as a direct result of the food stimulating the stomach *plus* (2) whatever was secreted before food reached the stomach (the "psychic secretions"). Pavlov wished to measure these two components of the curve separately.

In order to plot the curve of direct secretions only, Pavlov introduced food not through the dog's mouth but directly into its stomach through a tube, called a fistula. When food was introduced through the fistula into the stomach, the gastric secretion was much less than when food was eaten in a normal way. Curve (b) in Figure 2.1 shows the amount of secretion under this special condition. This, then, represented one component of the total secretion — the secretion that followed direct stimulation of the stomach by food.

The second component of curve (a) was determined by a method call *sham-feeding*. The dog ate food in the normal way, chewing and swallowing it, but the food was removed through another fistula before reaching the stomach. Despite the fact that no food reached the stom-

---

FIGURE 2.1 Measurements of three conditions in Pavlov's historic experiment on "psychic secretion." (a) Ordinary secretion when food is placed in the dog's mouth and eaten. (b) Secretion when food is placed directly in the dog's stomach. (c) Secretion when food is placed in the dog's mouth but not allowed to reach the dog's stomach. (d) The total secretion produced by conditions (b) and (c). [Data from I. P. Pavlov, *Work of the Digestive Glands* (London: Griffin, 1910). Translated by W. H. Thompson.]

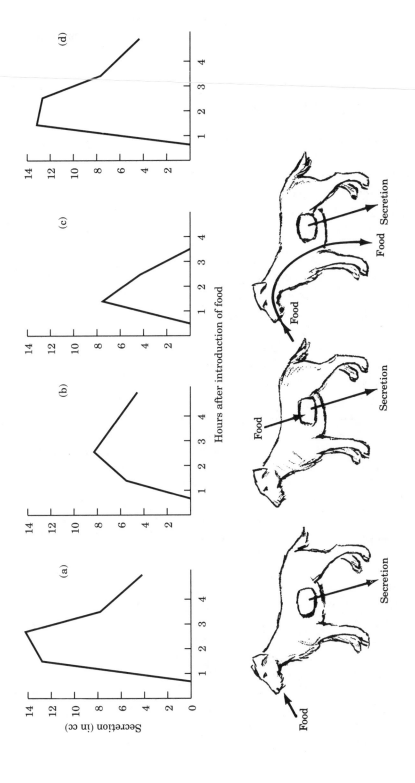

ach, there was a secretion of stomach acids as shown by curve (c). Curve (d), which is the sum of curves (b) and (c), is similar to curve (a). Thus, the experiment confirmed Pavlov's suspicion that total stomach secretion derived about equally from direct stimulation and psychic stimulation.

Now let us turn to another of Pavlov's experiments. Pavlov knew that his dogs began to salivate when they merely saw food, just as a hungry man begins to salivate when he enters a restaurant or passes a bakery. Pavlov wondered whether such premature salivation was caused only by the sight of food in particular or whether *any* stimulus, such as the sounding of a tone, would cause this premature salivation if followed often enough by actual eating.

To answer this question, Pavlov constructed the apparatus shown in Figure 2.2. A hungry dog was isolated from as many extraneous stimuli as possible. Then Pavlov struck a tuning fork, which produced a tone, and after a half-second he fed the dog. He repeated these pairings of tone and food several times, measuring salivation all the while through a tube leading from the dog's cheek to a small container. At first, the dog salivated only after the food was inserted into its mouth, but it gradually salivated earlier and earlier in the procedure, until salivation finally appeared somewhat *before* the dog was fed but after the tone. Pavlov found that such psychic secretions could be established in this manner for many kinds of stimuli.

It is important to recognize the difference between Pavlov's earlier experiment with sham-feeding and his later one with the presentation of a tone before feeding. In the first experiment, Pavlov observed a psychic secretion linked to food, a stimulus that had already been established and (for all Pavlov knew) could have been established even before the dog was born. In the second experiment, however, Pavlov observed a psychic secretion that followed a wholly new and arbitrarily chosen stimulus. This process — the forging of a connection between a new stimulus (like a tone) and an existing reflex (like salivation to food in the mouth) — Pavlov called *conditioning*.

Elements of Classical Conditioning

It is worth examining Pavlov's classical procedure more closely in order to learn the traditional nomenclature for its various elements.

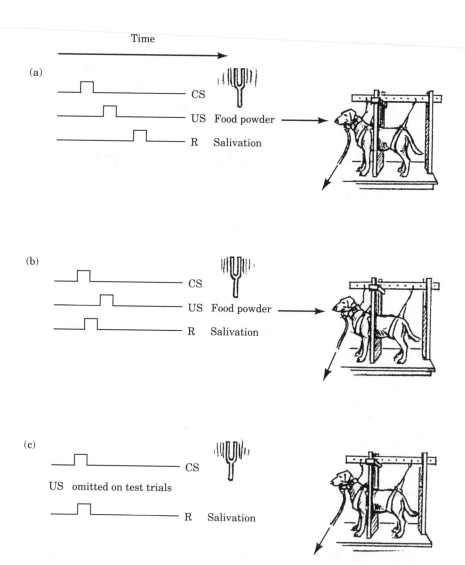

FIGURE 2.2 Classical conditioning. (a) Procedure to establish conditioning. (b) One test for conditioning: Does the response eventually precede the unconditional stimulus? (c) Another test for conditioning: Does the response occur in the absence of the unconditional stimulus? (CS = conditional stimulus; R = response; US = unconditional stimulus.)

The first necessary element is an established reflex. A reflex consists of a stimulus and a response that is reliably elicited by the stimulus. In Pavlov's experiment the response was salivation and the stimulus was the presence of food in the mouth. The stimulus part of this reflex — the presence of food in the mouth — is traditionally called the *unconditional stimulus* (US). The next requirement for classical conditioning is a neutral stimulus, anything that by itself will not cause the response before the experiment begins. This neutral stimulus is called the *conditional stimulus* (CS). Besides tones, Pavlov used lights, pictures, and other objects as CSs. Indeed, Pavlov himself became a CS for his dogs. (This was the bothersome effect that launched Pavlov's research into conditioning.) The US – response connection and the CS are the two basic components of any classical conditioning experiment. Figure 2.2 shows how they are related in time.

The result of the conditioning procedure is the *conditional reflex*. The conditional reflex in Pavlov's experiments was salivation in response to a previously neutral stimulus. Parts (b) and (c) of Figure 2.2 show two measurable effects of classical conditioning, both of which were studied by Pavlov. Part (b) shows the salivation response occurring progressively earlier until it occurs before the US; part (c) shows the occurrence of the response with the US omitted. In order for the response to occur with the US omitted, the sequence in (a) is presented repeatedly except that, according to a prearranged schedule, the US is occasionally omitted. As the experiment progresses, the usual observation is that the response without the US becomes almost but not quite as large in magnitude as the response with the US. Measurement of the effect shown in (b) emphasizes the latency of the response; measurement of the effect shown in (c) emphasizes the magnitude of the response. (As classical conditioning proceeds, one finds that the latency of the response to the CS becomes shorter and its magnitude becomes larger.)

Pavlov saw conditioning as the establishment of a new reflex by the addition of a new stimulus to the group of stimuli that are capable of triggering a response.

Classical conditioning, Pavlov believed, shed new light on the process of association. In association, as exemplified by Ebbinghaus's study with nonsense syllables, there are all the elements of classical conditioning. One syllable is presented to the subject first (the CS). Then another is presented to the subject (the US). These pairings are repeated, and finally the subject can say the name of the second syllable (the response) when he is presented with the first. Pavlov maintained that psychologists like Ebbinghaus who were studying association were really doing experiments in classical conditioning but with the stimuli and responses not as well controlled as they were in Pavlov's laboratory.*

Although Pavlov's original experiments used the secretion of saliva in response to food in a dog's mouth as the basic reflex, to which a neutral CS was attached, the classical conditioning procedure has since been carried out with many other kinds of reflexes. Mild electric shock has often been used as a US because it produces a host of measurable responses. For example, after electric shock, the rate of breathing increases, the heart rate increases, and the part of the body being shocked is withdrawn. In one experiment performed by H. S. Liddell at Cornell University, sheep were shocked briefly on the foreleg, causing them to breathe faster and deeper and also to raise the leg (even though the wires delivering the shock were attached to it). The experimenters decided to set a metronome ticking a few seconds before the shock was given. After this was done four or five times, a sheep would lift its leg and begin breathing faster as soon as the metronome started ticking. The shock was the US; the metronome ticking was the CS; the leg raising and faster breathing were responses.

The Conditional Response

Pavlov believed that the entire process of conditioning establishes a new connection in the brain, a connection between the conditional stimulus and the unconditional stimulus. After conditioning, presentation of the CS activates the representation of the US in the brain and that representation in turn activates its response (the unconditional response, or UR). Pavlov's view is called the *stimulus substitu-*

---

*Currently, even psychologists most involved in the study of mental events recognize that they must correspond to some processes in the brain. The modern discipline of *cognitive neuroscience* attempts to discover the physiological basis of such complex mental events.

tion hypothesis: The sight of a lemon reminds us of the taste of a lemon, so we salivate. This view comes down to us, through Pavlov, from the British associationists and Ebbinghaus, who asserted that the representations of the stimuli in the mind (the ideas) themselves become associated.

The fact that the conditional and unconditional stimuli now elicit a common response would only be an indication that the association of ideas has taken place. Pavlov believed that the representations of the stimuli are events in the brain, not the mind, but still the common response would be an indication that these representations had become associated.

Because the stimulus substitution hypothesis holds that the CS acts only *through* the original US, the response to the CS after conditioning (the CR) must, according to this hypothesis, be identical in quality to the original, unconditional response (UR).

Another view of classical conditioning says that something about the conditioning process causes the sight of the lemon to make us salivate — directly, not because it reminds us of the taste of a lemon. According to this second view, the conditional response may differ not only in strength but also in quality from the unconditional response; the CR may not even be similar to the UR. Often theorists who hold this view maintain that the CR differs from the UR by being preparatory. In Pavlov's salivation experiment the CR is salivation, because salivation prepares the dog for the food powder to be inserted into its mouth. As this example suggests, the *preparatory hypothesis* derives from functional psychology.

In most cases of classical conditioning, the response that prepares an animal best for the onset of the US is the same as the response to the US. For instance, an eyeblink is the response to a puff of air to the eye, and it is also the response that best prepares the animal for an oncoming puff of air if it is made before the air arrives. Salivation is the response to food powder in the mouth, and it is also the response that best prepares the animal for the presentation of food powder. Withdrawal is the response to electric shock, and it is also the response that best prepares the animal for an oncoming electric shock. All of these are common USs and Rs in experiments on classical conditioning. The response to the CS (the CR) in all of these instances is the same in form as the response to the US (the UR). Is this because the actual UR is excited by the CS, as the stimulus substitution theory would hold, or is it because the animal is preparing for the oncoming

US after being warned by the CS? The same response would be observed in either case.

In 1937 K. Zener investigated this question by conducting a conditioning experiment with dogs. Instead of restraining the dogs as Pavlov had done in his experiments, Zener let them move freely about in a cage. He presented them with periodic signals followed by food and took motion pictures of the dogs' behavior during and between the signals. he found that though the dogs' glandular response, salivation, was the same in preparation for food and in the presence of food, their motor responses were different. In preparation for food, the dogs engaged in exploratory behavior with much motor activity. In the presence of food, the dogs' behavior was confined to chewing; they did not move about. Moreover, the dogs engaged in exploration, sniffing, and barking during the signal but not in chewing. The stimulus substitution hypothesis would lead one to expect chewing, too; if the signal excites the same motor responses as the food, the dogs should chew as well as salivate during the signal.

Thus Zener's observations appear to constitute evidence against the stimulus substitution hypothesis. Until recently, however, most psychologists believed that motor responses (as opposed to autonomic responses such as salivation and the galvanic skin response) were not subject to classical conditioning techniques; consequently, Zener's findings did not seem relevant to classical conditioning. But many recent experiments have shown that classical conditioning of motor responses is possible and in some cases even easy to do. To the extent that classical conditioning is a general phenomenon, Zener's findings demonstrate its mechanisms.

The hypothesis that the CR and the UR are different has gained added support from analyses in salivary conditioning experiments showing that the chemical content of dogs' saliva during the preparatory period (when only the CS is present) is actually different from the chemical content when food is present. In heart rate conditioning, as we mentioned previously, the CR is often opposite in direction to the UR. In eyeblink conditioning as well, differences in blinking in response to the CS and US are observed. On the whole, then, the stimulus substitution hypothesis, at least in its strongest form as in Pavlov's brain model, has been disproved—the CR does not equal the UR. Whether the CR is wholly preparation for the US or whether another physiological mechanism modifies the UR to create the CR is still unknown.

Extinction

So far we have been talking about conditioning as if it were a one-way process. We have noted, for example, that by a procedure such as that shown in Figure 2.2 we can condition a dog's salivation response to a tone struck on a tuning fork. The dog salivates when it hears a tone. Is that dog then fated to salivate when it hears the tone for the rest of its life? No, it is not. Any response can be eliminated if the CS occurs a sufficient number of times without the US following. We recall that the CS was occasionally presented alone in the test trials of part (c) of Figure 2.2. However, it was isolated like an island amid a sea of conditioning trials, like those in part (a) of Figure 2.2 Suppose we arranged large blocks of trials in which the CS is always presented alone. What would happen to the response? We would find that the response would begin to decrease in magnitude so that eventually it would cease to appear. This process is called *extinction* of the response. A typical extinction curve is shown in Figure 2.3.*

The usual procedure for extinguishing a response is quite straightforward. The US is simply omitted from the normal conditioning procedure.

In order to clarify the process of extinction, let us pay an imaginary visit to Pavlov's laboratory. Suppose we bring a dog with us, one that has never been exposed to any laboratory conditioning procedure; if we prevail upon Pavlov to sound his tuning fork, our dog will not salivate. Suppose another dog, one of Pavlov's, was previously conditioned so that it salivated to a tuning fork tone but that its response was subsequently extinguished. When Pavlov sounds his tuning fork, his dog salivates as little as ours. It seems as though the conditioning of Pavlov's dog has been wiped away by the process of extinction and that no one could ever tell the two dogs apart on the basis of their behavior.

In fact, Pavlov found that he *could* distinguish between two such dogs if he presented the tone and then sounded a loud noise suddenly and unexpectedly. The dog with the extinguished response (Pavlov's,

---

*The galvanic skin response (GSR) of Figures 2.3 and 2.5 is a change in electrical resistance between one area of the skin and another. It is often measured between the front and the back of the hand (as shown in Figure 1.1). The GSR reliably follows electric shock and other painful stimuli and is frequently the measured response in classical conditioning experiments with humans.

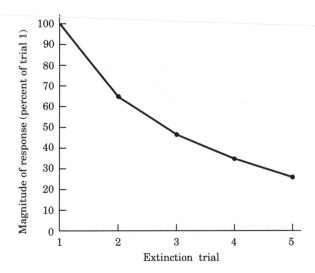

FIGURE 2.3 Typical extinction curve. Each extinction trial is a presentation of the CS (a tone) alone. In this case the curve shows the extinction of the galvanic skin response following 24 conditioning trials. Each point represents the average response of 20 human subjects. [Data replotted from C. I. Hovland, "Inhibition of reinforcement and phenomena of experimental extinction," *Proceedings of the National Academy of Sciences*, **22**, 1936, 430–433.]

in our example) would salivate, and the other dog (ours) would not. Pavlov reasoned that extinction did not eliminate conditioning but added another force equal and opposite to the force of conditioning. He called the force added by extinction an *inhibitory force*. He thought that the sudden loud noise somehow temporarily removed the inhibitory effect of extinction and allowed salivation to begin.

Pavlov had discovered that if the noise was sounded during conditioning it stopped salivation. In other words, the noise acted in the opposite direction to whichever process was going on. It could not do this if the processes of first conditioning then extinction were the same as no conditioning at all. Pavlov called the extinction process a form of *internal inhibition*. The action of the loud noise during extinction, which produced salivation, he called *disinhibition*, or the release of inhibition. The action of the loud noise during conditioning, which inhibited salivation, he called *external inhibition*.

The process of internal inhibition may be compared to a system of weights and counterweights. Imagine a weight attached to a block of wood (as in Figure 2.4) and tending to pull it toward the left (assume the weight of the scales themselves is insignificant). There are two ways to stop the block from moving toward the left. One is to cut the string or otherwise remove the weight (an analogy to wiping away conditioning). Another way is to add another weight on the other side

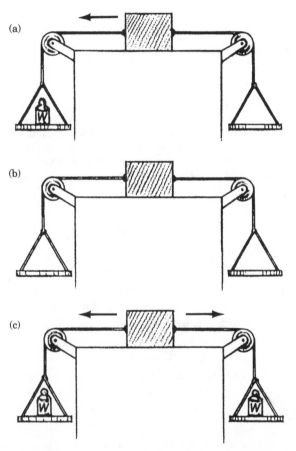

FIGURE 2.4 This system of weights shows how extinction might operate as either a negative or a positive process. (a) If conditioning is seen as the pull of a weight, extinction can be either (b) a negative process that simply removes the weight or (c) a positive process that adds a new weight to the system to counterbalance the effect of conditioning.

(an analogy to a force of inhibition). Both procedures produce a stationary block (extinction). If the weights and scales are hidden from view, how can you tell which system applies? You can distinguish between conditions (b) and (c) in Figure 2.4 by cutting one of the strings (an analogy to the disinhibitory effect of the loud noise). If this is done to the apparatus shown in (b), nothing will happen to the block. But if it is done to the apparatus in (c), the block will suddenly move in one direction (this is analogous to the reappearance of the response).

Generalization and Discrimination

There is bound to be some *generalization* when a new pattern of behavior is acquired. For instance, if a dog's behavior is modified in a laboratory so that the dog salivates when it hears a tone sounded by a tuning fork, another tone slightly higher or lower in pitch will also make it salivate. Generalization is also evidenced when a child, sometimes to the embarrassment of her parents, calls every man she meets "Daddy." Of course, the child will eventually learn to reserve the name "Daddy" for her male parent. When this occurs, we say she has learned to make a *discrimination*.

Let us consider an experiment performed in the United Sates in 1934 on the generalization of a classically conditioned response. The GSR (galvanic skin response) was conditioned in a group of college students; the US in the experiment was mild electric shock and the CS was a vibrating instrument applied to the skin. For some subjects the instrument was applied to the shoulder and for others to the calf. As training progressed, the amount of GSR measured on test trials (when the CS was presented without the shock) was seen to increase. Then, on later test trials, the instrument was occasionally applied at places on the skin *other* than where conditioning was originally established. The farther away from the original skin site that the instrument was applied on these later test trials, the weaker the response. Figure 2.5 shows the magnitude of the response as a function of the distance from the original point of application. The kind of curve shown in Figure 2.5 is called a *generalization gradient*.*

---

*The specific spot at which the vibrating stimulus was applied was not important in determining the gradient; what was important was the distance from the site of the original CS.

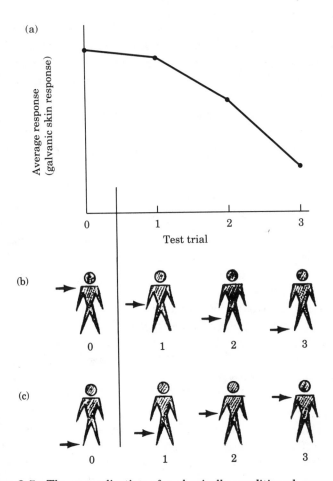

FIGURE 2.5 The generalization of a classically conditioned response. (a) The decline of a galvanic skin response to vibration as the vibration is moved farther from the original site of conditioning. (b) Some subjects were initially conditioned on the shoulder. (c) Some subjects were initially conditioned on the ankle. [Data from M. J. Bass and C. L. Hull, "The irradiation of a tactile conditioned reflex in man," *Journal of Comparative Psychology*, 1934, **17**, 47–65.]

Generalization gradients like the one in Figure 2.5 are by no means unalterable. Suppose we have set of similar stimuli, only one of which we want to be a CS. Suppose that even though we use only the desired stimulus as the CS in a classical conditioning experiment, we find that the subject generalizes and responds to the other stimuli, too.

How can we eliminate responses to these other stimuli but retain responses to the one we want to be a CS? We may try alternating conditioning trials that contain both the desired CS and the US with extinction trials that contain no US—only the unwanted stimuli. Our hope is that the animal will learn to discriminate the particular stimulus to which we want it to respond from the unwanted stimuli. This procedure works—but, significantly, it works only up to a point.

We know Pavlov's view that extinction is an active process of inhibition, not just a matter of wiping away old conditions but more like adding counterweights to a hypothetical system of weights (Figure 2.4). Keeping this in mind, consider the following a experiment, performed by one of Pavlov's students, Shenger-Krestovnikova. She trained dogs to salivate by a method similar to Pavlov's except that instead of a tone she used a circle drawn on a card as the CS. She found that after the salivation response had been conditioned in the presence of a circle, the response generalized to the extent that the dogs would also salivate when they saw an ellipse, like those in Figure 2.6. In order to condition discrimination between (a) and (b), (a) was presented with the US and (b) was presented without the US. Following this procedure, the dogs would salivate in response to (a) but not in response to (b). Then the same procedure was repeated with (a) and (c), then (a) and (d)—(d) being an ellipse very much like the circle.

According to Pavlov, this is what happened when (a) and (d) were discriminated:

In this case, although a considerable degree of discrimination did develop, it was far from being complete. After three weeks of work

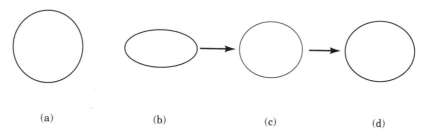

(a)   (b)   (c)   (d)

FIGURE 2.6 Shenger-Krestovnikova's stimuli. Dogs were conditioned to respond to a circle (a). Their responses to an ellipse (b) were extinguished. As the ellipse was gradually changed to look more like a circle, as in (c) and (d), the dogs' ability to discriminate broke down, and, in Pavlov's words, their behavior "presented all the symptoms of acute neurosis."

upon this differentiation not only did the discrimination fail to improve, but it became considerably worse, and finally disappeared
altogether. At the same time the whole behaviour of the animal
underwent an abrupt change. The hitherto quiet dog began to squeal
in its stand, kept wriggling about, tore off with its teeth the apparatus
for mechanical stimulation of the skin, and bit through the tubes
connecting the animal's room with the observer, a behaviour which
never happened before. On being taken into the experimental room
the dog now barked violently, which was also contrary to its usual
custom; in short it presented all the symptoms of acute neurosis. On
testing the cruder differentiations they were also found to be destroyed. [Pavlov, 1927/1960, p. 291]

One cannot help but draw a parallel to the behavior of humans
when they are required to perform for long periods of time at the limit
of their discriminative capacities. Humans can make just so many
discriminations until, like Pavlov's dogs, or rather like those of
Shenger-Krestovnikova, they start making mistakes and are unable to
perform tasks that were previously easy for them. In extreme cases
they may develop the "symptoms of acute neurosis" to which Pavlov
referred.

INSTRUMENTAL CONDITIONING

The Law of Effect

In 1898, Thorndike laid the groundwork for a simple but important
principle, which he named the "law effect." Here is a paraphrase of his
principle: One effect of a successful behavior is to increase the probability that it will occur again in similar circumstances. Thorndike
based this conclusion on experiments in which cats, dogs, and chicks
were repeatedly confined in puzzle boxes like the one shown in Figure
2.7. In order to escape from the box and get the food that was within
view, the hungry animal had to step on a lever, pull out a bolt, or
perform some other mechanical task. Thorndike found that the animal would eventually make the correct movement and get out of the
box. He measured the latency of the correct movement — how long it
took the animal to escape — and continued to measure latency for each
successive trial. Thorndike found that, in general, there was a negative

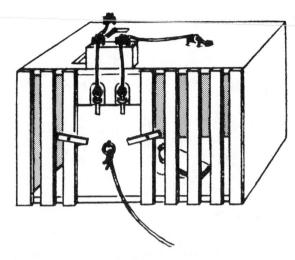

FIGURE 2.7 Thorndike's puzzle box. Cats that were placed inside this box learned to unbolt the door and then press the door outward to escape. [From E. L. Thorndike, *Animal Intelligence* (New York: Macmillan, 1911).]

correlation between the number of times an animal had escaped from the box and the length of time it took to escape — the more trials, the less time to escape. After many repeated trials, the animal would solve the puzzle and get out of the box almost immediately. The graphs in Figure 2.8 show how latency decreased with repeated trials.

Thorndike's puzzle box experiments were comprised of the following steps: (1) The experimenter provided a stimulus to the animal and observed the animal's behavior in its presence. (2) If the behavior was "appropriate," in the sense that it conformed to criteria set by the experimenter, he rewarded the animal. (3) This, in turn, increased the likelihood of the behavior recurring and producing more rewards. (In this sense, a reward to the organism is said to *reinforce* its behavior.) Today, Thorndike's experimental procedure is considered a major variant of *instrumental conditioning*, so called to distinguish it from Pavlov's classical conditioning procedure.

It is important to realize the purpose of the highly artificial situation in which Thorndike put his animals. He believed that the law of effect was not limited to such artificial situations but was a general law of nature. In his view the environment usually sets the conditions

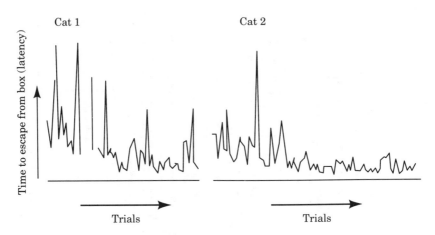

FIGURE 2.8 These two curves show the performances of two cats in Thorndike's box. [From E. L. Thorndike, *Animal Intelligence* (New York: Macmillan, 1911).]

of the puzzle for individual animals. Thorndike reasoned that a fox learns how to enter a barnyard in the same way that a cat learns to get out of a puzzle box. The reason Thorndike built his puzzle box was to isolate the phenomenon of learning and measure its progress. The conditions he set in the laboratory were meant to parallel the conditions of the environment but be less complicated. If the puzzle box seems to be an artificial way to study behavior, we should remember that all experiments are inherently artificial because they isolate from the complexity of the environment those particular variables that are of interest to the experimenter.

Much as the physicist prefers to work with an approximation to a vacuum when studying the behavior of falling bodies, thereby eliminating air resistance, Thorndike tried to isolate the mechanism of the influence of reward by removing environmental distractions.

The early experiments of Thorndike are important for many of the same reasons as are the early experiments of Ebbinghaus, which we discussed in the first chapter. Unlike the casual observations of their predecessors, the experiments of Ebbinghaus and Thorndike were systematic enough to be replicable. Their experiments have been repeated; as long as the same procedures have been followed, similar results have always been obtained.

Kinds of Instrumental Conditioning

There are four basic procedures used in instrumental conditioning, all of which are related to the evolution of individual behaviors. In capsule form, we can describe the four procedures as *reinforcement, punishment, negative reinforcement,* and *negative punishment.*

1. In the *reinforcement* procedure (also called *positive reinforcement* or *reward*), an act is followed by a positively valued stimulus or event. Thorndike's law of effect stated that positive reinforcement would increase the probability of the act.
2. In the *punishment* procedure (also called *positive punishment*), an act is followed by a negatively valued stimulus or event. Thorndike had also postulated a "negative law of effect," which stated that punishment would decrease the probability of the act.
3. In the *negative reinforcement* procedure (also called *escape*), an act is followed by the removal of a negatively valued stimulus or event. Negative reinforcement generally increases the probability of the act. For example, Thorndike found that his cats would often learn to solve the puzzle in the box even when they were not fed afterwards. In other words, they learned to escape confinement.
4. In the *negative punishment* procedure (also called *omission*), an act is followed by the removal of a positively valued stimulus. Like positive punishment, negative punishment tends to decrease the probability of the act.

Figure 2.9 is a diagram showing basic relationships among the four kinds of instrumental conditioning. (In Chapter 3, when we discuss the aversive control of behavior, we shall have something to say about which of these methods can best be used in a given situation to increase or decrease the occurrence of various kinds of behavior.)

CLASSICAL AND INSTRUMENTAL CONDITIONING COMPARED

How are classical conditioning and instrumental conditioning related? No definitive answer to this question is generally accepted by modern behaviorists. Without going into the details of the theoretical disputes

	Stimulus presented	Stimulus removed
Positively valued stimulus	Reinforcement	Negative punishment
Negatively valued stimulus	Punishment	Negative reinforcement

FIGURE 2.9 Four basic kinds of instrumental conditioning are classified by the consequences of a specific act. For example, if a specific act is followed by the presentation of a positively valued stimulus (a reward), the instrumental conditioning is classified as (positive) reinforcement.

in this area, we can observe that classical conditioning and instrumental conditioning are two closely related but distinguishable phenomena.

Differences between classical and instrumental conditioning experiments can be found in the animal's influence on reinforcement and in the classification of the behavior by the experimenter.

The Animal's Influence on Reinforcement

Let us take food as an example of a reinforcer. In a classical conditioning experiment, the animal's influence on the appearance of food is negligible. The experimenter decides the time for the delivery of food. By contrast, instrumental conditioning experiments are arranged so that the animal can produce food by a particular response. In Pavlov's experiments, food was presented on each trial regardless of what the animal did. If one of Pavlov's dogs had been trained with food withheld until salivation occurred, the classical conditioning experiment would have been transformed into an instrumental conditioning experiment.

If we consider the animal to be a single unitary system, we find that there are three elements in both the classical and instrumental conditioning procedures that cross the boundary of this system. (See Figure 2.10.) Because the US in classical conditioning and the reward in instrumental conditioning are corresponding elements, they share a common name—reinforcement. In both procedures the presence of reinforcement determines conditioning and its absence serves to define extinction. (In instrumental conditioning, we speak of the animal as being rewarded and of the response as being reinforced. We say, "The dog was rewarded for opening the latch" or "The latch-opening response of the dog was reinforced," not "The dog was reinforced" or "The response was rewarded."). When reinforcement is mentioned in connection with classical conditioning, the speaker is referring to the US. Thus, in classical conditioning, an unreinforced trial may be either a test trial, as in Figure 2.2b, or part of a block of extinction trials.

Whether reinforcement in classical conditioning functions similarly to reinforcement in instrumental conditioning is a question about which there is some dispute. Although Figure 2.10, which shows the animal as a system, reveals a similarity with respect to the inputs and outputs of the system, the difference between the two methods lies in the interaction between the animal and conditions in its environment.

Figure 2.11 shows the system in Figure 2.10 with the environment also diagrammed. The difference between the two parts of Figure 2.11 is the dotted feedback loop in the instrumental conditioning diagram. In classical conditioning, the temporal relation between the CS and US is determined by the experimenter in advance, and nothing the subject does will change it. In instrumental conditioning, on the other hand, reinforcement occurs only after the response is made.

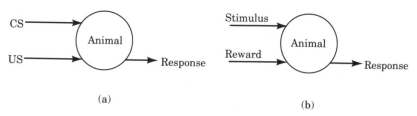

FIGURE 2.10 Inputs to and outputs from the animal in (a) classical conditioning and (b) instrumental conditioning.

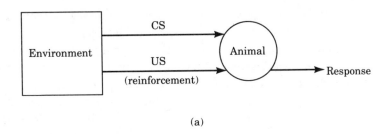

(a)

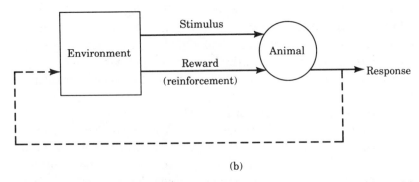

(b)

FIGURE 2.11 Interaction between the animal and its environment in (a) classical conditioning and (b) instrumental conditioning.

In some early experiments on conditioning this critical difference was not realized. Consider the two experiments diagrammed in Figure 2.12. In both experiments, a tuning fork is sounded and electric shock is delivered to the dog's paw. In one case, the circuit is arranged so that lifting the paw does not break the circuit; in the other, lifting the paw does break the circuit. The procedure shown at the bottom of the figure is instrumental conditioning: The subject's behavior here serves to determine the presence or absence of the shock. The procedure sketched at the top is classical conditioning: The subject's behavior has no effect on the shock, but the pairing between the tuning fork stimulus, the shock, and the withdrawal of the leg is always maintained.

We discussed extinction previously in relation to classical conditioning. Extinction consisted in eliminating the US (the reinforcer).

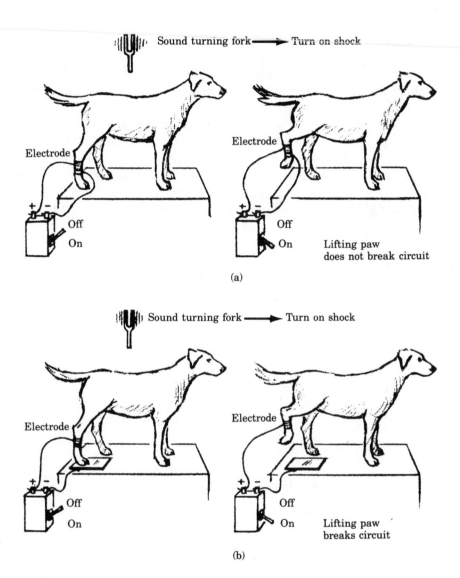

FIGURE 2.12 The difference between (a) classical conditioning and (b) instrumental conditioning illustrated by a minor change in an electric-shock circuit.

Extinction in instrumental conditioning also consists in eliminating the reinforcer. In order to extinguish an instrumentally conditioned response, we stop rewarding the animal for making the response. The results are the same for classical and instrumental conditioning—the probability that the response will recur decreases.

We have spoken of the *probabilities* that responses will recur. One difference between classical and instrumental conditioning can be seen in the different contingencies involved. A contingency is a set of conditional probabilities, the probability that, given one event, another event will occur. A contingency table that could apply to a classical conditioning experiment is shown in part (a) of Figure 2.13. It

(a)

	US	No US
Presence of CS	1.0	0
Absence of CS	0	1.0

(b)

	Reinforcement	No Reinforcement
Presence of response	1.0	0
Absence of response	0	1.0

(c)

	Elevator arrives within 2 minutes	Elevator doesn't arrive within 2 minutes
Button pushed	.8	.2
Button not pushed	.4	.6

FIGURE 2.13 Contingency tables for (a) a standard classical conditioning experiment, (b) a standard instrumental conditioning experiment, and (c) elevator arrivals versus button pushing. The values in the tables are conditional probabilities. In (c), for instance, .8 is the probability that a certain elevator will arrive within 2 minutes of pressing the button.

shows that when the CS is presented, the probability of the US is 1.0; when the CS is absent, the probability of the US is zero — that is, the US (the reinforcer) is completely dependent on the CS. With instrumental conditioning the contingency set by the experimenter is between the response and the reinforcer. The table in part (b) Figure 2.13 says that when a response is made, the probability of reinforcement is 1.0; when no response is made, the probability of reinforcement is zero — that is, reinforcement is completely dependent on the response. The reinforcer is omitted during extinction of both kinds of conditioning; in extinction, all the numbers in the left column of the table would be zero and all the numbers in the right column would be unity.

One advantage of this way of formulating the two types of conditioning is that other nonzero and nonunity values may be put in the table and their effect on conditioning studied. In everyday life we rarely find the complete dependencies shown in parts (a) and (b) of Figure 2.13. Responding that usually produces reinforcement sometimes fails to work, and nonresponding that usually fails to produce reinforcement sometimes produces reinforcement. Occasionally pushing the button and waiting fails to bring an elevator, and occasionally elevators arrive without any button pushing at all. The contingency of elevator arrivals on button pushing might be as shown in Figure 2.13c. Clearly, pushing a button makes elevator arrivals more probable but by no means certain.

Classifying Behavior

The ever-changing pattern of acts that comprise an animal's behavior are sometimes analyzed into relatively large chunks (like sleeping, resting, and eating) and sometimes into relatively small bits (like heartbeats, breaths, blinks, and nerve impulses). Obviously, there is no single correct way to classify behavior. How one classifies the behavior of a particular animal depends largely on one's point of view and on the degree of one's interest in the animal.

For most of us, a person's eye movements during sleep is a detail scarcely worthy of note; we are content with the observation that the person seems to be asleep. On the other hand, if we were studying the nature of sleep, we might attempt to keep a careful record of such bits of behavior, and eye movements and other muscular spasms might turn out to be significant classifications of behavior for our study.

If we observe someone, say a businessman, for a considerable period, how should we group the events we observe? Our businessman is always doing something — always breathing, for instance. Will that form an important part of our description? Should we describe in detail the nervous mechanism involved in each breath? Or should we ignore his breathing entirely and concentrate on molar actions, like his work or his eating? We also face the problem that at any given time our subject may be doing *many* things — breathing, writing, working, earning money, digesting his food, advancing his career, biting his upper lip, blinking, hoping, thinking, and sitting.

Consider how different observers might describe what the businessman did in a single day. Some descriptions might be relatively molecular in the sense that they go into some detail about bits of his behavior. Some might be more molar in the sense that they divide his behavior into relatively large chunks, but all could be fairly consistent and reasonable ways to look at what he is doing. The businessman's associates may describe his behavior in terms of his business activities. His wife may describe his behavior in terms of his domestic activities. His doctor, his insurance agent, his banker will each have a particular outlook. Each will describe the behavior of the man in terms of his or her interest in the man.

As psychologists, though, where do *we* draw the line? How can we bring some organization to this complex ongoing process? (Indeed, how shall we classify *all* the possible behaviors of *all* possible animals?) If we are interested in the *modification of behavior*, then we must find a way to classify behavior in terms of its modifiability.

We have described two methods of modifying behavior — classical conditioning and instrumental conditioning. What do they tell us about how to classify the businessman's behavior (and behavior in general)? Figure 2.14 shows how the contingencies of reinforcement in the two methods aid in classifying behavior.

In classical conditioning, reinforcement is the presentation of an unconditional stimulus that invariably elicits a response Thus, responses in classical conditioning must be grouped into a class, or category, on the basis of their common elicitation by a certain type of stimulus. (The stimulus thus defines the category.) As our hypothetical businessman goes through his day, some of the things he does fall into such stimulus-defined categories.

For instance, when a light is turned on, the man's pupils contract, and there is some electrical activity in the cortex of his brain. When he

(a)

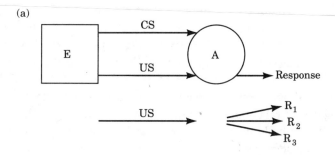

(b)

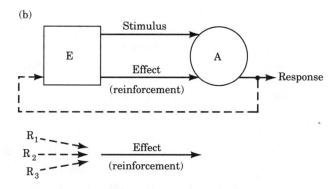

FIGURE 2.14 Classification of behavior according to classical conditioning and instrumental conditioning. (a) Classical conditioning. Any acts that are invariably elicited by a single stimulus can be grouped together. Thus we can identify "leg withdrawal following electric shock" and distinguish it, as a category, from other muscular movements. (b) Instrumental conditioning. Any acts that produce the same effect can be grouped together. Such a category is called an *operant*. An operant could include such diverse actions as pressing an elevator button with one's thumb, one's forefinger, or one's elbow or even asking another person to press the button—in short, any action that moves the button. (E = experimenter or environment; A = animal.)

hears a sudden loud noise, he withdraws from it, shows increased heart rate, and a group of other measurable phenomena. Each stimulus has a set of behavioral and physiological responses that follow it. With respect to classical conditioning, *the group of measurable phenomena elicited by a particular stimulus are classified together as the response to that stimulus.* Only a limited set of responses, however, can be so classified. Most of the man's behavior, especially that part that appears to be "voluntary," cannot be elicited by any particular stimulus. The techniques of classical conditioning are difficult to apply to such behavior. For instance, if our businessman were head of a construction company engaged in building a dam, we would be hard put to find any unconditional stimulus that elicited the behavior of dam building in the businessman.* Psychologists who are interested in classical conditioning do not talk about the response of dam building. If they want to describe dam building at all in terms of classically conditioned behavior, they must break the entire process down into smaller responses such as the movements of certain muscles, which are unconditionally elicited by known stimuli or which may be conditionally elicited. (As we said before, CRs may differ from URs.)

In instrumental conditioning, on the other hand, we need not limit ourselves only to behavior known to be elicited by certain stimuli. We are free to work with any behavior that the animal will emit. The only requirement is that we be able to measure the behavior so as to reward or punish the animal when the behavior is emitted. The dam building of our businessman can be measured, and reinforcement can be programmed for it. Dam building is thus a legitimate category of behavior for instrumental conditioning.

In order to measure a given class of behavior, all the members of that class must have some common environmental effect. For instance, all dam-building behavior must potentially result in a completed dam. The businessman's contract, which determines the conditions of his reward, sets forth only specifications of the completed dam. How the dam is built is up to the businessman. There might be an infinite number of ways in which this contract could be fulfilled. Similarly, an experimenter might be training a rat to press a bar. The experimenter programs reinforcement for bar-pressing but does not specify how the bar must be pressed. The rat may press the bar with its left paw, its right paw, its head, or its tail or in an infinite number of other ways. What these infinite different actions of the rat have in common is that they all change a certain portion of the environment in the same way — they all succeed in moving the bar through a certain angle, and they all may produce reward.

Any class of behavior that produces such a common effect on the environment is called an *operant*. The term was coined by the Ameri-

---

*However, in the case of certain animals like the beaver, dam building may be an innate pattern of behavior that can be elicited by certain stimuli.

can psychologist B. F. Skinner, who first proposed that instrumental behavior consists of *emitted* acts, which are classified according to their effect on the environment (as opposed to classically conditioned behavior, which consists of elicited acts, which are classified according to the stimulus that elicits them). In this chapter, we shall deal with several operants, including bar-pressing, key-pecking, door opening, the breaking of photocell beams, and even running from one place to another. All are operants in the sense that they are categories that describe an infinite set of individual acts that have a common effect on the environment.

Classical and Instrumental Conditioning in the Same Experiment

In a given situation, both classical and instrumental responses may be reinforced simultaneously. In other words, response A may be required to produce the reinforcer, and response B may be elicited by the very same reinforcer.

An experiment by Gaylord D. Ellison and Jerzy Konorski produced classical and instrumental conditioning with the same reinforcer and studied the two kinds of responses separately. In this experiment a dog was trained to press a lever while a light was on in order to produce a buzzer (CS) followed by food (not food directly). The experimenters could measure both lever-presses and salivation during the light and during the CS. When the light was introduced, the dog had to press the lever nine times. This turned off the light and produced the buzzer. Eight seconds later the food was automatically dispensed.

This somewhat complicated procedure enabled Ellison and Konorski to measure rates of salivation (classically conditioned) and bar-pressing (instrumentally conditioned) separately. First, they measured salivation and bar-pressing before all of the nine presses were made. (At this point, bar-pressing was the appropriate response, since it was required to produce the reinforcer.) Second, they measured salivation and bar-pressing after the nine presses were made (and after the CS was presented) but *before* the US (food) was presented. By then bar-presses had no effect, but the CS produced salivation.

Figure 2.15 shows their results. Bar-presses, the instrumental responses, were high during the light and low during the buzzer; salivation was high during the buzzer and low during the light. Thus,

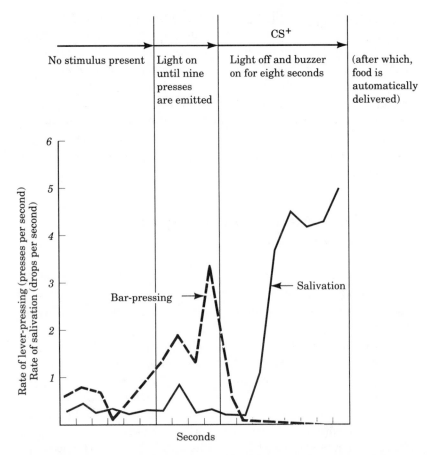

FIGURE 2.15 An instrumentally conditioned behavior (bar-pressing) and a classically conditioned behavior (salivation) occurring simultaneously in the same experiment. [Data from G. D. Ellison and J. Konorski, "Separation of the salivary and motor responses in instrumental conditioning," *Science*, 1964, **146**, 1071–1072. Copyright 1964 by American Association for the Advancement of Science.]

within a single experimental situation, both classical and instrumental responses can be measured separately and made to occur at maximum rate at different times depending on the conditioning procedure that generated them.

Stimuli in Classical and Instrumental Conditioning

In Figures 2.10 and 2.11 there are arrows labeled "Stimulus" in the instrumental procedure corresponding to the arrow labeled CS in the classical procedure. In instrumental conditioning, this stimulus is called a *discriminative stimulus*. In discussing classical conditioning, we spoke of the CS as eliciting a response; in discussing instrumental conditioning, where responses are supposed to be emitted, we cannot speak of a discriminative stimulus as eliciting a response. Instead, following the usage of B. F. Skinner, we say that the discriminative stimulus *sets the occasion* for the response to occur. For instance, a green traffic light (a discriminative stimulus) sets the occasion for crossing the street but does not elicit street crossing. In the Ellison–Konorski experiment, the light is a discriminative stimulus and sets the occasion for bar-pressing while the buzzer is a conditional stimulus and is said to elicit salivation.

Many theorists have claimed that there is only one kind of conditioning. Those who have said that all conditioning boils down to classical conditioning have claimed that discriminative stimuli are really conditional stimuli; those who have said that all conditioning boils down to instrumental conditioning (for example, those who maintain that the CR is a preparatory response that is instrumental in enhancing the positive value or ameliorating the negative value of the oncoming US) have claimed that conditional stimuli are really discriminative stimuli. We shall have much more to say about the role of conditional and discriminative stimuli in Chapters 5 and 6. However, the arguments among people who would reduce one basic type of conditioning to the other are beyond the scope of this book. We therefore retain the two separate concepts — classical conditioning and instrumental conditioning.

Anatomical Correlates of Classical and Instrumental Conditioning

Psychologists formerly believed that classical and instrumental conditioning were distinguishable by the part of the nervous system in which they can act. Classical conditioning is said to work better with autonomic functions such as glandular secretions, and instrumental conditioning is said to work better with nonautonomic responses such as muscular movements. Ellison and Konorski's experiment provides an example of this distinction. The classical component was autonomic (salivation), while the instrumental component was muscular (lever-pressing).

These anatomical boundaries, however, have been crossed many times. Classical conditioning experiments have been performed with muscular responses such as blinking, and Neil Miller and his students at Rockefeller University have instrumentally conditioned autonomic responses. For instance, when an animal whose heart rate is being measured is given reward (feedback) only when its heart rate varies within a certain range, the heart rate tends to stay within that range more than it does if rewards are delivered randomly. Apparently, the characteristic of autonomic behavior that normally makes instrumental conditioning difficult is lack of feedback to the behaving animal.

This area of research holds practical promise, since it implies that people can learn to keep blood pressure, stomach acidity, and so forth at nonharmful levels provided they have feedback informing them of the state of these autonomic functions. This is the goal of the emerging field of biofeedback, which uses electronic devices to enhance awareness and control of physiological processes.

PSEUDOCONDITIONING

Pseudoconditioning in Classical Experiments

Suppose we select a CS and a US and, after pairing them and testing the results as shown in Figure 2.2, find that the unconditional response is now elicited by the CS. Can we safely assume that conditioning has taken place? Unfortunately, no. In some cases, the US presentation may change the state of the animal so that the CS produces the response by itself without any necessary connection to the US. Consider, for example, an experiment using electric shock as the US and a vibratory tactile stimulus as the CS (see Figure 2.16). First vibrations are applied to one hand of a human subject. No effect is found. Then vibrations are paired with shock to the hand, and we observe a withdrawal of the hand. Then vibrations are applied alone, and again the hand is withdrawn. Is this effect the result of classical conditioning? The test is to get another subject, apply electric shock alone (unpaired with vibrations), then apply vibrations alone, and see if the hand is now withdrawn. If it is, we can be fairly sure that the shock merely made the hand more sensitive to the vibrations and that we did not observe classical conditioning in the first subject.

A critical test of classically conditioned behavior is to determine whether the *relation between the CS and US* is necessary to produce

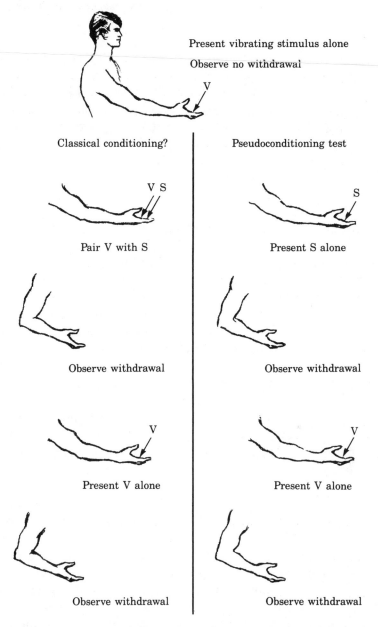

FIGURE 2.16 An example of a test for pseudoconditioning. If the results of these two procedures (left and right) are withdrawals similar in latency and extent, then it is possible that none of the withdrawals is a classically conditioned response. However, if there is no withdrawal after the test procedure (bottom right) even though there is a withdrawal after the classical conditioning procedure (bottom left), then the response at bottom left is a genuine classically conditioned response. In this case, V stands for a vibration and S stands for a shock.

the behavior. When we perform a classical conditioning experiment and observe what appears to be a conditional response but then find that the relation between the CS and US is not necessary to produce that response, we have merely observed *pseudoconditioning*. It is always important to test classical conditioning experiments to see if they can be explained on the basis of pseudoconditioning. Figure 2.16 shows the sequence of the pseudoconditioning test.

Pseudoconditioning in Instrumental Experiments

Consider the following hypothetical experiment. The experimenter puts a rat in a chamber, which has a bar protruding into it. Eventually, the rat, in the course of its normal movements about the chamber, will press the bar. When this happens the experimenter injects the rat with the drug adrenalin. This drug causes increased activity. The rat now moves more vigorously about the chamber. Because of this vigorous movement the rat hits against the bar sooner than before and the experimenter records a reduced latency of bar-pressing. After the second press, the experimenter again injects the rat with adrenalin, causing still more movement and hence an even faster rate of bar-presses. This continues until the rat is exhausted. Can we say that adrenalin is rewarding to the rat and that we have here a genuine case of instrumental conditioning of the bar-press response? We cannot until we have tested for pseudoconditioning.

How can we perform such a test? In order to test for pseudoconditioning we have to find out whether the same response would occur without the critical element, the relation between response and reward. In the case of the rat and the adrenalin, it would be easy to prove that adrenalin was not instrumentally conditioning bar-presses. We would merely take another rat and place it in an identical chamber. This time we would ignore the bar and just inject the rat periodically with adrenalin. Here no systematic relation of injections and bar-pressing would be established. If this rat's rate of pressing increased as much as the first rat's, we could assume that the increase in pressing we observed for the first rat was not a result of the pairing of responses with reinforcement but merely an artifact of the adrenalin itself. This, then, would be a case of pseudoconditioning.

THE HOW AND THE WHY OF BEHAVIOR

The basic concepts of conditioning have been introduced in this chapter in an historical context. It is time now to relate that history to modern behaviorism. Since the time of Pavlov and Thorndike, behaviorists have gradually come to abandon the concept of the *reflex* — the fundamental theoretical conception that tied these psychologists together in the first place as behaviorists. Both Pavlov and Thorndike believed that reinforcement acted to strengthen an internal stimulus – response connection — a reflex in the brain. But even as early as 1896 the American functionalist philosopher John Dewey (1859 – 1952) pointed out the oversimplicity of this conception.

Modern behaviorists generally agree that the main object of their interest is behavior itself (the *what* of behavior). But the underlying question typically addressed by modern followers of Pavlov differs from the one typically addressed by modern followers of Thorndike. Modern students of classical conditioning have abandoned the simple concept of reflex strength to focus on the *internal mechanisms* underlying behavior. Given that an animal behaves in a certain way, they want to know *how* that behavior comes about. Like Pavlov, they are interested in the antecedents of the behavior in question, but their conception of those antecedents (as the interaction of internal mechanisms) is much more complex than was Pavlov's. As we will see in later chapters, modern theories of classical conditioning are broader and therefore more applicable to everyday life problems than was Pavlov's theory. Recently Robert Rescorla, one of the most prominent of the many behaviorists studying classical conditioning, pointed out that the internal mechanisms underlying classical conditioning are similar to those thought by modern cognitive psychologists to underlie higher mental processes.*

Modern students of instrumental conditioning, led by B. F. Skinner, have also abandoned the simple concept of reflex strength to focus on the *external contingencies* governing behavior. Given that an animal behaves in a certain way, they want to know *why* it does so. Like Thorndike, they are interested in the consequences of the behavior in

---

*In a more advanced text by the author (see Suggested Readings), some cognitive models are explored in detail.

question, but their conception of those consequences (as a set of contingencies) is much more complex than was Thorndike's.

The remainder of this book will attempt to trace the development of these two lines of thought, one which asks *how* behavior occurs and looks to an internal mechanism for an answer, the other which asks *why* behavior occurs and looks to an environmental contingency for an answer. Obviously, both questions are valid. And, perhaps less obviously, answers to one question can throw light upon the other.

Suggested Readings

There are excellent translations of Pavlov's works that are easy to read and ought to be fully comprehensible to beginning students. I. P. Pavlov's *Conditioned Reflexes*, originally published in English in 1927 by Oxford University Press, is available as a paperback (New York: Dover, 1960).

The quotations from Locke, Mill and other historical figures were taken from R. J. Herrnstein and E. G. Boring (Editors) *A Source Book in the History of Psychology* (Cambridge, MA: Harvard University Press, 1965).

A comparison of instrumental and classical conditioning can be found in G. A. Kimble's *Hilgard and Marquis' Conditioning and Learning*. 2nd ed. (New York: Appleton-Century-Crofts, 1960) and in N. J. Mackintosh's *The Psychology of Animal Learning* (New York: Academic Press, 1974).

The best way to find out about a theoretical outlook is to read the original source. Here are some works by behavioral theorists:

Guthrie, E. R. *The Psychology of Learning*. Rev. ed. New York: Harper & Row, 1952

Hull, C. L. *A Behavior System: An Introduction to Behavior Theory Concerning the Individual Organism*. New Haven: Yale University Press, 1952.

Skinner, B. F. *The Behavior of Organisms: An Experimental Analysis*. New York: Appleton-Century-Crofts, 1938.

Skinner, B. F. *Science and Human Behavior*. New York: Macmillan, 1953.

Tolman, E. C. *Purposive Behavior in Animals and Man*. New York: Appleton-Century-Crofts, 1932.

The experiment of Ellison and Konorski that used classical and instrumental conditioning together may be found in G. D. Ellison and

J. Konorski's article "Separation of the salivary and motor responses in instrumental conditioning" (*Science*, 1964, **146** (No. 3647), 1071–1072). Konorski has also written a book about conditioning from a physiological viewpoint called *Integrative Activity of the Brain* (Chicago: University of Chicago Press, 1967).

Other works referred to in this chapter are:

Dewey, J. The reflex arc concept in psychology. *Psychological Review*, 1896, **3**, 357–370.

Rachlin, H. *Judgment, Decision and Choice: A Cognitive/Behavioral Synthesis*. New York: W. H. Freeman, 1989.

Rescorla, R. A. Pavlovian conditioning: It's not what you think it is. *American Psychologist*, 1988, **43**, 151–160.

3

Reinforcement and Punishment

One of the principal functions of science is to make valid predictions. Astronomers predict positions of heavenly bodies, physicists predict the behavior of physical objects; chemists predict the products of various combinations of elements. Science, to be meaningful, must go beyond the explanation of events after they have happened and make predictions about future events.

Since the very heart of the instrumental conditioning process is reinforcement, psychologists have concerned themselves with predicting whether a given stimulus will reinforce a given behavior. We have been talking loosely about positive reinforcers such as food for hungry animals or water for thirsty animals, but we have not specified any characteristic that food and water have in common to make them reinforcing. If we knew what this characteristic was, we could make true behavioral predictions; we would predict that a new stimulus with the characteristic would be reinforcing (that it would increase the probability of the behavior that it followed), while a new stimulus without the characteristic would not be reinforcing.

Theories of reinforcement in instrumental conditioning are attempts to specify this characteristic. Let us consider a few of them.

THEORIES OF INSTRUMENTAL REINFORCEMENT

Four of the influential theories of reinforcement that have emerged from the prolific speculation about the relation between reinforcer and animal are these:

1. *Need reduction.* This theory says that every reinforcer ultimately satisfies some vital need of the animal and "reduces the need" (that is, reduces the amount of the substance or thing needed) through a process of negative feedback.
2. *Tension reduction.* The tension reduction theory says that every reinforcer ultimately lessens some tension in the animal through a process of negative feedback.
3. *Brain stimulation.* According to this theory, every reinforcer ultimately stimulates certain parts of the brain.
4. *Response as reinforcement.* This theory holds that responses are reinforced by the ability to make other responses, for example, that bar-pressing is reinforced by the act of eating.

Before we discuss these four theories, we should note that each seems to contain at least a grain of truth but that none has succeeded, by itself, in accounting for all of the ways in which a response can be reinforced.

Need Reduction

Animals need certain things to survive, such as food and water, oxygen, and the appropriate temperature ranges. It is argued that all reinforcers must ultimately reduce one of these physiological needs. (In other words, if psychologists want to know whether a certain substance is rewarding to a certain animal, it would seem that all they have to do is call up the biology department of their university and ask whether the substance satisfies a physiological need. If so, then it must be rewarding. If the biologist tells the psychologists that a platypus needs the chemicals found in bananas in order to survive, then bananas must be rewarding to the platypus.)

Unfortunately, this theory is inconsistent with several well-known facts. Take the case of saccharin. There is no question that artificial sweeteners such as saccharin can be reinforcing. Rats will learn to run down the alley of a T-maze leading to a goal box with a saccharin solution in it although they have plenty of water available. They will also learn to press a bar to receive a saccharin solution. Similarly, humans will gladly put some coins in a slot to receive a cupful of carbonated water mixed with artificial flavoring and saccharin even when a water fountain is nearby. Yet such artificial sweeteners are passed through the body virtually unchanged. This is but one of many reinforcers that do not appear to satisfy any vital need.

Tension Reduction

Another theory, one closely related to need reduction, is that anything that immediately lessens tension of some kind in the animal is a reinforcer. Hunger, for instance, can be seen as a kind of tension that is lessened by eating. The trouble with this theory is that many things that seem to *increase* tension are reinforcing. For instance, it may seem like cruel and unusual punishment to allow a male rat to copulate with a female and then to remove him before he has a chance to ejaculate. Nevertheless, male rats will repeatedly run down the alley of a T-maze leading to such treatment rather than lack female rats altogether. Animals of all kinds will work hard at tasks that lead to no more startling reward than the sight of another animal or the opportunity to do a more complex task. For instance, monkeys will press a bar repeatedly to open a window that allows them to see activity in the laboratory. Monkeys will also solve puzzles with no reward involved other than the solution of the puzzle. It is difficult to classify all of these rewards in terms of tension reduction. If anything, some rewards seem to increase tension.

Of course, a tension reduction theorist could argue that *immediate* tension reduction is not necessary for reinforcement. All that is necessary is *eventual* tension reduction. Then each reinforcement could be traced to its eventual tension-reducing act. But the problem with such theoretical maneuvering is that when a theory is stretched and stretched — even to cover cases like these — it becomes nebulous and does not allow us to make predictions or to advance our understanding a great deal.

Brain Stimulation

In 1954 two physiologists, James Olds and Peter Milner, found that rats would press a lever in order to deliver a mild electric shock to a certain area of their brain. The experiment is shown in Figure 3.1. The rat was enclosed in a cage with a lever attached to an electrical switch that sent current through a wire to certain areas of its brain. Each time the rat pressed the lever, a very mild current (about 0.0001 amperes) was turned on for less than a half second. Olds found that rats would press the bar thousands of times an hour for periods of 12 hours or more to receive this stimulation. Evidently the current in the

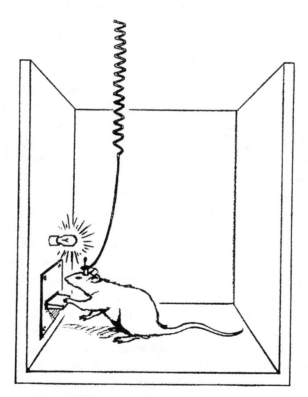

FIGURE 3.1 Old's self-stimulation experiment. [After "Pleasure Centers in the Brain," by James Olds. Copyright © 1956 by Scientific American, Inc. All rights reserved.]

rat's brain was reinforcing. This experiment led to the speculation that perhaps a common element in all rewards is an ability to stimulate certain locations in the brain. Olds called these areas "pleasure centers," reasoning that anything that stimulated them resulted in the feeling of pleasure.

Modern work with reinforcement by brain stimulation has failed to discover unique pleasure centers in the brain. Rather, stimulation in certain areas of the brain seems to engage internal mechanisms responsible for the reinforcing effects of normal motivational systems such as the food–hunger or thirst–water system. For instance, electrical stimulation in the lateral hypothalmus loses much of its power to reinforce a rat's lever-presses if the rat is not deprived of food. The main difference between brain stimulation reinforcement and normal food reinforcement seems to be the lack of a satiation signal (normally produced by food) with brain stimulation.

Response as Reinforcement

Although it is convenient to call a stimulus a *reinforcer*, some psychologists argue that it would be more accurate to designate responses with this term. (Thus they might prefer to say "eating the pudding is a reinforcer" to "the pudding is a reinforcer.") This theory, that reinforcement lies in the *act* of consuming a needed substance rather than in the substance itself, is called a *consummatory-response* theory. According to this theory, certain acts and the sensations involved in performing these acts are said to be innately reinforcing. The reason that bar-presses by a hungry rat will increase when they are followed by food is not because the bar-presses produce food but because they give the rat the opportunity to eat. Thus, *eating* and *drinking* are sources of reinforcement as opposed to food and water themselves.

This theory, unlike the need reduction theory, is consistent with the reinforcing powers of substances like saccharin, since the act of consuming saccharin and the sensations involved therein are the same as the act of consuming other substances that do reduce needs. Although sugar and saccharin are different with respect to their *need-reducing* powers, they are similar with respect to their *consummatory response*.

Another response theory of reinforcement, proposed by the psychologist David Premack, is called the *prepotent-response* theory. This theory is similar to the consummatory-response theory in the sense that responses are said to be reinforced only by the opportunity to make other responses. It differs from the consummatory-response theory, however, because it postulates no innate reinforcing responses (like eating and drinking). Instead, any response may be reinforcing. The power of one response to reinforce another is determined only by the relative strength of the two responses, the stronger response being capable of reinforcing the weaker. Relative strength, in turn, is measured by the relative time that the animal spends performing the acts if both acts are continuously available.

One of Premack's experiments illustrates the point. He allowed several children free access to candy and to pinball machines. He found that many of the children spent a greater proportion of time playing the pinball machines than eating candy. He reasoned that for these children playing with the machines was a stronger response than eating the candy. According to his theory, a stronger response should reinforce a weaker one. When he tested this by allowing the children to play with the machines only after they had eaten a certain amount of the candy, he found that eating candy increased. In other words, playing with pinball machines reinforced eating. Note that this is a reversal of the usual situation, where eating is the reinforcer and some other act is reinforced.

Premack's theory has two advantages. First, it takes the relative nature of reinforcers into account. It treats reinforcement as a *relation* between behavior and its consequences rather than an absolute fact; second, it provides an independent measure of reinforcing power by observing the relative time an animal is engaged in the reinforcing and to-be-reinforced acts.

The argument against both the consummatory-response theory and the prepotent-response theory is that reinforcement often can be achieved by bypassing any response. Normally when food is used as reinforcement, the presentation of food and eating of the food go together. It is possible, however, to separate them. When food is delivered without eating by injecting it directly into the stomach, the food is still reinforcing. Rats will learn to press a lever that results in the injection of food into their stomachs. Also, animals will learn to press a lever to get a higher proportion of oxygen to carbon dioxide in the air of a stuffy room despite the fact that more oxygen in the air causes less breathing — in other words, less responding (whether consummatory or prepotent). We must conclude, then, that animals can be rewarded in other ways than by making a response.

Premack might reply to this objection by saying that, as opposed to all the other theories, his is not a physiological theory at all but a behavioral one. His theory relates a choice test between two responses to the reinforcement paradigm (that is, the power of one response to reinforce the other). When a response is bypassed by injecting food directly into the stomach, the event is not a choice test, nor does it fit into the reinforcement paradigm. If an animal presses a bar to inject milk into its stomach, the entire sequence, consisting of bar-press plus milk injection, would be considered by Premack to be one consummatory response. This sequence as a whole (because it now contains a response) fits both the choice test model and the reinforcement paradigm.

Which Theory is Correct?

The above are only a few of the many theories about how positive reinforcers function. Even within the area of positive reinforcement we have not been able to arrive at a simple classification. These theories give us insight into how to choose reinforcers in specific instances, since they are all correct up to a point, and considered all together they cover most of the reinforcers we have found so far. The main point here, though, is that none of them by itself is sufficient to account for all known reinforcers. This means that the best way to tell if an event will reinforce a given response of a given animal is to try it out in an instrumental conditioning experiment.

One consolation for the lack of a unifying principle that would enable us to predict the things that are reinforcing is the general consistency in the way reinforcers act once they are known to be reinforcing. A reinforcer for one response will generally (but not always) be a reinforcer for other responses in the same animal. If you can teach your dog to give you its paw by rewarding it with a dog biscuit, you probably can also teach it to roll over with the same type of reward. But whether dog biscuits are rewarding in the first place can only be determined by trying them out.

REINFORCEMENT SCHEDULES

One of the earliest experiments relating to schedules of reinforcement was done more or less by accident by B. F. Skinner around 1932. In order to study the eating behavior of rats, he trained them to press a lever to receive a pellet of food and measured their rate of pressing, and hence their rate of eating, after various periods of food deprivation. One day Skinner found that his supply of pellets was low. This inspired him to set up the apparatus so that instead of reinforcing every press, he only reinforced one press a minute no matter how many times a rat pressed the lever.

Not only did the rats keep pressing the lever, but their rate of pressing was considerably higher than when every press was reinforced. This increase in rate of responding is evidence against the notion that less reinforcement simply produces less responding. Skinner inferred that the schedule (or rule) according to which reinforcement is presented could be a powerful way to control behavior and is a worthwhile subject of study in and of itself. The name for the particular reinforcement schedule used by Skinner is a "fixed interval" schedule. Let us now consider a method for measuring response rate and expressing the requirements of Skinner's schedule and the animal's performance with this schedule in graphic form.

Measuring Response Rate

In many forms of behavior, each response is preceded by a signal (or stimulus). The running of a race, for instance, is formally started by the sound of a gun. In that case, the proper measure of responding is the time between the signal and the completion of the response. Sometimes, however, a certain form of behavior is repeated many times in the presence of a single signal. For instance, suppose that a little girl begins to eat, lifting a forkful of food. The signal for this first forkful is a plate of food, which remains present during repeated instances of the same response. Although we can measure the latency of her first forkful of food, we must turn to *rate of response* if we want to quantify the rest of her eating. Her rate of eating may be expected to vary with her hunger and her food preferences. When she is hungry she needs no coaxing to eat heartily, but when she is not, she is likely to eat listlessly or not at all.

Perhaps the simplest way to measure rate of response in the laboratory is to measure how quickly an animal gets from one point to another. One device used for this purpose is called a *straight alley* and is, indeed, nothing but an alley with a box at either end. The animal runs from one box to the other, and its rate of running (its speed) can be measured automatically as it interrupts the light beams of a series of photocells. The straight alley is good for measuring the speed with which an animal runs toward a goal or away from a painful stimulus.

However, if we were interested in continuously measuring an animal's running speed one, two, and three hours after an injection of a drug such as caffeine, we would need an impossibly long straight alley to allow a rat to run as far as it could. In order to measure rate of running over such long periods, we use a device called a *running wheel* (Figure 3.2). As far as the animal (usually a rat) is concerned, the running wheel is an infinitely long straight alley; its convenience for the experimenter is that no matter how fast or far the rat runs, it remains in the same place. The rat's speed of running is easy to obtain by timing the wheel's revolutions.

A Skinner box (Figure 3.3) is frequently employed to study rate of response. To use this device for this purpose, we leave the signal on for a period of time and stipulate that, while the signal is on, pressing the lever will be reinforced. Figure 3.4a shows an event record of lever-presses by a rat when each lever-press was followed by a pellet of food. We can get a better picture of the changes in rate of response if we

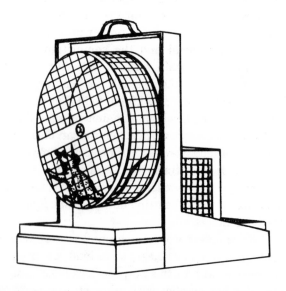

FIGURE 3.2 A running wheel. [Courtesy of Wahmann Manufacturing Co., Baltimore, Md.]

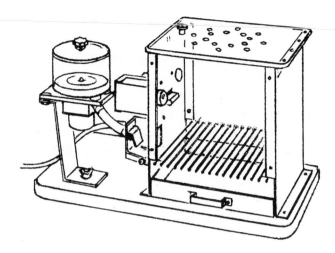

Figure 3.3 A lever box, or Skinner box. [Courtesy of Ralph Gerbrands Co., Arlington, Mass.]

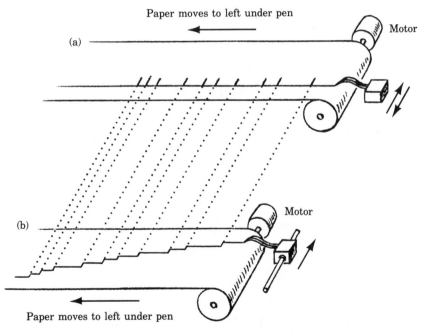

Paper moves to left under pen

(a)

Motor

(b)

Motor

Paper moves to left under pen

Figure 3.4 (a) An event recorder. A pen makes a regular tick for each response. (b) A cumulative recorder. A pen moves in one direction along a slide for each response and then automatically drops back to the starting position when it reaches the edge of the roll of paper.

transform the event record so as to plot the responses cumulatively as in Figures 3.4b and 3.5. In such a cumulative record, a steep slope represents a rapid rate of responding, and a shallow slope represents a slow rate of responding.

Fixed-Interval Schedules

In order to diagram fixed-interval (FI) schedules of reinforcement, we construct a graph with number of presses on the vertical axis and time

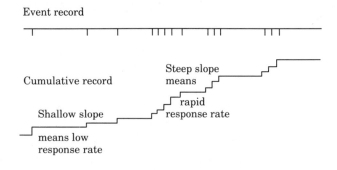

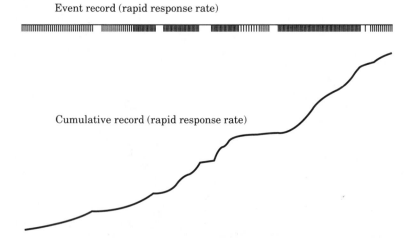

FIGURE 3.5 Event records and cumulative response records. When the response rate is rapid compared with the speed of the paper and the size of the steps, the cumulative recorder draws a relatively smooth line whose slope is proportional to the response rate at any instant.

on the horizontal axis, as in Figure 3.6a. Furthermore, we represent the conditions of reinforcement by a line on the graph. In Skinner's experiment, the requirement is that one minute elapse between reinforcers. After the minute has elapsed, the very next response is reinforced. Assuming that the rat presses the lever often enough, one response would be reinforced every minute. This could be represented by a vertical line at each minute on the horizontal axis. Starting at the origin, then, we can draw a cumulative record of the responses, as in Figure 3.6b, until they reach the required interval. Each response raises the cumulative record another step, and the width of the step indicates the time between responses. After the first minute has elapsed, reinforcement occurs (represented by a downward slash on the graph) after the next response, and so on for the other intervals. If we project the slashes across to the vertical axis, as in Figure 3.6c, we get a picture of the number of responses between reinforcers. In a 1-minute fixed-interval schedule (an FI-1′ schedule), the animal has to respond only once every minute to receive the maximum reward. Any additional responses during the minute have no effect.

The kind of behavior often observed with fixed-interval schedules, and shown by the cumulative records of Figure 3.6, is a pause after reinforcement and then an increase in rate of responding until a high rate is reached just as the interval is about to end. This pattern (called scalloping) is found with many animals for many responses. (An example of human behavior that conforms to the same pattern might be the frequency with which one looks at a pot of water when one is impatient for it to boil, or the frequency with which the oven door is opened to test the turkey while a hungry family is waiting.)*

Fixed-Ratio Schedules

Another kind of schedule much studied in the laboratory is the fixed-ratio (FR) schedule. Here the animal is rewarded only after making a certain fixed number of responses. For instance, a rat might be rewarded for every fourth press instead of for every press. Figure 3.7a shows a cumulative record of a pigeon rewarded with 3 seconds of access to food for every 50 pecks on an illuminated disk. (This is called

---

*Recent experiments have shown that in many fixed-interval schedules, the change from pausing to rapid responding is quite sudden.

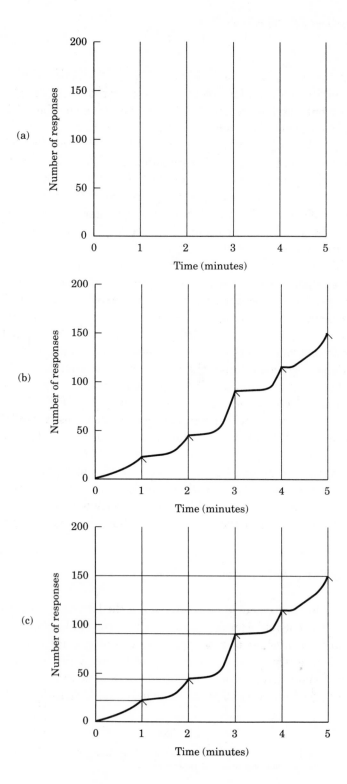

an FR-50 schedule.) The lines showing the locus of reinforcement are horizontal instead of vertical, reflecting the fact that fixed numbers of responses rather than intervals of time determine the availability of reinforcement. Each response raises the cumulative record a small step. When the step is reached corresponding to the ratio, reinforcement occurs, represented by a slash on the graph. If we project the slashes downward to the horizontal axis, as in Figure 3.7b, we get a picture of the rate of reinforcement in time. If the reinforcers are close together, they are occurring rapidly; if they are far apart, they are occurring slowly. Note that after each reinforcement, the pigeons pause before beginning to respond again. This pattern of a rapid burst of responding that fulfills the ratio and then a pause after reinforcement is found for pigeons pecking a disk, rats pressing a lever, monkeys pressing a disk, humans tapping a telegraph key, and innumerable other responses.

Variable Schedules

The fixed patterning of responses that occurs when fixed-interval or fixed-ratio schedules are imposed does not appear with variable-interval and variable-ratio schedules. A variable-interval (VI) schedule makes reinforcement of a response available sometimes after short intervals and sometimes after long intervals. Figure 3.8 shows cumulative records of pigeons pecking a key for variable-interval and variable-ratio schedules of reinforcement. When we refer to a fixed-interval schedule of 1 minute (FI-1'), we mean that a response will be reinforced only after a 1-minute interval. When we speak of a variable-interval schedule of 1 minute (VI-1'), we mean that the *average* of the intervals used in that schedule is 1 minute.

When variable-interval and variable-ratio schedules are used, responses usually occur at a fairly constant rate. Note that the rate of

---

FIGURE 3.6 Cumulative record of a rat's lever-presses reinforced on a 1-minute fixed-interval schedule. (Ticks indicate reinforcements.) (a) The vertical lines mark the locus of each reinforcer; a reinforcer is available once at the end of each minute no matter how many times the rat presses the lever. (b) Cumulative response rates, showing reinforcers received by the rat. (c) Projection of the results to the vertical axis. The distance between the horizontal lines shows how many responses occurred for each reinforcer.

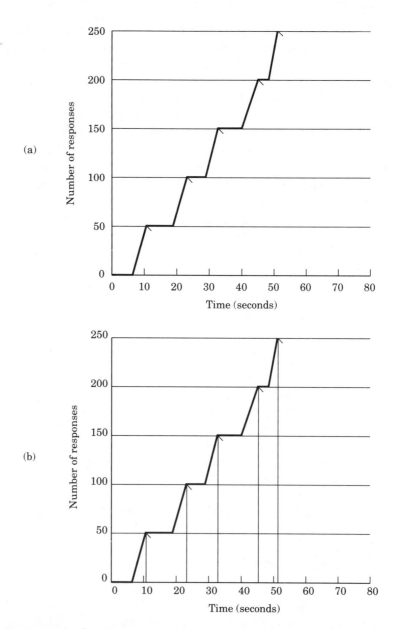

FIGURE 3.7 Cumulative record of a pigeon's pecks reinforced on a fixed-ratio schedule of 1 reinforcer for each 50 pecks. (a) Cumulative record with horizontal lines marking the locus of each reinforcement and ticks representing actual reinforcements. (b) Projection to the vertical axis showing time between reinforcements.

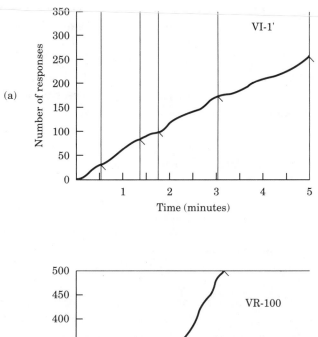

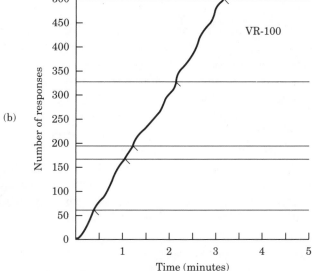

FIGURE 3.8 Loci of reinforcements and cumulative records for variable-interval and variable-ratio schedules of reinforcement of a pigeon's pecking. (Ticks indicate reinforcements.) (a) This graph shows a variable-interval schedule in which a reinforcement is available at the *average* rate of once per minute. (b) This graph shows a variable-ratio schedule in which a reinforcer is available at the *average* ratio of 1 per 100 responses.

responding with the variable-ratio schedule in Figure 3.8 is quite a bit faster than the rate for the variable-interval schedule. Because of the slow, steady rate of responding on variable-interval schedules, they are often used as baselines to gauge the effects of other variables on behavior. A rat on a variable-interval schedule, for instance, responds more rapidly after being given an injection of Dexedrine, a stimulant, than after being given an injection of pentobarbital, a depressant.

Extinction After Partial Reinforcement

We know that the withdrawal of reinforcement from an instrumental response extinguishes the response. In other words, its rate decreases. We might ask how extinction of responses that have been conditioned under the various schedules of reinforcement described above compares with extinction of responses conditioned under a schedule of continuous reinforcement (where each response is reinforced).

Our line of thinking might run as follows: The more reinforcement for a response, the stronger that response should be. The stronger a response is, the more it should resist extinction. The better a response resists extinction, the more responses one should observe after reinforcement has been withdrawn. This line of reasoning seems logical, but, as a matter of fact, exactly the opposite holds true. When a response has been continuously reinforced, extinction is usually much faster than when the same response has been reinforced only part of the time. This result so surprised psychologists that they called it "Humphreys' paradox" (after Lloyd G. Humphreys, the man who first demonstrated it experimentally). Yet, this seemingly paradox is a most reliable, reproducible, and significant effect.

Perhaps we can gain an insight into Humphreys' paradox from this example: There are two hypothetical Coke machines. One, in building A, produces a drink for every three quarters inserted. The other, in building B, is partially broken. Ocasionally when the quarters are inserted, nothing happens. The people in building B complain repeatedly but ineffectually about the situation; still, they seem to be willing to lose their quarters once in a while as long as they eventually get a Coke. Now, suppose both machines break down completely. Which one will receive more quarters before the quarters stop altogether? Probably the machine in building B, which has been only partially reinforcing the quarter-inserting behavior. It will take a while before the people in building B realize that the machine is completely inoperative. The people in building A, on the other hand, will immediately realize that there is something wrong and stop inserting their money.

To be more general, the Coke machine example shows that animals must learn to discriminate between conditions of reinforcement and conditions of extinction, and that anything that helps them to do this will speed up extinction. Partial reinforcement on some schedule is more like extinction than is constant reinforcement and hence harder to tell from extinction. To the extent that conditions of reinforcement resemble conditions of extinction, there will be more responses during extinction.

But when we say that an animal responds to conditions, that the conditions of extinction must be discriminated from the conditions of reinforcement, what do we mean? Simply that animals can discriminate between general situations as well as between particular stimuli. Once more, this is the problem of molecularity versus molarity. At the beginning of this chapter, we discussed the problem of categorizing an animal's behavior. Let us return to this problem and consider the following example: Two people might describe the behavior of the same man as "building a house" or as "laying bricks," depending on their point of view. One continuum upon which these descriptions could be located is that of molarity–molecularity. The molar view is broad and encompassing; the molecular view is narrow and detailed. In the same way that the experimenter (or the environment) may react to the molar or molecular aspects of the subject, so the subject may react to molar or molecular aspects of the environment. If a person moves from Alaska to Florida, he probably does not do so because it happened to snow in Alaska one day, but he might do so because it is generally snowy in Alaska. He is more likely to react to the *rate* of snowing than to an individual snowstorm. Similarly, any response may be sensitive to the *rate* of reinforcement or some other collective property of reinforcers rather than to each reinforcer as it occurs.

More direct evidence that the problem of extinction is actually one of discriminating between conditions of reinforcement and conditions of extinction is that, when cues are provided during extinction, the extinction process is sped up. For instance, in a Skinner box, if the color of the illumination of the test chamber is changed when reinforcement is withdrawn, extinction is faster. Any signal that is present during extinction and not present during conditioning will speed up extinction. Another piece of evidence is the fact that extinction is faster for fixed-interval and fixed-ratio schedules than for variable-interval and variable-ratio schedules. In the fixed schedules, disruption of the regular pattern of reinforcement signals extinction; in the variable schedules, there is no pattern to disrupt.

The assumption in the original reasoning that led to Humphreys' paradox is that strong conditioning of a response produces more responses in extinction. This assumption is based on the notion that latency of response, magnitude of response, and resistance to extinction are all measures of the same thing, namely, the "strength" of the response. Apparently responses in extinction are not exclusively determined by the strength of a response but also by a failure to discriminate between conditions of extinction and conditions of reinforcement. Where enough cues to this discrimination are provided, there are relatively few responses after reinforcement is withdrawn.

CONDITIONAL REINFORCEMENT AND CHAINS OF BEHAVIOR

It may have occurred to the reader by now that there are few human actions that are directly reinforced by unconditional reinforcers such as food. "Man does not live by bread alone," the saying goes. But then, what *does* he live by? At the risk of impiety, behaviorists must answer: Man lives largely by *conditional reinforcers*.

The idea of a conditional reinforcer is really quite simple and is based on common sense. In classical conditioning, a neutral stimulus (which beomes the CS) is followed by unconditional reinforcement (the US). In instrumental conditioning a neutral stimulus is always followed by unconditional reinforcement, provided the correct response is made in its presence. Thus from the subject's point of view it is sufficient to obtain the neutral stimulus in order to be sure of eventual unconditional reinforcement. If a child is fed (unconditional reinforcement) whenever she is seated in a certain chair (the neutral stimulus) she will soon learn to climb into the chair when she is hungry and direct her efforts to sitting in the chair. To a visitor who did not know that the child was fed in that chair, it would seem as if the chair itself was a reinforcer. The visitor would see the child strain to climb into it and then cry until she was placed in it. In this sense, the chair is a conditional reinforcer. (If the child's parent eventually stopped feeding her there, the chair would lose its conditional reinforcing properties.)

Conditional reinforcement bridges the gap between laboratory procedures and complex human and animal behavior. It is a process by which things and events that formerly did not reinforce behavior can become apparently reinforcing. A newborn baby's rewards are easy to enumerate: milk, a change of diapers, and a certain amount of fondling by its parents. As the baby grows up, the list of things that she will work to produce may be enlarged to include priase, money, fame, achievement, and so forth. A dollar bill may not be as rewarding to a baby as a shiny dime. As she grows older, though, the dirty green piece of paper may become relatively more sought after. It is reasonable to explain this change as a case of conditional reinforcement — the dollar has become linked to other reinforcers.

Wolfe's Experiment

An illuminating study of how conditional reinforcement becomes effective was done by John B. Wolfe in 1936. Chimpanzees, like babies, are initially quite indifferent to money, but Wolfe showed how money could come to reinforce behavior. The "money" used by Wolfe in his experiment consisted of poker chips. In a corner of the chimpanzee's cage was a vending machine that provided a grape every time the chimpanzee inserted a poker chip. After a chimpanzee learned to put a chip in the slot for the grape, Wolfe found that he could teach it to do other tasks, such as pressing a lever or pulling on a string in order to receive poker chips. Thus, the poker chips, to which the chimpanzees were initially indifferent, took on the properties of reinforcement. In fact, even when the vending machine was not present, the chimpanzees would continue to work to accumulate chips that they could use to operate the machine later.

One can think of various ways of extending Wolfe's experiment. Suppose the vending machine produced a grape only if a blue chip was inserted. We could install another vending machine that would produce blue chips but only if a red chip was inserted. We could install still another machine that would produce red chips if white chips were inserted. It is likely that the chimpanzees could then learn still another task to get the white chips. By such means highly complex instrumental behaviors are established.

The entire sequence, starting with the response that earns the white chip and ending with the response that earns the grape, is called a *chain of behavior*. We could reinforce each response in the chain only under certain specified conditions. For instance, the vending machines could be made inoperative except when a light is on above the slot. Then the chimpanzees would have to insert chips in slots only when the light was on above them. Figure 3.9 illustrates such conditions. Although this particular chain is discontinuous, with each step clearly signaled by a specific stimulus and clearly delineated from the step before, chains of behavior may become quite continuous. (For instance, the sequence of movements involved in playing the piano eventually become continuous.)

The important rule in establishing chains is to start with the last response—the one that is unconditionally reinforced. Wolfe *first* taught his chimps to put a token in the slot for the grape and *then* taught them to work for the tokens. If you want to teach a dog to fetch your slippers and drop them in front of you, *first* teach the dog to drop the slippers and *then* to fetch them.

Extinction of Chains of Behavior

If the final unconditional reinforcement is eliminated from the chain, the entire chain of behavior will often disintegrate and eventually cease to occur. But what happens if the chain is interrupted in the middle? In other words, what happens if one of the conditional reinforcers is eliminated? In Figure 3.9 suppose that the lever and vending machine 1 remained operative but that vending machine 2 got clogged so that even when its light went on, depositing a red chip produced nothing but the loss of the chip. Our own experience in such situations tells us that the chimpanzee, after hitting the machine or shaking it or sticking its finger as far into the slot as it will go, will eventually stop depositing red chips. Soon after, the chimp will stop operating the lever to produce the white chips. In other words, all behavior leading to the point at which the chain is broken will be extinguished. But what about the behavior after the point at which the chain is broken? This, generally, will remain intact. After the above extinction process was carried out, the chimpanzee would probably reject a red chip but,

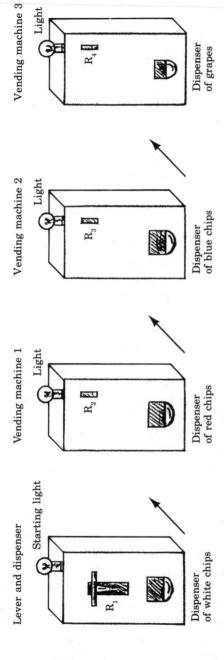

FIGURE 3.9 Hypothetical extension of Wolfe's experiment to produce an extended chain of behavior. The light on the dispenser at left signals to a chimpanzee that a white chip is available. The chimp responds (first response, R_1) by pulling a lever. The light on vending machine 1 signals the availability of a red chip. The chimp now responds (R_2) by inserting the white chip in machine 1. When the light on vending machine 2 comes on, the chimp responds (R_3) by inserting the red chip into the machine. The chimp receives a blue chip that may then be inserted (R_4) into vending machine 3 when its light signals that a grape is available.

if given a blue chip, would insert it in vending machine 3. Thus the chimp's behavior in the chain after the point of the interruption would not have been extinguished.

LEARNING WITH DELAYED REINFORCEMENT

What happens when the temporal relation between response and reinforcement is varied so that reinforcement is delayed? The answer is that in almost all cases a delayed reinforcement is worth less than immediate reinforcement during the acquisition of a habit. Let us consider the power of delayed reinforcement to strengthen an individual response.

The main problem for an experimenter is to define experimentally the delay interval and its attributes. She must decide what sort of thing she wants to happen during the delay period. One point of view says that nothing at all should happen during the delay. But if nothing happened—if in a strict sense all motion of any kind was suspended and all processes halted—then by definition delay could have no effect. Any effect it would have must be the result of some process (be it "forgetting" or "interference by other responses") during the delay period. In other words, to say that nothing must happen during the delay period is to say that the delay period can have no effect. It is as if you were instantly to freeze the universe in its motion for the delay period and then allow it to move again when the delay was over.

An alternative would be to allow many events of all kinds during the delay period. For instance, let us go back to the chain of responses illustrated in Figure 3.9. Suppose we consider the first response in the chain, pressing the lever to receive a white chip, as a response that is ultimately reinforced by the grape delivered at the end of the chain. The other responses, the placing of the various chips in the slots, would merely be ways of filling up the delay period between the lever-press and its reinforcement.

One criticism of this kind of experiment is that there really would be no delay of reinforcement even for responses at the beginning of the chain. The various poker chips would serve as conditional reinforcers that could effectively signal the coming of food. Since poker chips had been repeatedly associated with food, the chimpanzee's behavior would be reinforcd as much by the sight of the poker chips as by the sight of the food. The chimpanzee in this situation is much like the television quiz show winner who is presented with a check instead of prizes. Although the check is only a piece of paper, the recipient is no less happy than the person who receives a refrigerator or television set, because he will be able to cash the check and get the prizes in the future. We may therefore say that the poker chip reduces *uncertainty* about whether food will be presented. Even should we cause a delay between acquisition of the poker chip and its insertion in the machine, the chimpanzee would still have the poker chip (the promissory note) in its hand during the delay period. When Wolfe did cause such a delay (Figure 3.10b), the chimpanzees responded just as fast to get poker chips as when there was no delay. However, when Wolfe caused a delay between insertion of the poker chip and delivery of the food (Figure 3.10c), when the chimpanzee has to wait during the delay period with no poker chip in hand, responding for poker chips fell off sharply.

Experimenters have tried to eliminate conditional reinforcement from delay-of-reinforcement experiments. G. Robert Grice (1948) provided food to rats in a device similar to a T-maze.* The floor of one arm was white and the floor of the other arm was black. The arms were occasionally reversed so that the white and black arms were not consistently associated with the same sides. After running down either arm, the rats were kept in one of a pair of identical grey delay boxes for varying periods for different groups of rats. Then they were allowed into a goal box. If they had originally run down the white arm, they were then fed in the goal box. If they had originally run down the black arm, they were not fed. Figure 3.11 shows Grice's experiment. When there was no delay, the rats learned fairly easily to go in the direction corresponding to the white arm. However, when the delay was longer than 5 seconds, none of the rats in the delay group could learn to run consistently down the white arm to food.

Like the chimps in Wolfe's experiment (Figure 3.10c) the rats in Grice's experiment (Figure 3.11b) had nothing during the delay period that signaled reinforcement to come. When Grice provided one delay box following a choice of white and a distinctly different box following

---

*A rat in a T-maze runs from a start box, at the foot, to a "choice point," at the end of the stem, and then down one of the two arms to a goal box at the end.

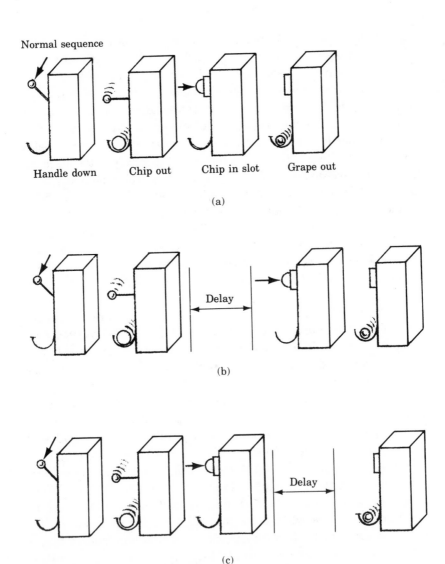

FIGURE 3.10 How the point of delay affected lever-pressing in Wolfe's experiment. (a) Normal sequence without a period of delay. (b) Delay between collecting chip and inserting it in slot. In this sequence, the chimp has the chip during the delay, and the delay does not slow down the chimp's lever-pressing. (c) Delay between placing poker chip in slot and collecting grape. In this sequence, the chimp has no chip during the delay, and the delay does slow down lever-pressing.

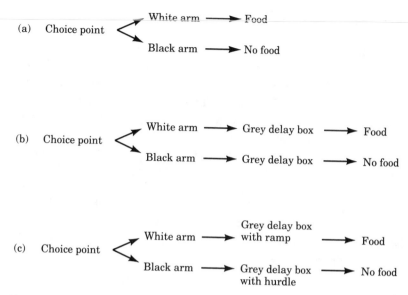

FIGURE 3.11 Grice's experiment. (a) No-delay group, which learned to go to the white arm. (b) Delay group, which could not learn to go to the white arm when delayed longer than 5 seconds. (c) Conditional-reinforcement group, which learned to go to the white arm.

a choice of black (Figure 3.11c) the performance of the rats improved considerably, even with longer delays than the original 5-seconds.

The reason the rats in the conditions of Figure 3.11b did not learn the maze is that no stimulus in the grey delay box was reliably correlated with either alley. An animal could, however, provide such correlated stimuli by its own actions.

A human child in circumstances similar to those shown in Figure 3.11b might learn to put his hands in his pockets whenever he turned in the direction of a white passageway and keep them there until he was finally permitted to enter the goal room. Correspondingly, he could put his hands on his head whenever he turned down the black passageway and keep them there until he entered the goal room. He would soon learn that he was rewarded whenever he had his hands in his pockets and unrewarded whenever he had his hands on his head. This mediating response would serve to connect the situation at the choice point with that in the goal room and enable the child to make the correct response easily. In other words, he could provide differential cues for himself like those Grice provided for some of his rats (Figure 3.11c).

Many of the mediating responses that humans use to bridge gaps between response and reinforcement are verbal. Instead of putting our hands in our pockets or on our heads, we would probably solve the problem by saying to ourselves, "I'll go to the white side now" or "I'll go to the side opposite to the white now." If, when reinforcement came, we had been saying some such phrase, we would be likely to remember what we were saying the next time we reached the choice point and to use the phrase to guide our choice behavior. The use of repeated verbal responses is a common technique for bridging gaps in time. The shopping list repeated over and over again by a child as he walks to the store or the phone number repeated over and over again between the telephone book where we have looked it up and the telephone where we dial it are examples.

PUNISHMENT AND NEGATIVE REINFORCEMENT

So far in our discussion of reinforcement, we have been dealing mostly with positively valued reinforcers, stimuli or objects that most animals will approach, such as food, water, and sexual partners. These are shown in the top two boxes of Figure 2.9, where the types of instrumental conditioning are diagrammed. The bottom boxes of the figure show processes using aversive stimuli, stimuli that most animals will escape from or avoid. Control of behavior with such aversive stimuli can be just as effective as control with positive stimuli. If we spend less time on aversive control, it is because we have already covered basic principles applicable to both aversive and positive control, not because aversive control is unimportant.

Before we begin a discussion of experimental findings, let us repeat a few definitions made earlier. Figure 3.12 shows a particular way of looking at the behavior of an animal in a laboratory situation. Suppose the animal is a rat in a Skinner box with a lever. The entire large circle of Figure 3.12 represents all the behavior of which the rat is capable: scratching, biting, jumping, and so forth. The small white circle within the large one represents a particular portion of the total —pressing a lever. This portion is what we have previously defined as

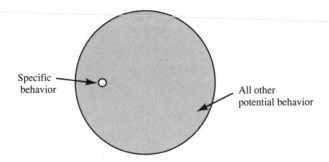

FIGURE 3.12 Specific and nonspecific definitions of behavior.

an operant—it represents a class of still more specific kinds of behavior, all of which somehow depress the lever. If pressing the lever is followed by aversive stimulation, the process is called punishment. If anything the animal does *except* pressing the lever is followed by aversive stimulation, the process is called negative reinforcement.

For example, referring to Figure 3.12, if we shocked the rat for behavior included in the small white circle (after each lever-press), we would be punishing the lever-pressing behavior. If we shocked the rat for all behavior included in the large grey part of the circle (that is, all behavior *except* a lever-press), we would be negatively reinforcing the lever-press. Punishment will tend to decrease the rate of lever-pressing and negative reinforcement to increase it. According to common usage, when we refer to positive reinforcement, we frequently just say "reinforcement," when we refer to negative reinforcement, we always say "negative reinforcement." (A similar convention exists with respect to positive and negative numbers. We often say "three" for "positive three" but we always say "negative three.") If we shocked the rat for all behavior in the big circle including that in the small circle, we would be delivering shock independently of the behavior of the rat.

The problem of defining an aversive stimulus is analogous to the problem of defining the nature of positive reinforcement, and the attempted solutions have also been analogous. Just as there is a need reduction theory of positive reinforcement, there is a need increase theory of aversive stimulation. Just as there are response theories of positive reinforcement, there are response theories of aversive stimulation. Defining aversive stimuli as "painful" and positive reinforcers as "pleasurable" does not help. Such definitions suffer from the same drawbacks as other mentalistic concepts — they give us no guidelines to tell what is painful or pleasurable to another animal.

It would be pointless to trace through a series of "aversive-stimulation theories" because our conclusion would be similar to the one we reached about positive reinforcement: There is no unifying principle that enables us to predict the things that are aversive. Our consolation, however, is also the same; a stimulus that proves to be aversive in one situation will generally be aversive in others. If beating a dog with a rolled-up newspaper is an effective punishment for defecating in the house, chances are it will also be effective punishment for jumping on the laps of guests. If electric-shock punishment reduces the rate of bar-pressing in rats, it will also reduce the rate of wheel-running.

Punishment

Just as positive reinforcement tends to increase the rate at which a behavior is emitted, punishment tends to decrease the rate. Figure 3.13a shows a cumulative record of the lever-presses of a rat in a Skinner box where lever-presses have no effect. The low slope of the line means that the rat occasionally presses the lever even with no positive reinforcement, but the rate of pressing is very low. Figure 3.13b shows a cumulative record of presses that are *positively* reinforced according to a variable-interval schedule. The steep slope of the line shows that the rate of pressing is much more rapid for positive reinforcement than for no reinforcement at all. Figure 3.13c shows cumulative records when lever-presses are rewarded *and* punished. In this case, the punishment was a brief electric shock following each press. The particular intensity of punishment used caused a slowdown, or suppression, of the rate of pressing shown by a slope between that for the rate of pressing for reward only and slope for the rate of pressing for neither reward nor punishment. Figure 3.14 shows how

---

FIGURE 3.13 The effect of punishment on a rat's rate of bar-pressing for food. (Ticks in cumulative records, at bottom, mark reinforced responses.) (a) Lever-presses have no effect on reinforcement. (b) Lever-presses are positively reinforced on a VI-1' schedule. (c) Lever-presses are positively reinforced on a VI-1' schedule, and each press is punished with an electric shock. (E = experiment; A = animal; S^D = discriminative stimuli).

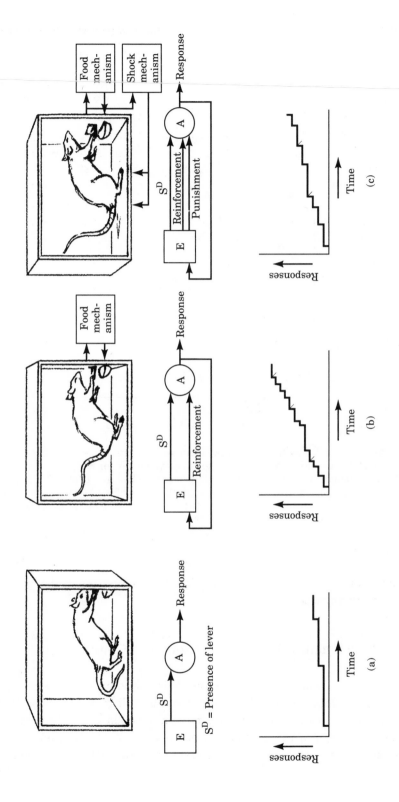

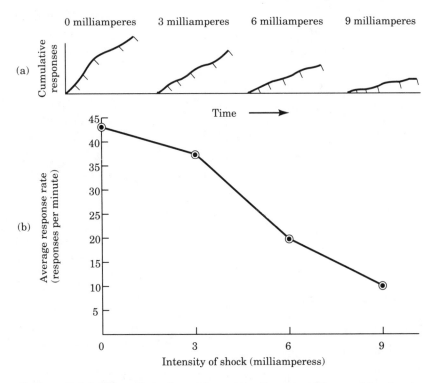

FIGURE 3.14 The effect of punishment on the rate of key pecking in pigeons. (a) Cumulative records of pigeons pecking a key for reinforcement on a VI-1′ schedule. (Ticks indicate reinforcements.) The graph at left shows a no-shock condition; the remaining graphs show the effect of varying intensities of shock. (b) A function showing that the rate of responding decreased as the intensity of the electric shock increased.

the intensity of punishment determines the suppression in the rate at which pigeons peck a key.

Is Punishment a Form of Instrumental Conditioning?

In the last chapter, we discussed pseudoconditioning. We introduced pseudoconditioning in instrumental conditioning experiments with the hypothetical example of an adrenalin injection as a reinforcer for bar-pressing in a rat. The test of adrenalin as a pseudoreinforcer is whether the same increases in bar-pressing occur when the injection of adrenalin is dependent on and independent of a bar-press. If the drug causes just as many bar-presses when it is delivered randomly as when it follows each bar-press, then we do not have a case of instrumental conditioning.

It is also possible that the process of punishment may not be a form of instrumental conditioning. With positive reinforcement we are trying to train the animal to *do* something. With punishment we are trying to train the animal *not* to do something. When a hungry animal is presented with food, the behavior that one observes is eating. In order to get the animal to perform some act other than eating (like pressing a bar), the food must be made dependent on the bar-press. When an animal is shocked, the behavior that one observes is jumping or running or freezing in position, but *not* bar-pressing. In other words, shock can itself produce "nonperformance" of bar-pressing, the very effect we are trying to obtain. In order to get the animal to *stop* pressing a bar, all one needs to do is shock the animal. But we said previously that true instrumental conditioning must involve a *relation* between responding and its consequences, not simple presentation of those consequences. It is at least conceivable that to reduce responding there may be no need to shock the animal in any relation to its responses.

The question then becomes: Will aversive stimulation delivered independently of responding suppress behavior as much as aversive stimulation delivered only when a response is made? If it does, then punishment does not have the properties of instrumental conditioning. If it does not — if aversive stimulation must follow responding to have its maximum effect — then punishment does have the properties of instrumental conditioning. Many experiments have been performed to answer this question, and their answer has almost been unanimous — aversive stimulation delivered independently of responding has some suppressive effect to be sure, but nowhere near as much as when it follows immediately after each response. To the extent that there is a difference between the effects of response-produced aversive stimulation and response-independent aversive stimulation, punishment is a form of instrumental conditioning.

Curve B in Figure 3.15 shows the rate at which a pigeon pecked a key where pecks were reinforced with food on a 1-minute variable-interval schedule and inescapable shocks were delivered twice per second. As the intensity of shock increased, the rate of pecking decreased slightly. Curve A in Figure 3.15 is the same graph as in Figure 3.14b,

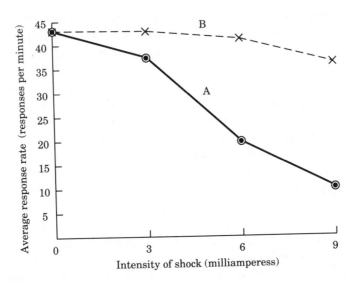

FIGURE 3.15 Curve A is the same as in Figure 3.14, showing the rate of response as punishment increases. Curve B shows the rate of response under the same conditions of reinforcement but with the shocks delivered independently of the responses. The rate of delivery of the independent shocks was 120 per minute.

showing the rate at which another pigeon pecked a key when pecks were reinforced with food on the same schedule but shock was delivered only when the pigeon pecked the key. As the intensity of shock increased, the rate of pecking decreased drastically. The difference in the slopes of these two curves shows the instrumental effect of shock.

What implications for human behavior can we draw from these empirical findings? Does it mean that our grandparents were right when they said, "Spare the rod and spoil the child"? Is modern child rearing, with its deemphasis on punishment, all wrong? Not necessarily. There is no question that punishment works—the trouble with punishment may be not that it doesn't work but that it works only too well. A single intense shock to a pigeon following a peck on a key can suppress key-pecking permanently without disturbing other behavior. If we severely punish a child for "being fresh," we must ask ourselves whether we want to suppress the child's outspokenness completely and permanently. Another implication to be drawn from this research is that random presentation of aversive stimulation has little positive effect. Consider parents who constantly spank, shake, or slap their children for reasons that are only tenuously related to their specific acts. Such parents will never understand why their children are so naughty despite constant attempts at discipline. If children are to be spanked, they should be spanked immediately after the offense. Otherwise, any acts performed between the offense and the spanking are liable to be suppressed along with or instead of the act the parents intend to suppress. If a child is innocently reaching for a lollipop at the moment it occurs to his mother that he ought to be punished for something he did an hour before and she suddenly slaps his hand, it may be a long time before he again reaches for a lollipop.

Furthermore, one must be certain that "the punishment fits the crime." The classic example of an inappropriate punishment is spanking a child for crying. The spanking generates still more crying, which, in turn, is punished by still more spanking, and so on, until the child or the parent becomes exhausted. (Such vicious circles may indeed be responsible for some otherwise inexplicable cases of child abuse.)

In general, with regard to both reward and punishment, the more specific and discrete the response, the more likely it is that reward and punishment will work. Punishment of a child for "being a bad boy that day" or reward for "being a good boy that day" will be much less effective than an immediate punishment for carelessly breaking a vase or an immediate reward for saying "please." When you want a specific response from a fellow animal, it is far more effective to reward the occurrence of the behavior than to punish its absence. When you want an animal *not* to do something specific, it is more effective to punish the occurrence of the behavior than to reward its absence. Referring to Figure 3.12, it is usually more effective to apply either reward or punishment to the operant represented by the small white area of the circle than to the large grey area. When reward and punishment are applied to the grey part, it is hard for the animal to distinguish the situation from one in which reward and punishment are applied to white and grey together — in other words, a situation in which reward and aversive stimulation are independent of any response. In the next sections on escape and avoidance, we will look at what happens when punishment is applied to large, general classes of behavior such as those represented by the large grey part of Figure 3.12.

Escape (Negative Reinforcement)

In the typical escape-conditioning experiment, an aversive stimulus is presented and the experimenter waits until the subject performs some act that the experimenter has specified in advance. When the act is performed, the aversive stimulus is removed. For example, a dog may be placed in a shuttle box (one with a hurdle in the middle that the dog can leap over). When the dog is on one side of the box, it may be shocked until it leaps over the hurdle. Dogs in such situations quickly learn to jump over the hurdle.

Negative reinforcement is a synonym for escape. Although the word *escape* vividly describes what is happening in a typical negative reinforcement experiment, we shall use the phrase "negative reinforcement" to remind us of the relation between this process and that of positive reinforcement. Both kinds of reinforcement will strengthen whatever acts they follow. Positive reinforcement reinforces by adding a positively valued stimulus; negative reinforcement reinforces by taking away an aversive stimulus. The line between these two processes is not always easy to draw. (Is turning on the heater on a cold day a reinforcer because it gives us warmth or because it removes our feeling of cold?)

One theory of reinforcement (the need reduction theory that we mentioned previously) holds that all reinforcement is negative reinforcement. The eating of food, for instance, is thus "escape from hunger" and the drinking of water is "escape from thirst."

Nevertheless, the behavior of animals when exposed to aversive stimuli is different from that of animals who are deprived of food or water. A pigeon that is being shocked will jump around the area in which it is confined and flap its wings; a pigeon deprived of food will engage in more deliberate searching and pecking motions. It may be that one difference between an aversive stimulus (such as electric shocks or loud noises) and such feelings as hunger or thirst is that the former originate suddenly outside the animal while the latter originate gradually within it. Because of the violent behavior generated by aversive stimuli, it is difficult to train an animal to perform delicate, subtle, or complicated acts to escape them. It is difficult, for instance, for animals to react nonviolently to aversive stimuli even though, in many cases, nonviolence may be the best means of escaping them. Only a great deal of previous training enables people in a crowded auditorium to keep from running to the exits to escape a fire. Similarly, although it is easy to train a pigeon to peck a key to obtain food, it is difficult to train a pigeon to perform the same act to escape from electric shock. (On the other hand, it is easy to train a pigeon to flap its wings, to run around a cage, or to raise its head to escape electric shock.)

A great deal of patience is required to train an animal to react to aversive stimuli in nonviolent ways. One must find the precise value of intensity that will be aversive enough to facilitate escape, yet not so intense as to trigger violent reactions. In everyday life, we are often faced with similar problems. Perhaps prisons should be aversive enough relative to the outside world so that people do not want to stay in them, yet not so aversive that prisoners become more bitter or violent than they were before their incarceration.

It is possible to train an animal to perform an act it would not ordinarily perform under aversive stimulation. For example, the cockroach will ordinarily run away from light, yet this photonegative insect can, in the course of repeated trials, learn to go to a dark box situated under a light. Figure 3.16 diagrams the experiment. The roach is placed in one end of an alley with a very weak light above a covered box at the other end. In order to get to the box, which is in complete shade, the roach must move toward the light. If the light is made very bright initially, the roach will stay at the end of the alley where it is put and not move. However, if the light is very dim, the roach will adapt to the light and move down the alley and find the dark box. Once the roach learns to run to the dark box when the light is dim, the intensity of the light can be increased slowly. The roach will eventually learn to approach a bright light to get to the dark box. The roach has thus learned to escape the bright light by running towards its source.

Avoidance

An experiment by Richard Solomon and L. C. Wynne illustrates the relation of avoidance to escape. They trained dogs in the shuttle box diagrammed in Figure 3.17. When the dogs were on side A, they were severely shocked. The electricity remained on until the dogs jumped to side B. However, 10 seconds before each shock, a light in the box went out. Gradually the dogs came to jump when the light went out but *before* the shock came on, thus avoiding the shock altogether.

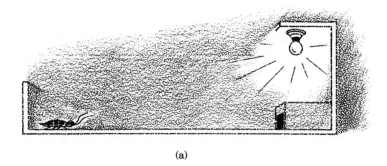

(a)

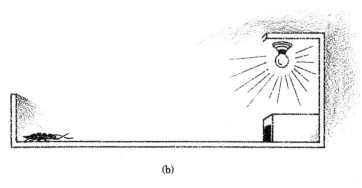

(b)

FIGURE 3.16 Teaching a cockroach to approach a bright light. (a) The roach learns to go to the dark box. The intensity of the light is gradually increased over many trials until (b) the roach goes to the dark box in spite of a bright light.

The relation between avoidance and escape bears a certain similarity to the relation between conditional reinforcement and unconditional reinforcement. In conditional reinforcement experiments, we concluded that one of the values of conditional reinforcers is that they signal to the animal "when unconditional reinforcement is due." Avoidance procedures perform a similar function; they tell the animal when aversive stimulation is due. In both conditional reinforcement and avoidance situations, the signal makes a certain kind of behavior appropriate. Conditional reinforcing signals are part of a chain culminating in positive reinforcement. Avoidance signals are part of a chain culminating in nonpresentation of an aversive stimulus.

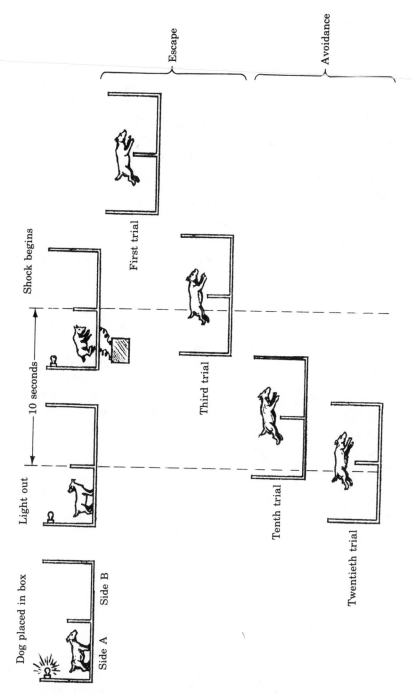

FIGURE 3.17 Solomon and Wynne's avoidance experiment. First trial: Dog jumps over barrier long after shock begins. Third trial: Dog jumps immediately after shock begins. Tenth trial: Dog jumps between signal and shock. Twentieth trial: Dog jumps immediately after signal starts.

If we look upon animals as reacting to overall molar features of the environment, we can see how avoidance behavior may easily come about. One person may react to the fact that the sun is shining and dress accordingly, while on the same morning another may react to the fact that it is the month of April and hence carry an umbrella even if the sun is shining at that particular moment. This second person is, in essence, avoiding getting wet, just as Solomon and Wynne's dogs avoided shock by responding even when shock was not present at the moment. For some of Solomon and Wynne's dogs, the transition from escape of shock (reaction to the shock itself) to avoidance of shock (reaction to the stimulus that indicated shock was to come) was rapid (Figure 3.18, dog A); for other dogs this transition was more gradual (dog B).

The invariable correlation between the light-out signal and the shock in Solomon and Wynne's experiment is not always paralleled in everyday life "avoidance situations." Just because it is April, it will not necessarily rain. Sometimes the man who responds to the more molecular aspects of his environment, who leaves his umbrella home on sunny days even in April, is better off than his more foresighted brother. People obviously have to strike a general balance between a molecular and molar view of life, and sometimes this can be difficult.

It is generally true that children find it difficult to respond to the molar conditions of their environment. As we grow older, we sometimes have difficulties in the other direction. The woman who can never take a vacation, for instance, or who worries and cannot enjoy herself while her children are away at camp are examples of people who are responding to aversive molar aspects of their environment at the expense of the molecular. To put it another way, there are those who cannot see the forest for the trees and those who cannot see the trees for the forest.

Extinction of Escape and Avoidance

When extinction of escape and avoidance is carried out in a way parallel to extinction of positively reinforced behavior, the reinforced response disappears quite rapidly. For instance, suppose one of Solomon and Wynne's dogs learned to jump over a barrier to escape—and then to avoid—shocks. Suppose we want to extinguish this behavior. During extinction the jumps would no longer be reinforced by escape

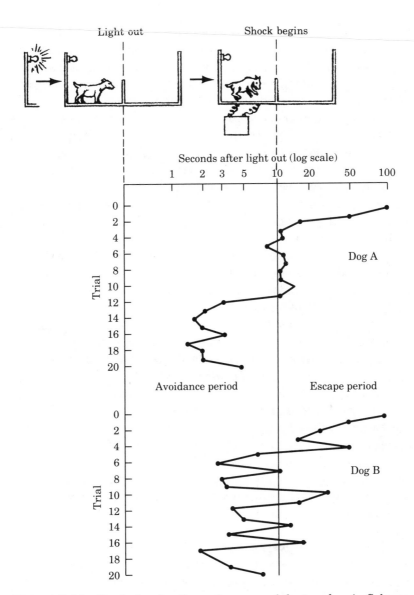

FIGURE 3.18 Graph showing the performance of the two dogs in Solomon and Wynne's experiment. (Each point represents a jump over the barrier.) Dog A shifted rapidly from escape to avoidance, while dog B shifted gradually. [Data from R. L. Solomon and L. C. Wynne, "Traumatic avoidance learning: Acquisition in normal dogs," *Psychological Monographs 67*, 1953, (No. 354).]

or avoidance—we would shock the animal no matter what it did. When this procedure is followed, the jumps eventually stop. In fact, responses extinguished in this manner are often extinguished so thoroughly that it is difficult to get the animal to respond again, even when extinction is discontinued and conditioning is reinstated.

There is another procedure for reducing the rate of avoidance behavior that produces exactly the opposite results. Suppose again that an animal has learned to jump over a barrier to avoid shocks, as in the Solomon and Wynne study. Then, suppose the experimenter maintains the same conditions—the same box, the same signal, and the same jump before the shock comes on—except that the shock apparatus is unplugged. When Solomon and Wynne tried unplugging their electrical apparatus, they found that the dogs kept jumping; the dogs would jump literally hundreds of times after shock had been discontinued. Eventually the avoidance behavior will slow down and stop under these conditions, but the process is a lengthy one, especially when compared with the normal extinction procedure.

It is easy to understand why the second extinction process is so inefficient if we remember what was said about extinction of positively reinforced responses: *The easier it is to discriminate the reinforcement situation from the extinction situation, the faster extinction will be.* In the case of the two extinction processes for avoidance, the first is easily distinguished from reinforcement. As soon as the dog makes the previously reinforced jumping response and the shock is maintained nevertheless, the conditions of reinforcement are obviously at an end. However, in the second procedure, when the dog jumps and is not shocked, the conditions are identical to those of reinforcement. With the second method of extinction, as long as the reinforced response is maintained, the conditions of reinforcement and extinction are identical.

To illustrate the two methods of extinction, consider the behavior of two children who learn to hit or otherwise interfere with the pleasure of other children in order to prevent the other children from taking their toys. One child is then put among older children who take his toys regardless of how aggressively he behaves. The other child is put among younger children who do not take his toys, no matter how meekly he behaves. It is reasonable to suppose that the aggressive behavior of the first child will stop while that of the second child will continue; a model example, perhaps, of how a neighborhood bully is created.

In fact, the slow, inefficient extinction of avoidance is seen by some behavioral therapists as a major factor in much adult human neurotic behaviors. As children, people learn many avoidance behaviors. Sometimes, as adults, they continue to perform these behaviors even though the sources of aversive stimulation have long been absent. For instance, if a girl is punished in her youth for open displays of emotion, as an adult she is likely to inhibit such display, perhaps inappropriately, to the detriment of her relations with her husband and children. In this case, a therapist might encourage his or her patient to express her emotions openly in a permissive atmosphere in the hope of extinguishing the heavy-handed childhood conditioning.

Suggested Readings

Books on the nature of reinforcement usually have the word *motivation* in the title. The sections on motivation and reinforcement in the books by Kimble and Mackintosh (previously cited) are excellent. The implications of Premack's theory for human behavior are traced in Rachlin (cited in the Suggested Readings of Chapter 2).

The parameters of reinforcements — schedule, delay, conditional reinforcement, and so forth — are discussed in detail in the Kimble and Mackintosh books and in a collection of original essays edited by W. K. Honig and J. R. Staddon, *Handbook of Operant Behavior* (Englewood Cliffs, NJ: Prentice-Hall, 1977).

Punishment and aversive control are treated only sketchily in the Kimble book but are more fully covered in the Mackintosh book and in the Honig-Staddon collection. A systematic account of the investigation of parameters of reinforcement and punishment can be found in a paperback by F. A. Logan and A. R. Wagner, *Reward and Punishment* (Boston: Allyn & Bacon, 1965).

The Wolfe and Grice experiments are described in Kimble's book, but it is instructive to read Wolfe's own descriptions of his experiments, which are found, unfortunately, only in J. B. Wolfe, "Effectiveness of token-rewards for chimpanzees," *Comparative Psychology Monographs*, 1936, **12** (No. 60). The Solomon and Wynne experiment has been reprinted extensively and is described in most texts on learning. The original source is *Psychological Monographs* 1953, **67** (No. 354).

4

Patterns of Behavior

The word *evolution* literally means "act of unfolding or unrolling"; it may be applied to any process of development, formation, or growth. Darwin's theory of evolution by natural selection (described in Chapter 1) shows how the environment shapes the structure of a species (such as the giraffe) from generation to generation.

The present chapter considers how *patterns of behavior* (as opposed to the structure of species) may evolve. First we consider the shaping of patterns of behavior within the lifetime of an individual organism. Second, we consider how such shaping may interact with patterns of behavior inherited by the animal through Darwinian selection.

LEARNED PATTERNS (SHAPING)

Consider the following hypothetical experiment.

Suppose we construct a puzzle box like Thorndike's (see Figure 2.7) except that we make the ceiling somewhat higher. Then suppose that we put a cat into the box, but that instead of letting it out after it solves a puzzle, we simply observe its behavior, particularly its jumping. (Thorndike reported that one common behavior of a hungry cat in a box is jumping.) If we measure the heights of the jumps and plot them as a distribution (see the lower left portion of Figure 4.1), the curve will probably be bell shaped, showing some very low jumps and some very high jumps but mostly medium jumps. Suppose that we open the door to the box after each jump greater than some arbitrary height, a little above average, say 13 inches, and feed the cat before putting it back into the box. At first, we find the usual number of 13-inch jumps. But as the experiment progresses, we find more and more jumps of 13 inches and above. In fact, the distribution will pobably change to one resembling that on the lower right of Figure 4.1.

Thorndike, who helped lay the foundation of instrumental conditioning, saw a direct connection between individual adaptation — the selection of successful behaviors from an animal's repertoire — and species adaptation. Indeed, the "law of effect" is simply natural selection at work within the life history of a single animal.

Both the structures and behaviors of species evolve. If the environment changes slowly and is the same for all members of the species, evolution from generation to generation works well. The spider's web spinning and the social interaction of bees, ants, and other insects are behaviors that have been brought about by natural selection.

But this evolutionary process, which takes generations to do its work, is too slow to solve some of the problems faced by some species. Take foxes, for example. If a farmer devises a new fence for his barnyard, a particular fox must change its behavior to get past that particular fence. If the fence is too high to jump over, the fox must learn to climb over it, tunnel under it, or gnaw through it. Since there are many foxes, many farmers, and many kinds of fences, there is little chance for the evolution of a whole breed of foxes whose specific "fence-climbing behavior" would be just suited to the peculiarities of any single fence. If such a breed of foxes did come into being, the farmer would replace the fence with another fence that the new breed could not climb over, and the process would have to begin again. In other words, given their relatively changeable environment, the only hope for foxes lies in adaptation by the individual rather than by the species. Each fox must respond to its own specific environmental conditions.

Individual adaptation, the ability of an animal to change its behavior in relation to changes in the environment, is nothing more or

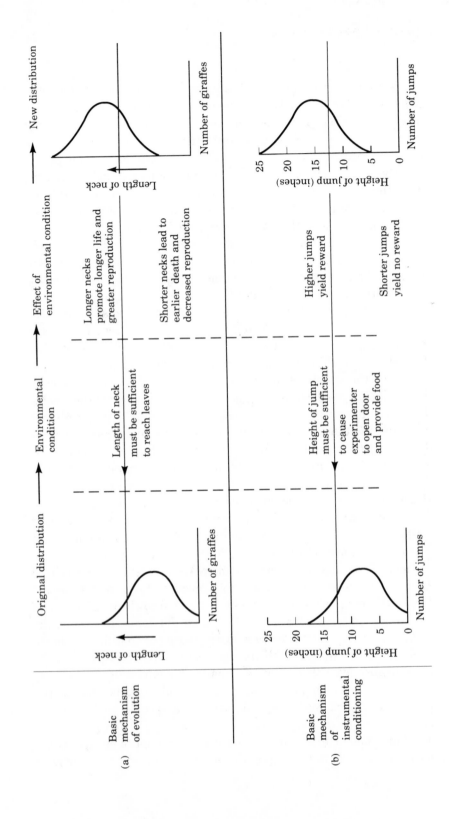

Basic
mechanism
of evolution

(a)

Original distribution → Environmental condition → Effect of environmental condition → New distribution

Length of neck

Number of giraffes

Length of neck must be sufficient to reach leaves

Longer necks promote longer life and greater reproduction

Shorter necks lead to earlier death and decreased reproduction

Length of neck

Number of giraffes

Basic
mechanism
of
instrumental
conditioning

(b)

Height of jump (inches)

Number of jumps

Height of jump must be sufficient to cause experimenter to open door and provide food

Higher jumps yield reward

Shorter jumps yield no reward

Height of jump (inches)

Number of jumps

less than learning. This relatively rapid adaptability of individual behavior complements the more gradual adaptability of species structure and species behavior we find in the long-term evolutionary process and is itself a product and a part of that process.

Shaping of Complex Behavior

Because an action cannot be rewarded or punished unless it occurs, the mechanism of the law of effect can only strengthen acts that *already* occur. This being the case, how could a man teach a dog to run to the closet and fetch his slippers? The man would probably have to wait a long time before this rather complex behavior occurred fortuitously so he could reward it. Instead, he must begin by rewarding the dog for simple acts already within its repertoire. As these simple acts are strengthened, other acts will appear in the repertoire more like the desired final behavior.

The law of effect works rather subtly and rather slowly on complex patterns of behavior; these complex patterns evolve from simpler patterns, just as complex species structures evolve from simpler structures. In our hypothetical experiment with the jumping cat illustrated in Figure 4-1, we would have to wait a very long time for a jump over 20 inches from when the cat is first put into the box. Thus, if we tried to strengthen 20-inch jumps by reinforcing them initially, we might not succeed. If, however, we first reinforced 13-inch jumps, we see from the revised distribution at the lower right of Figure 4.1 that 20-inch jumps would become fairly frequent. *Then*, if we rewarded 20-inch jumps, we would be likely to succeed in strengthening them. By this method of *successive approximations* to our goal, we could finally train the cat to consistently jump at the very limits of its capacity.

FIGURE 4.1 The basic mechanism of evolution compared with the basic mechanism of instrumental conditioning. The two examples used are (a) the natural selection of long-necked giraffes and (b) the jumping-cat experiment.

The Evolution of Functional Human Behavior
in the Clinic

In the laboratory we are concerned with complex contingencies of reinforcement and with quantifying the variables that control behavior. We tend to take for granted the basic principles by which such control is obtained, the principles outlined in this book. At several institutions, however, researchers have been resolutely applying these principles to the treatment of dysfunctional human behavior. These applications have been successful compared with more traditional methods of treating behavioral disorders.

One way to look at dysfunctional behavior is to regard it as behavior tht has evolved "out of synchrony" with changes in the environment. According to this view, when the environment changes too suddenly or drastically, an animal may not be able to "keep up"—to compensate adequately.

Someone who is unhappy about his behavior may seek help from a therapist. It is up to the therapist to provide the appropriate environmental gradations that will reward the patient for approximations to the desired behavior.

Sometimes it is society, rather than the individual himself, that desires a change in his behavior. Murder is an obvious example of a dysfunctional behavior that harms human society. Then there are those individuals who cannot function in the particular society in which they live. Some cannot hold a job; some cannot interact with other people; some cannot communicate rationally; others cannot even eat or attend to their own bodily needs without constant assistance. The basic question regarding such a person is: Do we want to use the most effective means we know to change his behavior for the better (that is, to bring it into conformity with the environmental contingencies)? If we refuse to try, we will continue to expose the inmate to the contingencies of reinforcement in our present institutions. This course of action often does provide a crude but effective means of modifying behavior—for the worse.

The techniques used in behavior modification are varied. At present, behavior modification outside the laboratory is more of an art than a science; each therapist evolves his or her own techniques for applying behavioral principles. Let us consider an example involving a verbal response of a catatonic schizophrenic patient who had been completely mute for 19 years prior to the incidents reported here. To say the least, the patient, referred to as S (for *subject*), was withdrawn and exhibited little psychomotor activity. This case history is not unique. It is from a report published in 1960 by Wayne Isaacs, James Thomas, and Israel Goldiamond of Anna State Hospital in Illinois.*

The S was brought to a group therapy session with other chronic schizophrenics (who were verbal), but he sat in the position in which he was placed and continued the withdrawal behaviors which characterized him. He remained impassive and stared ahead even when cigarettes, which other members accepted, were offered to him and were waved before his face. At one session, when E removed cigarettes from his pocket, a package of chewing gum accidentally fell out. The S's eyes moved toward the gum and then returned to their usual position. This response was chosen by E as one with which he would start to work, using the method of successive approximation. (This method finds use where E desires to produce responses which are not present in the current repertoire of the organism and which are considerably removed from those which are available. The E then attempts to "shape" the available behaviors into the desired form, capitalizing upon both the variability and regularity of successive behaviors. The shaping process involves the reinforcement of those parts of a selected response which are successively in the desired direction and the nonreinforcement of those which are not. For example, a pigeon may be initially reinforced when it moves its head. When this movement occurs regularly, only an upward movement may be reinforced, with downward movements not reinforced. The pigeon may now stretch its neck, with this movement reinforced. Eventually the pigeon may be trained to peck at a disc which was initially high above its head and at which it would normally never peck. In the case of the psychotic under discussion, the succession was eye movement, which brought into play occasional facial movements including those of the mouth, lip movements, vocalizations, word utterance, and finally verbal behavior.)

The S met individually with E three times a week. Group sessions also continued. The following sequence of procedures was introduced in the private sessions. Although the weeks are numbered consecutively, they did not follow at regular intervals since other duties kept E from seeing S every week.

Weeks 1, 2. A stick of gum was held before S's face, and E waited until S's eyes moved toward it. When this response occurred, E as a consequence gave him the gum. By the end of the second week, response probability in the presence of the gum was increased to such an extent that S's eyes moved toward the gum as soon as it was held up.

---

*In case histories, the subject is often referred to as S, the experimenter as E.

Weeks 3, 4. The E now held the gum before S, waiting until he noticed movement in S's lips before giving it to him. Toward the end of the first session of the third week, a lip movement spontaneously occurred, which E promptly reinforced. By the end of this week both lip movement and eye movement occurred when the gum was held up. The E then withheld giving S the gum until S spontaneously made a vocalization, at which time E gave S the gum. By the end of this week, holding up the gum readily occasioned eye movement toward it, lip movement, and a vocalization resembling a croak.

Weeks 5, 6. The E held up the gum, and said, "Say gum, gum," repeating these words each time S vocalized. Giving S the gum was made contingent upon vocalizations increasingly approximating gum. At the sixth session (at the end of Week 6), when E said, "Say gum, gum," S suddenly said, "Gum, please." This response was accompanied by reinstatement of other responses of this class, that is, S answered questions regarding his name and age.

Thereafter he responded to questions by E both in individual sessions and in group sessions, but answered no one else. Responses to the discriminative stimuli of the room generalized to E on the ward; he greeted E on two occasions in the group room. He read from signs in E's office upon request by E.

Since the response now seemed to be under the strong stimulus control of E, the person, attempt was made to generalize the stimulus to other people. Accordingly, a nurse was brought into the private room; S smiled at her. After a month, he began answering her questions. Later, when he brought his coat to a volunteer worker on the ward, she interpreted the gesture as a desire to go outdoors and conducted him there. Upon informing E of the incident, she was instructed to obey S only as a consequence of explicit verbal requests by him. The S thereafter vocalized requests. These instructions have now been given to other hospital personnel, and S regularly initiates verbal requests when nonverbal requests have no reinforcing consequences. Upon being taken to the commissary, he said, "Ping pong," to the volunteer worker and played a game with her. Other patients, visitors, and members of hospital-society-at-large continue, however, to interpret non-verbal requests and to reinforce them by obeying S. [from Isaacs, W., Thomas, J., Goldiamond, I. "Application of operant conditioning to reinstate verbal behavior in psychotics," *Journal of Speech and Hearing Disorders*, 1960, 25, pp. 8–12.]

Isaacs, Thomas, and Goldiamond succeeded in their attempt to change the behavior of a schizophrenic patient. But will a successful treatment in a mental hospital (or therapist's office), where the environment is largely under control, persist when a person returns to the normal complex environment outside of the institution? The arrow in Figure 1.21 labeled "external conditions" (called the "disturbance" in engineering) must not change too drastically. A herd of giraffes could not evolve so as to adapt to a sudden transfer to central Park in New York City, and a fox could not adapt to the area surrounding a modern poultry "factory." Similarly, behavioral modifications wrought in an institution could easily fail in other environments. Clearly, it is important that appropriate behavior continue to be rewarded in the "outside world."

Often dysfunctional behavior seems to be subject to the effect of positive feedback. For some reason a man has a mild behavioral disturbance; his relatives and friends overreact to the mild disturbance and upset him; this increases the disturbance, which, in turn, provokes stronger reactions. A behavioral therapist's treatment of such behavior would be designed to break this pattern in a direct fashion. Relatives who have refused to have a patient home for visits because they are upset by the patient's strange appearance or behavior may change their attitude when the patient's appearance and behavior are less strange. Their changed attitude may well strengthen normal behavior outside the institution.

The example of behavioral shaping in the clinic illustrates the changeability of behavior — its sensitivity to environmental contingencies. The concept of shaping is borrowed from sculpture where material is shaped into a form. As in sculpture the form of behavior ultimately shaped depends on the initial material. Just as wood must be shaped in conformance to its grain so behavior must be shaped according to its underlying pattern. We return now to consider innate behavioral patterns — we have to know what they are like before considering further how they may be shaped.

INNATE PATTERNS OF RECEPTIVITY

After a duckling is hatched, there is a period of a few days, called a *critical period*, when it will attach itself faithfully to almost any large moving object. In nature this object is almost always its mother — which explains the strings of ducklings trailing after their mothers around a pond. But the duckling will follow the moving object if it is a goose or even a human being, instead of a duck. Ducklings tend to follow round objects more readily than square objects, but they will follow square objects, too. In laboratory experiments ducklings have even followed painted blocks of wood. Whatever the duckling follows during its first few days it is likely to continue to follow, rejecting all other followable objects. If a duckling once starts to follow a human being, it will usually continue to follow that same person even though other people or other animals, including its natural mother, are available. This phenomenon, called *imprinting*, was first identified and studied extensively by the ethologist Konrad Lorenz. Lorenz found that if a duckling was imprinted with a goose during the early critical period and then removed after several weeks and put among other ducks, the next year it would direct its mating activity towards geese (the species with which it had been imprinted) rather than ducks, its own species, with which, moreover, it had spent all of its life except the first few weeks.

Some of these observations about imprinting fit neatly into the conditioning paradigms discussed previously. The first few days of life are bound to be upsetting, to say the least, and it is not unreasonable to suppose that any behavior would be reinforced that provides environmental stability (visual and otherwise). This would include, presumably, a duckling following its mother so as to maintain a single object in its visual field. When, as in nature, this object is also associated with food and warmth, it is not hard to understand why following occurs early in life, why the object followed is a source of reinforcement, and why the reinforcement might be expected to be strong and persistent.

Recently increasing attention has been paid to the development of bird song. Different species of birds have distinctly different songs, which they learn while young and eventually use to attract and respond to members of the same species for mating. Even within a species, different subspecies have different "dialects" — minor variations in the basic pattern. Birds that are crossbred (raised by parents with a different song) may develop songs that are mixtures of the song patterns of their biological and their adoptive parents.

The discovery of critical periods for animal learning has given rise to speculations that similar critical periods also exist for human learning. For instance, is there a critical period for the acquisition of language, prior to which language is impossible to learn and subsequent to which it is very difficult to learn? Does experience during some critical period determine once and for all whether we will be basically heterosexual or homosexual? As we have indicated pre-

viously, American psychology has been largely empiricist in orientation and has tended to answer these questiuons negatively. Acquisition
of language, reading, sexual preferences, and other types of human
behavior have been thought to be mostly due to experience — their
predictability being attributed more to similar experience than to
similar developmental processes.

One explanation for the existence of critical periods in imprinting, consistent with the basic principles of conditioning discussed in
previous chapters, considers the hormonal state of the animal during
the critical period. It is a hoary plot device in novels and movies that
an event experienced when a person is in a certain external or internal
state (when drunk, for instance) may be forgotten when that state is
no longer present (when sober) and then recalled when the state is
restored (when drunk again). Regarding external conditions, many of
us tend to regress to childhood attitudes and behaviors if we have been
living away from our parents for some time and then revisit them. Old
patterns and memories come flooding back when the stimulus conditions under which we learned those patterns are restored. In the case
of imprinting, the chaotic internal state of early life may return during
adolescence due to hormonal changes (in ducks or in people) and
thereby facilitate recall or predispose us to given patterns, or "tem-
plates," of reinforcement.

WARNING

Many of the topics discussed in this chapter originated as
challenges to the generality of the standard classical and instrumental paradigms presented in Chapters 2 and 3. Over the
last 20 years, however, these topics have become incorporated
into the standard paradigms. This incorporation has benefited
the psychology of learning in two ways. On the one hand, it
has been recognized that the standard conditioning paradigms
can be understood only within their biological context. On the
other hand, procedures and discoveries that once seemed to be
exceptions to the standard paradigms — exceptions to "general laws of learning" — are currently seen as points along a
continuum. For example, approximations to the long CS–US
delays obtainable in taste aversion learning (to be discussed
shortly) have been achieved with maze learning as well. And
the autoshaping procedure (also to be discussed shortly), far
from being an exception to general laws, has become a stan-

dard classical conditioning paradigm used for the discovery of general principles.

INNATE MOTOR PATTERNS

Thorndike's experiments with cats in a puzzle box illustrate the sensorimotor aspects of *belongingness*. In most of his experiments Thorndike trained cats to pull strings or press levers to get out of the box. In one experiment, however, Thorndike trained a cat to yawn to get out of the box. This training proved to be exceedingly difficult. Finally, when Thorndike succeeded, the yawn produced by the cat was an artificial parody of what a yawn should be. The cat opened and closed its mouth but did not really yawn. Evidently yawning and getting out of a box do not "belong together." Thorndike met with similar failures in trying to train a cat to scratch itself to get out of the box. The problem may have been that Thorndike's cats did not naturally yawn or scratch when confined. Rather, they tended to explore the cage and poke their paws and noses into corners. Because the cats did not yawn or scratch, Thorndike might have had difficulty teaching them these acts with *any* reward.

Negative Reinforcement

Since Thorndike, similar phenomena have periodically turned up in the psychological literature. Rats can be trained to jump forwards to escape shock to their rear paws and backwards to escape shock to their front paws, but not to jump in the opposite directions which in nature would be into instead of away from the place of danger. In avoidance studies it has been found easier to train rats to turn a wheel to avoid shock than to press a lever (Figure 4.2). Turning a wheel resembles the scrambling a rat would do to get out of the box, whereas pressing a lever involves orientation towards the source of the shock in the lower part of the box.

The movements an animal would normally make to escape from shock or other painful stimuli have been called, by the psychologist Robert Bolles, *species-specific defense reactions*. Each species has a repertoire of such responses ranging from freezing in place to running

(a)
Rat's natural reaction to shock
is to climb over the wall of its
box.

(b)
Turning a wheel is similar to
climbing and, hence, an easy
avoidance response to teach
and stable once taught.

(c)
Pressing a bar is not similar to
climbing and, hence, a difficult
avoidance response to teach and
unstable once taught.

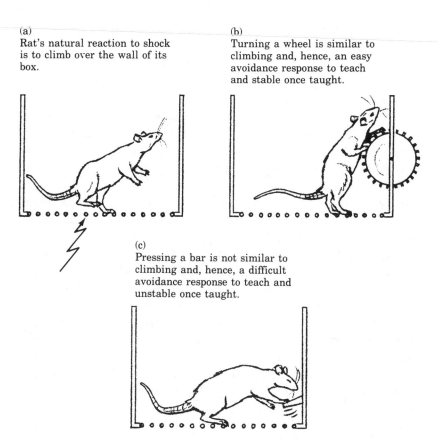

FIGURE 4.2 Why is it easier to teach a rat to escape and avoid shock by turning a wheel than by pressing a bar?

away to attacking. Bolles speculates that the responses corresponding to those the animal would normally emit in the presence of the aversive stimulus are the ones that can be taught as avoidance responses. If one attempts to teach an animal to avoid an aversive stimulus by making a response it would not ordinarily make in the presence of such a stimulus, the animal will learn the avoidance response only very slowly, the response will be unstable, and the performance of the response will look artificial, like the cat's yawning. When the response in an avoidance task is actually antagonistic to a species-specific defense reaction, it will be impossible or nearly impossible to teach.

It is no accident, Bolles argues, that many avoidance studies deal with dogs or rats jumping over hurdles to avoid shock. Jumping over a hurdle is just what these animals would naturally do to escape a painful stimulus. However, it should be realized that the association between jumping and avoidance of shock is far from arbitrary, and that any results obtained with this species-specific reaction must be scrutinized carefully before they can be generalized to other responses or other species.

It was once part of the lore of the animal conditioning laboratory that pigeons could not learn to escape or avoid aversive stimuli. What was meant was that pigeons could not be taught to escape or avoid shock by pecking an illuminated disk (a key). Pigeons can avoid certain stimuli very effectively, as anyone can testify who has tried to catch one on the street. But pecking a key was a convenient response to use with positive reinforcement (we shall see why in a few pages when we discuss autoshaping), and there did not seem to be any reason that pigeons should not learn to escape or avoid shock as they had learned to obtain food.

If instrumental conditioning were simply a matter of associating an arbitrarily chosen response with an arbitrarily chosen reinforcer, it would indeed be a mystery if pigeons could not learn to escape or avoid shock by pecking a key. But the mystery disappears as soon as it is realized that the typical species-specific defense reaction of pigeons to sudden shocks, such as those used in escape or avoidance experiments, is running or flying away. Thus it was found that head raising (a movement preparatory to flying) could be taught to pigeons as an escape or avoidance response. Similarly, pigeons could be taught to escape shock by walking to the other side of the chamber.

Pecking remained an impossible response to teach until shock was increased gradually instead of applied suddenly. When pulses of shock are introduced gradually, the species-specific defense reaction of pigeons is different from their reaction to sudden shock. With sudden shock the pigeons flee; with a gradual shock they attack. When shock is introduced gradually, it is in fact unnecessary to specifically train pigeons to peck a key to turn it off. If the key is suddenly illuminated after the shock reaches its maximum value, pigeons will attack the key. Figure 4.3 shows one pigeon pecking the key (actually a button

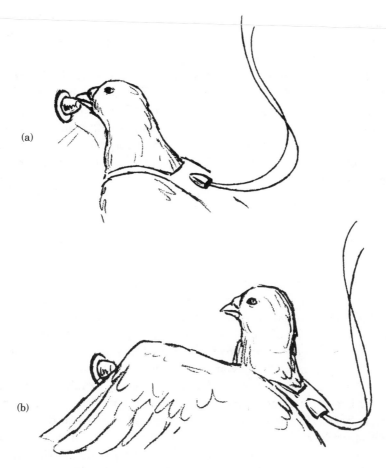

(a)

(b)

FIGURE 4.3 Pigeon escaping shock by (a) pecking key and (b) hitting key with wing.

illuminated and extended slightly into the chamber) and another hitting the key with its wings. Both of these responses occurred without any specific training. When the response in question is actually instrumental in turning off the shock, it tends to occur earlier and earlier (at less intense shocks) and to be made more efficiently. Instead of attacking the key, the pigeon now calmly brushes the key with its wings (if wing flapping was the initial response) or calmly pecks the key (if pecking was the initial response). The response undergoes a metamorphosis from a natural species-specific defense reaction to an instrumental response that resembles the initial reaction only superficially (as the instrumental yawn of Thorndike's cats resembled a real yawn only superficially).

The species-specific defense reactions described by Bolles are a subcategory of what the ethologists call fixed-action patterns. The species-specific defense reactions are fixed-action patterns that occur in the presence of aversive stimuli. According to Bolles, any responses learned to escape or avoid aversive stimuli are derived from these fixed-action patterns. One need not accept entirely this strongly nativist view to recognize the significant role that fixed patterns of behavior play in negative reinforcement.

Positive Reinforcement

In positive reinforcement, fixed patterns of behavior also play an important role in determining what behavior will be easy or difficult to modify. As in negative reinforcement, these patterns can help or hinder the process of conditioning, depending on whether the conditioning is or is not in harmony with the patterns. Let us first consider how fixed patterns of behavior may hinder conditioning.

After receiving training at Harvard University in animal learning, Keller Breland set out to apply in a practical setting the principles he had learned. He and his wife Marian trained animals to do various tricks for advertising purposes and for exhibits at state fairs, shopping centers, and the like. The training was accomplished with the use of instrumental conditioning principles. For instance, one exhibit, activated by a customer putting a quarter into a slot, consisted of a chamber containing a chicken, a miniature basketball basket located a miniature foul shot away from the chicken, and a short vertical tube a few inches in diameter located between the chicken and the basket. About a second after the chamber was illuminated, a continuous stream of air started from the tube and a ping pong ball popped out of the tube and hung suspended in the airstream. The chicken pecked at the ping pong ball and sent it in the direction of the basket, more often than not into the basket, scoring a point and receiving a short delivery of food from a hopper in the rear of the cage. After three points were scored, the chamber darkened and the show was over. After several such exhibitions the satiated chicken was retired for the day, and a hungry one replaced it. Tricks such as these, taught not only to chickens but also to reindeer, cockatoos, porpoises, and whales, helped confirm the principles discovered in animal laboratories.

In 1961, however, after about 15 years of this sort of endeavor, the Brelands published a paper called "The Misbehavior of Organisms," in which they recounted some of their failures. The failures all took the same form: An animal would be taught some simple act and learn the act quickly, but later another response would intrude into the act, becoming more and more frequent until it dominated the animal's performance so strongly that the food reward was delayed or not attained at all. For instance, consider the Brelands' description of the behavior of a pig:

> Here a pig was conditioned to pick up large wooden coins and deposit them in a large "piggy bank." The coins were placed several feet from the bank and the pig required to carry them to the bank and deposit them, usually four or five coins for one reinforcement. (Of course, we started out with one coin, near the bank.)
>
> Pigs condition very rapidly, they have no trouble taking ratios, they have ravenous appetites (naturally), and in many ways are among the most tractable animals we have worked with. However, this particular problem behavior developed in pig after pig, usually after a period of weeks or months, getting worse every day. At first the pig would eagerly pick up one dollar, carry it to the bank, run back, get another, carry it rapidly and neatly, and so on, until the ratio was complete. Thereafter, over a period of weeks the behavior would become slower and slower. He might run over eagerly for each dollar, but on the way back, instead of carrying the dollar and depositing it simply and cleanly, he would repeatedly drop it, root it, drop it again, root it along the way, pick it up, toss it up in the air, drop it, root it some more, and so on.
>
> We thought this behavior might simply be the dilly-dallying of an animal on a low drive. However, the behavior persisted and gained in strength in spite of a severely increased drive — he finally went through the ratios so slowly that he did not get enough to eat in the course of a day. Finally it would take the pig about 10 minutes to transport four coins a distance of about 6 feet. The problem behavior developed repeatedly in successive pigs. [from Breland, K. and Breland, M. The misbehavior of organism. *American Psychologist*, 1961, 16, pp. 681–684.]

The Brelands describe the interfering behavior of the pigs as *instinctive drift*. By this they mean that the pigs instinctively root (dig in the ground with their snouts), that the experimental situation with food and small wooden objects provided the conditions for exhibiting this behavior, and that the instinctive behavior came to predominate over the instrumentally reinforced behavior. We might call the rooting of the pigs a *species-specific appetitive reaction* to parallel the species-specific defense reaction described by Bolles. Both the appetitive and defense reactions are subcategories of fixed-action patterns.

Now let us turn to situations where fixed patterns of behavior work for, rather than against, conditioning. In Chapter 2 we discussed the concept of instrumental pseudoconditioning. In the example cited there, an injection of adrenalin delivered after each bar-press caused the rat to be more active and hence press the bar more often—so adrenalin, although it increased bar-presses, may not have done so via the mechanism of instrumental conditioning. But suppose the reward used is truly rewarding (when tested against a pseudoconditioning control) and also elicits some behavioral pattern that enhances measured responding. This is often the case with food—the behavior elicited by feeding enhances the particular response that food is supposed to reinforce.

With pigeons, periodic free presentation of food generates pecking of one kind or another, usually pecking at the wall of the cage. If there is an illuminated key on the wall and periodic reinforcers are dependent on pecking the key (as with a fixed-interval schedule of reinforcement), many of the pecks on the key can be attributed to the periodic food presentations themselves rather than to the instrumental dependency of the food presentations on pecking. In other words, in many instrumental conditioning situations a positive feedback process is at work. The food causes a pattern of behavior, which (as the experimenter has arranged) will produce more food, which in turn produces more of the behavior, and so on.

An experimental procedure that shows vividly how fixed patterns of behavior can interact with instrumental responding is the procedure called *autoshaping*. Autoshaping clearly shows that behavior can be "shaped" rapidly when species-specific reactions are brought into play. Not only do pigeons tend to peck when food is presented freely, but they will also direct their pecks at a response key if illumination of the key is paired with food. In 1968 Paul L. Brown and Herbert M. Jenkins published the first report of the phenomenon. Their basic finding was that when a hungry pigeon was exposed to periodic free presentations of food, each preceded by a brief (3- or 8-second) illumination of the response key, most pigeons would peck the key after about 40 to 50 such presentations.

In ordinary instrumental conditioning experiments, animals are trained to respond by a process called shaping. After the animal orients towards the response manipulandum, (the thing being manipulated—the rat's lever, for instance, or the pigeon's key) the experimenter presents food. This increases the probability of such orientation in the future. The next time the experimenter observes the orientation, he or she withholds food until the animal comes somewhat closer to the manipulandum, then closer and closer in successive approximations until the desired response is emitted. Figure 4.4a shows how a pigeon's behavior is shaped to peck a key. Shaping is the same sort of procedure as previously described to train a cat to jump higher and higher. Figure 4.4b shows how autoshaping is used to get a pigeon to peck a key by automatically pairing the key illumination with food and thus without observing the pigeon at all.

The process shown in Figure 4.4c is called *negative autoshaping*. It was first reported by David and Harriet Williams. Until the first peck at the key, the process is exactly the same as positive autoshaping shown above it. When the pigeon pecks the key, however, food is not delivered. Thus, there are two processes working in opposition in negative autoshaping. Pecking is stimulated by the autoshaping procedure, which acts as long as the pigeon does not peck. When the pigeon does peck, however, food is withheld—an instrumental contingency equivalent to *negative punishment*, which tends to decrease pecking. The result of the negative autoshaping procedure is that pigeons peck (as they do with the positive autoshaping procedure) and continue to peck at a slow rate, sometimes going for many trials without food because they pecked the key. Evidently autoshaping is a strong process since it overcomes the negative punishment contingency and keeps the pigeon pecking the key.

How does autoshaping work? At first, it was thought that successive approximations to a key-peck were being adventitiously reinforced by the food presentations. (The word *autoshaping* is derived from this theory. It connotes an automatic shaping of the response. We shall, however, use the word to refer to the procedure, not the theory.) But this simple instrumental conditioning theory cannot really account for autoshaping because the obvious test—looking to see whether the pigeon is moving closer and closer to the key on successive trials—fails. There is also some evidence that the duration of the key-peck (the time that the pigeon's beak is in contact with the key) in autoshaping, especially negative autoshaping, is shorter than

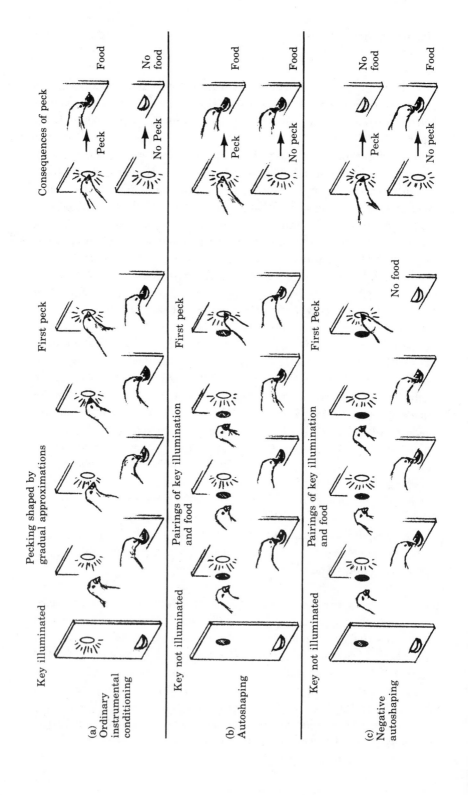

Consequences of peck

Key illuminated   Pecking shaped by gradual approximations   First peck

Peck — Food

No Peck — No food

(a)
Ordinary
instrumental
conditioning

Key not illuminated   Pairings of key illumination and food   First peck

Peck — Food

No peck — Food

(b)
Autoshaping

Key not illuminated   Pairings of key illumination and food   First Peck

No food

Peck — No food

No peck — Food

(c)
Negative
autoshaping

in regular instrumental conditioning. Another line of evidence against this theory is that in negative autoshaping pecking persists after the first peck. To explain such maintenance the adventitious instrumental reinforcement that is supposed to reinforce pecking would have to overcome the explicit instrumental contingency arranged to (negatively) punish pecking. It seems unlikely to most experienced researchers that this could be the case. Whatever maintains pecking in this situation would have to be stronger than adventitious reinforcement would be.

A better explanation for the pigeons' behavior in this situation is an innate tendency to peck in a situation where food is probable. The onset of the key light just before food delivery provides a signal delineating the period of high food probability. This signal acts as what ethologists would call a *releaser* for the peck.* To some extent the signal is a *learned* releaser; in classical conditioning, a signal (a conditional stimulus) by virtue of pairing with the unconditional stimulus comes to cause a response ordinarily elicited by the unconditional stimulus. This would explain the pigeon's tendency to peck during the signal (as it does at the food itself), but it does not explain why the pigeon directs its peck at the key. To some extent the onset of the key light must also be an *innate* releaser for pecking (provided there is an already established tendency to peck). The key itself perhaps resembles the food to some extent and releases pecks just as, in nature, the sight of a grain of food releases pecks.

Autoshaping, easy as it is to establish, depends on a number of conditions:

1. The pigeon should be hungry. Although autoshaping may work with relatively satiated pigeons, it works better with hungry ones.

---

*By *releaser* ethologists imply that the whole pattern of the response is ready to be performed but is normally inhibited. A releaser removes inhibition.

FIGURE 4.4 Contingencies of acquisition and maintenance of key-pecking behavior in a pigeon with ordinary instrumental conditioning, autoshaping, and negative autoshaping.

2. Food should be presented occasionally in the situation. Turning the key light on and off does not work if no food is present.

3. The key light must be turned on and off. Continuous illumination does not work even with food present.

4. The key light should signal a high probability of food; that is, it should come on just before the food, and it should be on for a brief time relative to the time it is off (the intertrial intervals). As the key light loses its power to signal reinforcement (by being left on too long, for instance), it also loses its power to autoshape pecking.

Autoshaping works with water reward as well as food. The peck at the key with water reward has a different topography from that with food reward: The pigeon seems to be sipping at the key instead of pecking at the key as it does with food reward. Autoshaping also works with electric-shock reduction. Pigeons will peck at a key when the key light is turned on just before electric shock is reduced. This may be because the shock, turned on gradually, elicits attack at the lit key. Responses of animals other than pigeons can also be autoshaped. Monkeys, for instance, have been trained by autoshaping to press a lit panel. Rats have been conditioned by autoshaping to press a lever with a light directly over it.

Autoshaping is a phenomenon that is being studied intensively now in several laboratories. New information may change the picture, but it seems now as if the autoshaped peck emerges from a combination of innate patterns of behavior, innate releasing stimuli, and classical conditioning. In recent years autoshaping has become an accepted method for studying the process of classical conditioning (as an association between the light and food).

Why is autoshaping important? It may seem as if we have spent too much time on this phenomenon. Why worry about the responses of a seemingly insignificant animal in an artificial environment? But autoshaping is important for several reasons. On one hand, it has shown psychologists that the supposedly simple case of a pigeon pecking a key in a Skinner box is actually much more complicated than it at first appears. The activity of pigeons studied in the Skinner box is not purely instrumental but is superimposed on the innate behavior patterns of the pigeon and "contaminated" by classical conditioning effects. On the other hand, autoshaping offers a unique opportunity to study how these various types of conditioning interact with each other and with the animal's behavior patterns under conditions in which behavior is more easily observed and measured than in most other experimental environments and certainly more than in the natural environment. The Skinner box offers the possibility of studying the interaction of the various components of behavior and evaluating the contribution of each component. Finally, autoshaping is worth studying because it involves the basic components of all learning, human and otherwise: innate patterns shaped to a greater or lesser extent by environmental contingencies.

ADAPTIVE AND MALADAPTIVE ASSOCIATIONS

In classical conditioning the CS–US relationship gives rise to an altered response. In instrumental conditioning the response–reinforcer relationship gives rise to an altered response. The limitations we have been discussing so far refer to the influence of the situation in which learning takes place on the alteration of the response. Motor reactions to the situation either facilitate or hinder the response. Now we turn to a more fundamental type of limitation — a limitation of the associability inherent between the CS and US and between response and reinforcement.

It turns out that associations, like motor reactions, are by no means arbitrary. That this is so can perhaps best be illustrated by describing an experiment by John Garcia and Robert A. Koelling published in 1966. In previous experiments it had been found extremely easy to train rats to form an association between sickness (usually caused by X-radiation) and taste (that is, rats would avoid the food they had eaten before becoming sick), but it had been difficult to train rats to form an association between sickness and visual or auditory stimuli. These experimental results fitted in with what was known about rats' natural avoidance of poisons. For centuries man has been trying to get rid of rats by poisoning them but without much success. For instance, if the basement of a butcher shop containing barrels of salted meats were infested with rats, the owner might poison a small dish of sugar and leave it out for the rats. But the rats would each eat only a drop of the sugar (even though it tasted good), become sick, and thereafter avoid sugar. They would keep eating the meat, they would not die, and they would not leave the cellar. This phenomenon, of tasting a bit of new food and then, if becoming sick, avoiding it thereafter, is known as bait shyness. It is an annoying habit of rats, which on their part is quite adaptive since it makes them difficult to poison. What Garcia and Koelling wanted to investigate was the relative ease with which rats associated sickness with taste but not with sights or sounds.

Garcia and Koelling tested four groups of rats in classical conditioning experiments. All the rats were given the same CS, what the experimenters called "bright-noisy-tasty water." By means of a drinkometer each lick at a tube was counted and followed by a brief flash of light and a click. The water in the tube was flavored with saccharin (or salt for some of the rats), so each lick was followed by a gustatory, a visual, and an auditory stimulus. This combined CS was then paired with different aversive stimuli (USs) for the four groups of rats. Two groups were given aversive stimuli that made them sick; one sickness group was given X rays while it was drinking, and the other was given the poison lithium chloride in the drinking water. The other two groups were shocked—one immediately after each lick and the other after a slight delay. Interspersed with the conditioning trials (each conditioning trial consisted of a 20-minute daily period of drinking paired with the aversive stimulus) were trials on which plain water was presented, without the aversive stimulus. In addition, prior and subsequent to the pairing of CS and US, each group was tested with the tasty water and bright-noisy water separately.

Figure 4.5 shows the results for the X-ray sickness group and the immediate-shock group (the other groups followed suit). During the pretest, the rats in both groups drank large quantities of both the bright-noisy water and the tasty water in about equal proportions. During the experiment proper, both groups of rats gradually came to stop drinking the bright-noisy-tasty water (although on alternate days they drank plenty of plain water). Evidently both sickness and shock caused the rats to stop drinking. But on the posttests, the rats that had been made sick did not drink the tasty water and did drink the bright-noisy water, and the rats that had been shocked did not drink the bright-noisy water but did drink the tasty water. Although both sickness and shock suppressed drinking, each became associated with

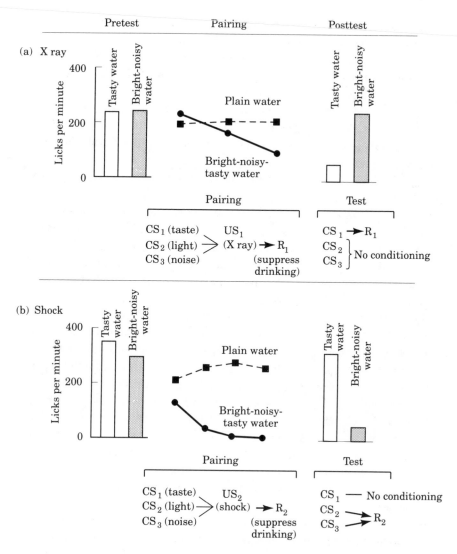

FIGURE 4.5 Garcia and Koelling's association experiment, with X ray and shock used as the aversive stimuli.

only some of the stimuli accompanying drinking. Sickness became associated with taste (and not with lights and sounds), whreas shock became associated with lights and sounds (and not with taste.)* These results clearly show that one cannot simply pair CSs and USs arbitrarily and expect conditioning to occur. Whether conditioning occurs will depend on which CSs are paired with which USs. For the rat, tastes and sickness "belong together."

Other experiments have shown that for other animals the belongingness of taste and sickness is not so strict as for rats. For instance, quail and guinea pigs both quite readily associate visual stimuli with sickness. This makes sense from a biological point of view. How an animal searches for food in its natural environment may determine which stimuli will be most easily associated with illness for that species. Both quail and guinea pigs forage in the daytime using their eyes. If quail and guinea pigs had to depend on taste to avoid poisonous food, they would have a great deal of difficulty surviving. Rats, on the other hand, typically forage at night using taste and smell. Thus it is these very senses that warn rats about poisonous food.

A peculiarity of taste–sickness associations is that they are best formed with novel tastes. Rats can learn to associate familiar tastes with sickness, but only after many trials and with a difficulty commensurate with that of associating sights and sounds with sickness.

Perhaps the most remarkable difference between taste–sickness association and the other types of learning that have been studied is the long delay possible between CS and US with the taste–sickness effect. To give an idea of the difference, Figure 4.6 shows, in parts (a) and (b), two standard delay functions, the first for classical and the second for instrumental conditioning, and in part (c) a delay function for taste–sickness learning. With many classical conditioning procedures, the optimum delay between CS and US may be as brief as about 0.5 second: in instrumental conditioning, immediate reinforcement is necessary. (When reinforcement has operated with a delay, it has

---

*Garcia has recently speculated that the relatively high incidence of anorexia nervosa (self-starvation) among teenage girls may be partially a form of taste aversion. The bodies of girls in their teenage years typically begin to produce the hormone estrogen. This hormone in large amounts makes people nauseous (hence the "morning sickness" common among pregnant women whose bodies also produce large amounts of estrogen). It may be that for some girls nausea becomes associated with various kinds of food. This pairing, in combination of course with the social pressures especially salient in those years, may be enough to start and maintain the behavioral pattern of anorexia nervosa.

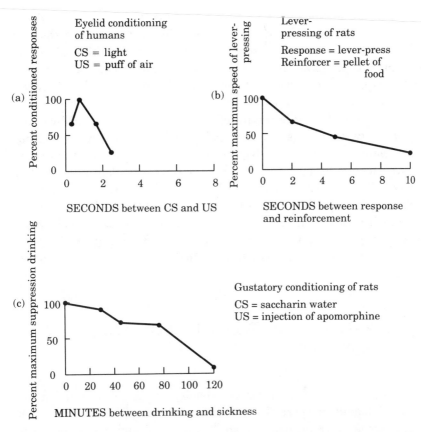

FIGURE 4.6 How delay affects conditioning with classical, instrumental, and gustatory procedures. (Data for (a) from B. Reynolds, "The acquisition of a trace conditioned response as a function of the magnitude of the stimulus trace," *J. Exp. Psych.*, 1945, **35**, 15–30. Data for (b) from C. T. Perin, "A quantitative investigation of the delay of reinforcement gradient," *J Exp. Psych.*, 1943, **32**, 37–51. Data for (c) from J. Garcia, F. R. Ervin, and R. A. Koelling, "Learning with prolonged delay of reinforcement," *Psychonomic Science*, 1966, **5**, 121–122.)

generally been assumed that the delay is bridged by conditional reinforcers — stimuli associated with primary reinforcement — which themselves follow immediately after the response). The delay function in Figure 4.6c, published by Garcia, Ervin, and Koelling, is of quite a different order, with conditioning at a high level even after a 1-hour delay. In this study each group of rats was given a sweet solution and then made sick later after a period indicated on the abscissa. There were five pairings of taste and sickness for each rat. Then the rats were tested for how much sugar solution they would drink. Even the group with a 3-hour delay drank less than the controls. Subsequent studies have found taste–sickness conditioning with delays between CS and US of up to 6 or 8 hours.

As we said at the beginning of this section, there is typically a long delay between tasting a poison and becoming sick. If rats could not associate the taste of the bait (in the butcher's cellar, for instance) with sickness, they would not have survived as plentifully as they have. The peculiar properties of taste aversion learning (the long delays, the rapid acquisition by rats) seem well suited to help them deal with poisons in their own ecological niche. Thus, to understand taste aversions (or, for that matter, any kind of learning), you have to take into account the evolutionary history of the species you are studying.

INTERACTION BETWEEN INNATE AND LEARNED PATTERNS

In many situations, patterns of behavior are established and maintained mainly by periodic environmental stimuli. A fairly obvious example is the traffic light, which signals "stop" and "go" according to a predetermined pattern and which governs behavior accordingly. However, just as environmental stimuli intrude to influence many naturally occurring biological rhythms, so do biological factors influence behavior governed by periodic environmental stimuli.

In institutions such as jails and army posts, where significant events are rigidly scheduled, behavior takes correspondingly rigid forms. When people leave the institution, their behavior continues to conform to the schedule for a while: They wake up, go to sleep, eat, rest, and exercise at the times determined by the institution until gradually a combination of variable exigencies of everyday life and variable biological rhythms takes over again. The old soldier who cannot adapt to civilian life may be unable to adjust his rigid behavior to more flexible rhythms. He feels lost if food is not provided at fixed times every day, and he wakes up at 6:30 each morning even though he has nothing to do at that hour.

An important study of environmentally induced periodic behavior was done by John Staddon and Virginia Simmelhag at Duke University. The researchers studied the behavior of pigeons that were allowed access to food at short, periodic intervals. Outside of the experimental chamber, the pigeons were fed only enough to maintain their weights at 80 percent of normal, or free-feeding weight, but permitted to drink water freely and swallow grit (small stones that a pigeon eats to help digest food). After being taken from their home cages and weighed, the pigeons were introduced separately into the experimental chamber. There a tray containing food was made available every 14 seconds for 2 seconds at a time. In the condition that currently interests us, the pigeons did not have to make any particular instrumental response to get food — the tray just came up for 2 seconds every 14 seconds regardless of what the pigeons did.

It was the pigeons' behavior during the 12 seconds between food presentations that Staddon and Simmelhag wanted to study. Specifically, they wanted to see whether any behavioral patterns would emerge. One wall of the experimental chamber had a window through which the pigeon could be observed. The researchers were able to discern 16 types of behavior exhibited by the pigeons in this relatively sterile environment. They ranged from "R_1 — magazine wall — an orientation response in which the bird's head and body are directed toward the wall containing the magazine [the food tray]" through "R_9 — preening — any movement in which the beak comes into contact with the feathers or the bird's body" to "R_{16} — locomotion — the bird walks about in no particular direction."

Whenever a pigeon engaged in one of the 16 activities, the observer would press a button corresponding to that activity on the recording device and hold it down until the activity stopped.

Two patterns emerged. Some responses started with low probability right after food delivery and became more and more probable during the 12 seconds of the cycle — at the end of the cycle, just before food delivery, these responses were most probable. Other responses reached maximum probability early in the cycle and then decreased to zero about halfway through the cycle. Figure 4.7 illustrates, in an idealized form, the two types of responses. The first kind were labeled *terminal responses*; the second kind were labeled *interim responses*. Figure 4.8 shows actual data for one pigeon.

The responses that turned out to be terminal responses were usually an orientation toward the wall of the chamber where the food

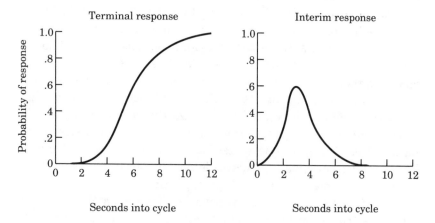

FIGURE 4.7 Idealized forms of terminal and interim responses in Staddon and Simmelhag's experiments.

tray would appear (R_1) and a pecking movement of the head (R_7); the terminal responses of all the birds were almost identical. Orienting toward the source of food and pecking seem appropriate, moreover, to the coming of the food, and these responses became highly probable as the food was about to appear. Interim responses, on the other hand, varied considerably from bird to bird. These involved locomotion, pecking the floor (where stray grains of food sometimes fell), flapping wings, preening, and so on. It is the theory of Staddon and Simmelhag that each cycle is divided into two periods — an early period, when food is improbable, and a later period, when food is highly probable for the pigeons. During the early period, when food is improbable, the tendency of the pigeons is to escape the chamber and seek food elsewhere. Since they are prevented from doing this, they seek reward from other sources. Thus, they look on the floor for food, they preen, they flap their wings. If there were another pigeon in the chamber, this is when they would perform aggressive or sexual acts. If there were water in the chamber, this is when they would drink. As the time for food approaches, however, their behavior becomes stereotyped — they engage in a fixed action pattern appropriate to a high probability of food.

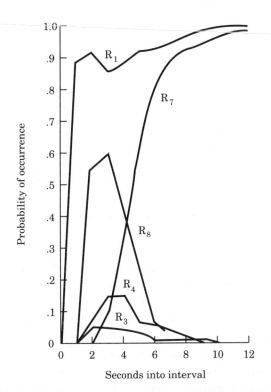

FIGURE 4.8 Probability of each behavior in one of Staddon and Simmelhag's pigeons as a function of postfood time averaged over three sessions of steady-state responding. (Each point gives the probability that a given behavior occurred at that second of postfood time.) R_1 = *Magazine wall* (an orientation response in which the bird's head and body are directed toward the wall containing the magazine.) R_3 = *Pecking floor* (pecking movements directed at the floor.) R_4 = *Quarter circle* (a response in which a count of one quarter circle would be given for turning 90° away from facing the magazine wall, a count of two for turning 180° away, three for 270°, and four for 360°. R_7 = *Pecking* (pecking movements directed toward some point on the magazine wall. This point generally varied between birds and sometimes within the same bird at different times.) R_8 = *Moving along the magazine wall* (a sidestepping motion with breastbone close to the magazine wall; a few steps to the left, followed by a few steps to the right, etc. Sometimes accompanied by (a) beak pointed up to ceiling, (b) hopping, (c) flapping wings.) [From Staddon, J. E. R., and Simmelhag, V. L. The superstition experiment: a reexamination of its implications for the study of adaptive behavior. *Psychological Review*, 1971, **78**, 3–43. Copyright 1971 by the American Psychological Assn.]

Adjunctive Behavior

Adjunctive behavior is another term for interim activities. Adjunctive behavior occurs when a strong environmental stimulus such as food (or electric shock) is presented at fixed or variable intervals. In the sparse environment of Staddon and Simmelhag's experimental chamber, few such activities were available. But in everyday life — where the fixed pattern of meals and the sleep–wake cycle occur — many other activities are simultaneously available. What happens when other activities are made available in the experimental chamber? Obviously we cannot consider every conceivable activity, so let us briefly consider one (aggression) that has been studied in some detail.

It was discovered by a group of psychologists (Nathan Azrin, Donald Hake, and R. Hutchinson) at Anna State Hospital in Illinois that when two animals of the same species are placed together in a cage and subjected simultaneously to a brief but severe electric shock, they turn on each other and fight, often severely injuring one another. When only one of the animals is shocked, that animal attacks the unshocked animal.

This attack behavior occurred reliably after each shock, and Azrin and his colleagues as well as other psychologists investigated it. They found that many species of animals, including rats, monkeys, pigeons, turtles, and people, exhibit aggression when exposed to a painful stimulus in the presence of another animal. Animals also attack models of other animals and even inanimate objects. The reliability and severity of the aggression depends on the intensity of the painful stimulus. For some animal species aggression is also found when food is presented cyclically. When an animal is fed part of the time and not fed another part of the time, it will often attack another animal during the period when the presentation of food is improbable.

From an anthropomorphic view, it migh seem that the animal was fooled into thinking that the other animal was hurting it (or removing its food) and so it retaliated by attacking the other animal so that the other animal would stop its pain-inducing behavior. In that case the aggression would be a reasonable way to reduce pain. But this view of aggression does not appear valid. When rats are trained to press a lever to escape shock, they tend to ignore the lever when another rat is present and spend their time attacking the other rat (which does nothing to reduce the shock) instead of pressing the lever that would reduce the shock. Thus, rats actually will tolerate greater pain in order to attack another rat. It has also been found that a shocked pigeon will work to produce a model of another pigeon and then attack the model. The model that the shocked pigeon attacks serves as a reward, similar to the food which a hungry pigeon eats.

So it seems as if animals have a very strong tendency to attack something, almost anything, between shocks or between food presentations. If an attackable object is available, they will attack that object even at the cost of more pain. If nothing is available to attack, they will seek something to attack and do work (peck a key, for instance) in order to get it.

Some experimentation has also been done on ways to reduce this sort of aggression. Certain drugs will decrease aggression, but it is not clear whether they reduce aggression directly or only the effective intensity of the pain. It has been found possible to reduce aggression somewhat if each aggressive response is followed by a severe punishment—another shock. In this case, the punishment shocks, although they may augment the strong instinctive tendency to attack, effect a learned inhibition of attack. As we have seen, severe punishment is one of the most powerful—though not necessarily one of the most useful—ways to modify behavior.

Another very vivid type of adjunctive behavior is polydipsia. It was discovered by John L. Falk (who coined the term, *adjunctive behavior*). When a rat is exposed to periodic food presentations, and water is simultaneously available, the rat will drink large amounts of water (much more, in fact, than it would ordinarily drink). As with aggression, the rat will do work in order to get the opportunity to drink; also, the temporal pattern of drinking is the same as that of aggression. Still other activities that follow the adjunctive behavior pattern are pica (eating wood and other nonfood material), wheel running, and sexual behavior.

In the experimental chamber we may observe a few terminal and interim activities by making one significant event (such as the availability of food) periodic and restricting the availability of other activities (such as drinking or aggression). In everyday life many significant events occur periodically and may overlap, and many other activities are continuously or intermittently available.

A Theory of Behavior and Evolution

Evolution depends on two kinds of principles. First, there are the principles of *variation*, such as the laws of genetics, which ensure phenotypic diversity. These principles are responsible for the shapes of the original population distributions in Figures 1.18 and 4.1. Then there are the principles of *selection*, which, operating through the population's interaction with the environment, permit certain members and not others to survive.

Staddon and Simmelhag, in their complex experimental and theoretical article, draw an analogy between the processes of evolution and learning. It has been noted many times that reinforcement promotes learning of instrumental responses in much the same way that natural selection promotes the survival of adaptive organisms (see Figure 4.1). But Staddon and Simmelhag carry the analogy further. Pointing out that behavior and the mechanisms by which it is modified are part of biological inheritance, they suggest that evolutionary principles may underlie both the production and selection of behavior.

From their observations and those of similar experiments with other animals, Staddon and Simmelhag classified the sorts of behavior likely to be interim and terminal, and speculated on the function of these two classes of behavior. The sorts of behavior likely to be interim are those that will produce *some* reinforcement when a principal source of reinforcement is improbable.

Data from studies of adjunctive and aggressive behavior, in which the subjects — usually pigeons or rats — have been provided opportunities for other interim behaviors, show that during such interim periods acts such as drinking, fighting, and sex increase markedly. In the absence of these opportunities pigeons try to escape from the situation. When escape is impossible, the pigeons groom or hunt on the floor or in the hopper for stray pieces of food. In other words, interim behavior with respect to one reinforcer (food in this case) consists of the search for other reinforcers during the period when the first reinforcer is improbable. Terminal behavior, on the other hand, usually consists of responses appropriate to the principal reinforcer. When the reinforcer is food, pigeons peck during the terminal period.

At the beginning, the pigeons shifted several responses from the interim to terminal periods and back again. It was almost as if they were trying out various terminal responses. Once pecking was selected as a terminal response, however, it remained the most frequent terminal response for the rest of the experiment, with only occasional brief shifts to other terminal responses.

The alternation between interim behavior during periods of low probability of reinforcement and terminal behavior during periods of high probability of reinforcement, Staddon and Simmelhag claim, corresponds to genetic laws of variation of biological evolution. That is, the natural variation in interim and terminal responding corresponds to the natural variations of genes in the reproduction of species.

What, then, is left for the other evolutionary principles, analogous to natural selection, which Staddon and Simmelhag call the *principles of reinforcement?* Very little indeed. When reinforcement is made dependent on some particular behavior, it can act only to prevent that behavior from being shifted from a terminal response to an interim response. The reinforcement contingency does not strengthen the response, according to Staddon and Simmelhag. It simply prevents that response from being shifted into the interim category (it props up the response), just as natural selection does not directly stregthen any trait but merely prevents that trait from dying out. When reinforcement is made dependent on a naturally occurring terminal response, as when a pigeon's peck is reinforced, training is easy. When reinforcement is made dependent on another response, such as preening, which would normally occur only during the interim period, training is more difficult. Followng a behavior like preening by food reinforcement makes it ipso facto a terminal response. On one hand, making food dependent on preening tends to preserve preening as a terminal response according to the principles of reinforcement. On the other hand, the principles of variation will act to substitute another, more appropriate terminal response such as pecking. This conflict makes training much more difficult than when food is dependent on pecking in the first place.* When, as with negative autoshaping, food is dependent on not pecking, the conflict is extreme, with pecking and not pecking alternating as the principles of variation and reinforcement compete. (Recall also the Brelands' misbehaving pigs. Rooting is a terminal response; a pig will root just prior to eating whether the pig's trainers like it or not.)

Extinction occurs automatically when reinforcement is withdrawn, according to Staddon and Simmelhag, because the prop that was keeping the response from being shifted out of the terminal category is removed. With reinforcement dependent on a terminal re-

---

*But not impossible in all cases. If simply making reinforcement dependent on an interim response (like preening) does succeed in making that former interim response a stable terminal response, we can expect to observe a new set of interim responses. This may be how we generate wholly new behavior such as that involved in "insight."

sponse, behavior during the terminal period will vary less widely. Only the reinforced response will be a terminal response. With reinforcement maintained but the relationship of reinforcement to behavior removed, terminal responding will still occur but will be more variable; responses other than those previously reinforced will more or less frequently appear during the terminal period. With reinforcement removed entirely, only interim responding will occur and behavior will be still more variable. When we observe previously reinforced responses to decrease during extinction, we are observing the increase in variability. Other responses appear as well as the one previously reinforced.

Thus the Staddon and Simmelhag theory ties together the facts of instrumental and classical conditioning with the ethological and biological acts discussed in this chapter.

Suggested Readings

Two collections of articles about biological patterns and learning are:

Seligman, M.E.P., ed. *Biological Boundaries of Learning.* New York: Appleton-Century-Crofts, 1972.

Hinde, R.A., and Stevenson-Hinde, J., eds. *Constraints on Learning: Limitations and Predispositions.* London: Academic Press, 1973.

An article explaining some of the biological factors discussed in this chapter from a general evolutionary viewpoint of learning is:

Logue, A.W. Taste aversion and the generality of the laws of learning. *Psychological Bulletin,* 1979, **86**, 276–296.

An article by Philip Teitelbaum, entitled "Levels of integration of the operant," organizes the material in this chapter in an interesting way. It appears in the Honig–Staddon volume cited in Chapter 3. However, the most influential and penetrating discussion of how constraints on learning fit into an evolutionary framework is the article by John Staddon and Virginia Simmelhag discussed at the end of this chapter, "The supersitition experiment: a reexamination of its implications for the study of adaptive behavior." (*Psychological Review,* 1971, **78**, 3–43).

The following is a list of articles referred to in this chapter:

Azrin, N.H., Hutchinson, R.R., and Hake, D.F. Extinction-induced aggression. *Journal of the Experimental Analysis of Behavior*, 1966, **9**, 191–204.

Bolles, R. Species-specific defense reactions and avoidance learning. *Psychological Review,* 1970, **77**, 32–48.

Braveman, N.S. Poison-based avoidance learning with flavored or colored water in guinea pigs. *Learning and Motivation,* 1974, **5**, 182–194.

Breland, K., and Breland, M. The misbehavior of organisms. *American Psychologist,* 1961, **16**, 681–684.

Brown, P., and Jenkins, H. Auto-shaping of the pigeon's key peck. *Journal of The Experimental Analysis of Behavior,* 1968, **11**, 1–8.

Garcia, J., Ervin, F., and Koelling, R. A. Learning with prolonged delay of reinforcement. *Psychonomic Science,* 1966, **5**, 121–122.

Garcia, J., and Koelling, R. A. Relation of cue to consequence in avoidance learning. *Psychonomic Science,* 1966, **4**, 123–124.

Thorndike, E. L. *Animal Intelligence.* New York: Macmillan, 1911.

Williams, D., and Williams, H. Auto-maintenance in the pigeon: sustained pecking despite contingent non-reinforcement. *Journal of the Experimental Analysis of Behavior,* 1969, **12**, 511–520.

5

Stimulus Control
and Animal Cognition

Virtually any meaningful act of any animal takes time to occur. Even a rat's lever-press may be broken down into approaching the lever, raising a paw, centering the paw over the lever, lowering the paw, applying force, releasing the force, and so forth. Human actions like singing an aria, building a house, or playing baseball endure longer still. How can long-duration actions be analyzed? Figure 2.14 suggests two ways. Figure 2.14a, illustrating classical conditioning, shows a response elicited by antecedent events (the CS or US); long-duration actions could be analyzed in terms of a string of such events. A string of conditional stimuli (CSs) might elicit a string of responses that together constitute a complex act.

Organized instinctive patterns as well as individual acts are subject to classical conditioning. Male Japanese quail, for instance, normally engage in a relatively complex sequence of actions constituting copulatory behavior when a female (the US) is present. If a wooden model (the CS), which normally does not elicit copulatory behavior, is paired a sufficient number of times with the sight of a female quail, however, the complex series of actions that constitute copulatory behavior will be directed to the model. Copulatory behavior itself may then be analyzed as a set of more discrete responses (approaching, displaying, mounting, etc.), each with its own unconditional and conditional stimuli.

But the inner causes of our complex actions are difficult to analyze in this straightforward way. Large parts of the string of conditional and unconditional stimuli that elicit each component of singing an aria, for instance, are buired deep within the singer's nervous system — eventually discoverable, we hope, but at present beyond the grasp of neurophysiology.

Another way of analyzing complex acts is suggested by Figure 2.14b, where responses are categorized not in terms of their antecedents but in terms of their consequences. The act of building a house, for instance, may be viewed in terms of its consequence (a completed house) and analyzed into components (laying a foundation, putting up the supports, attaching the walls, etc.), each classified by its own characteristic consequence. These subacts, in turn, may be analyzed into sub-subacts such as hammering nails, pouring cement, and laying bricks, each again classified in terms of its consequences. If you were writing a book on house building, you would probably organize it this way — in terms of a set of actions with goals, subgoals, and sub-subgoals.

Figure 5.1 shows a set of nested acts that a house builder might perform. In each solid box is just one of the subacts that might be a component of the higher-level act in the box that encloses it. Next to each act, in a dotted box, is its feedback. For example, the consequence of hammering one nail is the sight and feel of a set-in nail, which in turn reinforces the hammering. But hammering this nail is only one of several acts that comprise fastening a board, which in turn is only one of several acts that comprise building a floor, which is only one of several acts involved in erecting the structure, and so on, to building the house, earning a living, and raising a family. The shelter the house provides (or the money paid to the builder) might constitute feedback for and (hence reinforcement of) building the house. Similarly, raising a family is reinforced by good social relations with family and community.

At the same level as raising a family are being a good citizen, being a good son or daughter, and being a good friend. Together these might comprise being a good person, which is (according to some philosophers) its own reward. The important point about Figure 5.1 is

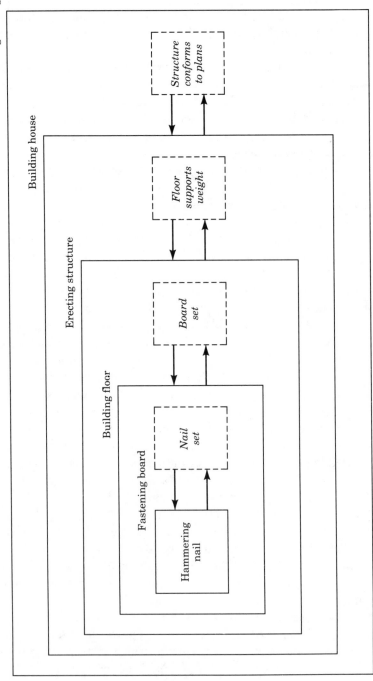

that each higher-level act is more abstract, takes longer to perform, is more difficult to discern, and is less directly related to its feedback than the one inside it.

The stimuli that guide complex behavior of this kind do not simply elicit a response. Rather, in Skinner's terms, they "set the occasion" for a member of the class of behavior (an operant) that defines the response. That is, they signal the presence of a contingency relating actions to consequences. A book on house building, for instance, together with a bank statement signaling available resources and indications of a tight housing market, does not elicit the act of house building, but it does set the occasion for building a house.

Human language may be used as such an occasion-setting class of stimulation. Language is often said to mirror the world (nouns stand for things, verbs for actions), but language does not *just* mirror the world; when we use language to describe things and actions (as a house-building book describes the behavior of building a house), we almost always do so for a practical purpose — *to guide the behavior of other people and ourselves.*

This chapter begins with a brief discussion of stimuli in classical conditioning (as are represented in Figure 2.14a) and goes on to explore the more complex case of the role of stimuli in instrumental conditioning (Figure 2.14b). We reserve discussion of language as a form of stimulus control for the next chapter.

STIMULUS CONTROL

Stimulus control is another term for stimulus discrimination. If an animal comes to respond one way in the presence of a stimulus and another way in its absence, then that stimulus is said to "control" the animal's behavior much as a red light controls traffic.

FIGURE 5.1 Nested activities and feedback (dotted boxes) comprising part of the set of activities in building a house. Still more abstract categories of action are indicated at upper right.

Stimulus Control in Classical Conditioning

We have already discussed stimulus control (discrimination) in classical conditioning. Recall the experiment of Shenger-Krestovnikova with circles and ellipses as stimuli for dogs (Figure 2.6). The circle (CS) was followed by food powder; the ellipse was not. At first dogs salivated when circles or ellipses were presented; they later came to salivate only when circles were presented (except when the circles and ellipses were almost identical). From one point of view, the dogs learned to discriminate between the circles and ellipses. From another point of view, the circles gained control of the dog's salivation.

The most common form of discrimination conditioning consists of alternating two stimuli (like the circles and ellipses), with only one followed by the US. Because this form of discrimination conditioning is so common, there are special terms for the stimuli; the stimulus followed by the unconditional stimulus (the circle) is called the CS + ; the stimulus not followed by the unconditional stimulus (the ellipse) is called the CS − .

There are, however, other ways to obtain stimulus control in classical conditioning. For example, instead of circles followed by food (and ellipses followed by no food), Shenger-Krestovnikova's experiment might have had circles followed by more food and ellipses by less food. The dogs might then have come to respond during exposure to both circles and ellipses, but to respond more to circles. Alternatively, Shenger-Krestovnikova might have adjusted the amount of food proportionally to the roundness of the ellipse. (In Figure 2.6, (b) would have been followed by the least food, (c) by more food, (d) by still more food, and (a) by the most food.) The dogs might then have come to salivate in proportion to the roundness of the stimulus. Still another possibility would have been to follow circles by food and ellipses by electric shock to the paw. Then circles might have come to elicit salivation, and ellipses, withdrawal.

Stimulus Control in Instrumental Conditioning

In instrumental conditioning the relation between behavior and reinforcement (or punishment) is very important; however, *signaling stimuli* (which are neither reinforcers nor punishers in themselves) can also play an important role. In classical conditioning the CS is correlated with reinforcement; in that sense the stimulus plays a primary role. In instrumental conditioning, however, nonreinforcing stimuli play only a secondary role: They indicate changes in the correlation between behavior and reinforcers (or punishers). A good example of a stimulus serving such a secondary function in human behavior is an out-of-order sign on a Coke machine. This sign tells us about the relationship between coins and Cokes but is not itself directly associated with either. Signs that signal a relation between responses and reinforcers are called *discriminative stimuli.*

As in classical conditioning, the most common instrumental discrimination procedures involve alternate presentation of two stimuli; in the presence of one stimulus, responses are reinforced; in the presence of the other, responses are not reinforced (or are reinforced less frequently). As with classical conditioning, the stimuli for this special discrimination procedure also have special names. A discriminative stimulus that signals a relatively high positive correlation between responses and reinforcers is called an S^D ("ess dee"). A discriminative stimulus that signals a relatively low correlation between responses and reinforcers is called an S^Δ ("ess delta"). Figure 5.2 shows this common discrimination procedure with the two types of conditioning.

It is important to note that alternation of stimuli signaling reinforcement and no reinforcement at all (as in Figure 5.2) is only one of many discrimination procedures — only one form of stimulus control. A discriminative stimulus may signal any relation between responses and reinforces. In practice the negative discriminative stimulus, S^Δ, is defined relative to the positive discriminative stimulus, S^D. That is, if two stimuli signal different relationships between responses and reinforcers, the one signaling the higher positive correlation is called the S^D and the other is called the S^Δ. The color of the sky in the morning, for example, gives an indication of whether a trip to the beach that afternoon will be reinforced by the opportunity to swim. But blue skies in the morning do not guarantee fair weather, nor do grey skies guarantee rain. Blue skies signal one relation between response and reinforcement, grey skies another. Thus, while we may refrain from going to the beach on a grey morning, it is *possible* that our response (going to the beach) would be reinforced (nice weather at the beach). Nevertheless, a grey sky would be considered an S^Δ for going to the beach.

As we said in previous chapters, classical and instrumental conditioning may be viewed in corresponding ways. Note that the only

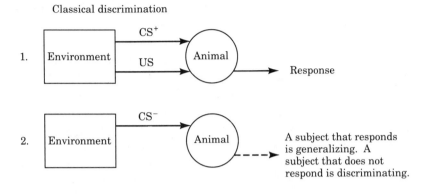

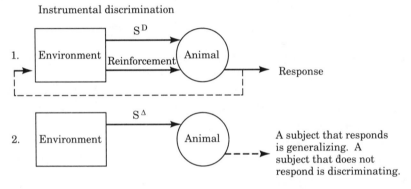

FIGURE 5.2 Discrimination procedures for classical and instrumental conditioning.

operational difference between the upper and lower diagrams of Figure 5.2 is the dashed feedback line in the lower figure. Theorists who believe that a stimulus cannot become a CS + unless there is some sort of feedback (some sort of consequence of the conditional response) say, "Classical conditioning is nothing but a form of instrumental conditioning; consequently, a CS + is really a kind of S^D." Other theorists believe that the critical relationship in the lower figure is that between the S^D and the reinforcer; the feedback contingency, they believe, is irrelevant except as it affects the S^D–reinforcer relationship. These theorists say, "Instrumental conditioning is nothing

but a form of classical conditioning; consequently, an S^D is really a kind of CS + ."

Many modern behaviorists fall into one of these camps. There is a tendency in recent writing to avoid argument by using the symbol S + for either a CS + or an S^D and to use the symbol S − for either a CS − or an S^Δ. However, regardless of *theoretical* view, classical and instrumental conditioning differ as *procedures*, and the presence or absence of explicit feedback has very strong effects on behavior. It is therefore important for the student to be able to distinguish between a CS + as illustrated in the upper diagram and an S^D as illustrated in the lower diagram of Figure 5.2 and correspondingly between a CS − and an S^Δ.

Successive Discrimination and Simultaneous Discrimination

Within the confines of instrumental conditioning, discrimination has been studied in two ways. One way, called *successive discrimination*, alternately presents two different discriminative stimuli. The other way, called *simultaneous discrimination*, presents two discriminative stimuli together.

The alternating green and red of a traffic light, telling us to go (respond) in the presence of the green and stop (not respond) in the presence of the red is an example of successive discrimination. The adjacent green and red lights marking open and closed toll booths on a highway or bridge are an example of simultaneous discrimination. They tell us not whether to go or stop, but whether to go one way or another. In general, simultaneous discrimination situations can produce finer distinctions in responses to stimuli than successive discrimination situations.

There are two reasons for this greater sensitivity of simultaneous discrimination. First of all, the stimuli themselves are easier to tell apart when presented simultaneously. It is easier, for instance to tell a dark from a light shade of grey when the two greys are side by side than when they are seen at different times. Second, even when the stimuli are clearly distinguishable, the properties of simultaneous procedures tend to create greater differences in performance than the properties of successive procedures. In successive discriminations, responding appropriately to one stimulus when it appears does not preclude responding appropriately to the other when it appears.

In simultaneous discriminations, on the other hand, when the animal is responding appropriately to one stimulus, it is losing time during which it might be responding appropriately to the other.

It is easy to see how simultaneous discrimination is more sensitive than successive discrimination in everyday life. At home, when dinner is put before someone, she often only has the choice of eating it or not. Observing a person's eating habits at home may tell you little about her preferences for food, since many people will eat whatever is put in front of them. In a restaurant, however, a choice is available, and eating one food often precludes eating another. Here, the same person is liable to be more discriminating.

Connections

In classical conditioning, the conditional stimulus (the CS) is said to cause the response; in instrumental conditioning the stimulus is said to set the occasion for the response.

The CS in classical conditioning is like an air raid siren signaling an event to come and generating a direct response. The discriminative stimulus of instrumental conditioning is like the "Open" sign in a store window signaling that *if* we were to turn the knob of the door, the door would be unlocked.

This distinction rests on the distinction we previously made between elicited and emitted responses. During classical conditioning, responses are preceded by the US and are said to be elicited, or caused, by the US. After conditioning has taken place (when responses begin to occur after the CS), the responses are, by extension, said to be elicited or caused by the CS. During instrumental conditioning, on the other hand, responses are not preceded in any strict way by any stimulus. They are said to be emitted by the animal. The discriminative stimulus never invariably indicates reinforcement. It may indicate that reinforcement is available *provided* some response is made. Thus, when responding increases in frequency during the discriminative stimulus, we do not say that the stimulus elicits or causes the responses, but that the stimulus *sets the occasion* for the responses to occur.

Accordingly, when pecking by pigeons at a key is reinforced when the key is green and unreinforced when the key is dark, and the pigeon pecks more frequently at the green key, we say that the green key sets the occasion for the response as opposed to the notion that the green key *causes* the response. Similarly, when a man is paid for working on weekdays and not for working on weekends, we say that the stimuli that tell him what day of the week it is (for example, checking a calendar) set the occasion for his work. It would be awkward to say that a calendar *causes* the man to work. We also realize that these stimuli, while controlling whether the man works or not, do not exert exclusive control. It is rare to find a one-to-one correspondence of weekdays and working.

Testing for Control by S^D and S^Δ

Let us return to the procedure illustrated in the lower part of Figure 5.2.) Two discriminative stimuli are alternated. One (the S^D) signals a positive correlation between responses and reinforcers; the other (the S^Δ) signals in this case a zero correlation, with no reinforcement programmed regardless of responding. The behavior usually observed under these conditions is straightforward: responding during the S^D and no responding during the S^Δ.

A particular instance of such a discrimination, involving a pigeon and a key, is illustrated at the top of Figure 5.3. The pigeon's pecks are reinforced when the key is green (S^D) and not reinforced when the key is white with a vertical bar (S^Δ). After alternate exposure to the two discriminative stimuli, the pigeon comes to peck at the key when it is green and not when it is white with a vertical bar.

What has the pigeon learned about the two discriminative stimuli? Consider these three alternatives:

1. The pigeon learns to peck when the key is green (S^D).
2. The pigeon learns not to peck when the key is white with a vertical bar (S^Δ).
3. The pigeon learns to peck when the key is green *and* not to peck when the key is white with a vertical bar.

A parallel set of questions can be raised about virtually any discrimination. A child may be rewarded for kissing its parents and not rewarded for kissing strangers. Does the child learn (1) to kiss its parents, (2) not to kiss strangers, or (3) both?

Which alternative is learned depends on what the child already does. If prior to learning the child kisses nobody, it must learn to kiss

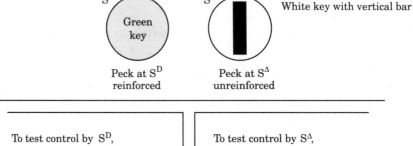

S^D Green key

Peck at S^D
reinforced

S^Δ White key with vertical bar

Peck at S^Δ
unreinforced

To test control by S^D,
present

Red key

If pigeon pecks less at red key
than at green key, green key has
exerted control over responding.

To test control by S^Δ,
present

White key with
horizontal bar

If pigeon pecks more at horizontal
bar than at vertical bar, vertical bar
has exerted control over not
responding.

FIGURE 5.3 Procedures for testing control by S^D and S^Δ.

its parents and need learn nothing specific about strangers. If prior to learning the child kisses everybody, parents and strangers, it must learn not to kiss strangers but nothing specific about its parents. If the child prior to learning sometimes kisses some people, it must learn to kiss its parents *and* not to kiss strangers. The same sort of reasoning applies to the pigeon. If it ordinarily does not peck, it must learn to peck the green key. If it ordinarily pecks, it must learn not to peck the white key with the vertical bar. If it sometimes pecks, it must learn both.

Whether alternative 1, 2, or 3 applies in any given case depends on the animal (both its species and its previous experience), the stimuli, the reinforcer, the response, and the relation between the reinforcer and the response. The question that concerns us here is how to test the alternatives.

Alternatives 1 and 2 imply that one of the stimuli has no effect: Alternative 1 implies that the S^Δ has no effect, and alternative 2 implies that the S^D has no effect. One way to test either of these alternatives is the hypothetical experiment shown in Figure 5.4. The rationale for the tests follows a somewhat complicated argument. The stimulus that is supposed to have no effect is varied. If it is argued, as it is in alternatives 1, and 2, that one of the stimuli has no effect, then its variation also ought to have no effect. If, on the other hand, varying either stimulus has the effect of producing variation in behavior, then alternative 3 must have been correct.

An important practical point of the tests is that the S^D and S^Δ must be varied separately along different continua. In the illustration in Figure 5.4, the continuum is color for the S^D and angle of the bar for the S^Δ. Suppose otherwise, that the S^D and S^Δ varied along the same continuum — that the S^D was a simple white key and the S^Δ was a grey key (and the continuum is brightness). Then in the test phase, any new stimulus (a new shade of gray) would be a variation of both the S^D and the S^Δ. If the pigeon pecked less during the new stimulus, there would be no way of knowing whether it was because the stimulus was less like the S^D or more like the S^Δ. In the example in Figure 5.4, on the other hand, where the S^D and S^Δ are on two continua, we can be fairly certain that while the red key is not like the S^D, it is no more like the S^Δ than the green key was.

Another practical problem with the procedure in Figure 5.4 is what to do about reinforcement while the test stimuli are presented. For tests of the efficacy of S^D, for instance, the usual solution is to stop reinforcement altogether during the test and alternate the original S^D and a group of test stimuli varying along the same dimension (color, in the case of the example in Figure 5.4). This would be a simple generalization experiment where responding would be expected to fall off as the stimuli became more different from the original S^D, provided the S^D had an effect, that is, provided either alternative 1 or 3 were true. Otherwise (if alternative 2 were true), responding would not drop off but would remain at a high value as the color of the stimulus was varied.

For tests of the efficacy of S^Δ, a corresponding procedure is followed. Reinforcement is discontinued, and the original S^Δ is alternated with test stimuli varying along the same dimension (tilt of the bar across the white key in Figure 5.4). This experiment, shown in Figure 5.4 (bottom curve), would test generalization of the S^Δ. Responding would be expected to increase as the stimuli became more different from the original S^Δ provided the S^Δ had an effect (provided

Training

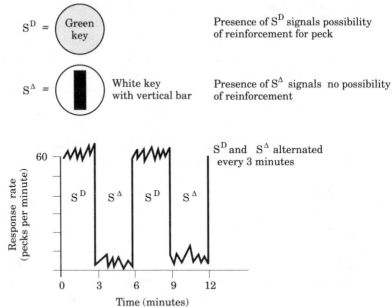

S^D = Green key   Presence of S^D signals possibility of reinforcement for peck

S^Δ = White key with vertical bar   Presence of S^Δ signals no possibility of reinforcement

S^D and S^Δ alternated every 3 minutes

Response rate (pecks per minute)

S^D S^Δ S^D S^Δ

Time (minutes)

Test phase   Reinforcement discontinued. Stimuli alternated. Average rate of responding measured during exposure to each stimulus.

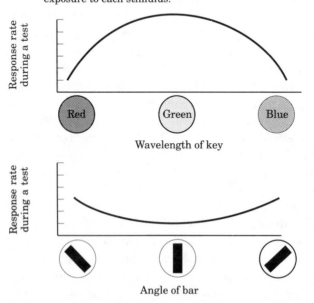

Response rate during a test

Red   Green   Blue

Wavelength of key

Response rate during a test

Angle of bar

FIGURE 5.4 Hypothetical experiment to test discrimination.

either alternative 2 or 3 were true). Otherwise (if alternative 1 were true), responding would not increase but would remain at the same low value as the angle of the bar was changed.

While the specific hypothetical experiment of Figure 5.4 has not been performed exactly as described here, enough similar experiments have been performed for us to be certain that in the case described (pigeons pecking a key), alternative 3 is correct. Both S^D and S^Δ gradients have been found. Figure 5.4 shows a hypothetical S^D and S^Δ test phase gradient. Usually S^Δ gradients are somewhat shallower than S^D gradients. Some experimenters have speculated that this is because the S^D is the only stimulus signaling a positive relationship between responses and reinforcers, while the S^Δ shares the property of signaling nonreinforcement with the myriad other stimuli in the pigeon's environment. Since the S^D is unique and the S^Δ somewhat more general, the pigeon is likely to respond in the presence of a new stimulus as if it were another of the general, more common S^Δ's. In the generalization test, therefore, the particular S^Δ of training does not produce as much discrimination in responding as the S^D of training. This is another way of saying that while alternative 3 is correct, alternatives 1 and 2 are not equally incorrect. There is some truth to alternative 1 in the case of Figure 5.4.

Some psychologists interpret the test phase gradients shown in Figure 5.4 as reflections of processes inside the animal. The S^D gradient is said to mirror an excitatory process inside the animal. The excitation is a continuous state said to underlie emissions of discrete responses. The S^Δ gradient is said to mirror an inhibitory process inside the animal. The inhibition is said to underlie the nonemission of the response.* It is arguable whether the concepts of excitation and inhibition are necessary to mediate between environment and behavior.

Complex Discriminations

Most experiments in the laboratory use discriminative stimuli of a simple kind—they use tones, lights, bars, and so forth. Yet we know that humans and animals are capable of much more complex discrimi-

---

*The notion that inhibition is associated with nonreinforcement comes from Pavlov's conception of extinction as a positive inhibitory process (see Figure 2.4).

nations. We recognize the faces of our relatives, the handwriting of our friends, and their voices. Nonhumans are also capable of making complex discriminations of this kind. Dogs recognize their masters' faces, and the famous RCA trademark reminds us that a dog can recognize his master's voice as well.

Pigeons have been taught to discriminate (rapidly and accurately) between slides containing the presence and absence of people, bodies of water, fish, trees, other pigeons, manufactured objects, particular individuals, the cartoon character Charlie Brown (versus other Peanuts characters), oak leaves (versus leaves of other trees), and trucks (versus cars).

As an illustration of the complex discriminations that are possible, consider the following experiment with pigeons and pictures of trucks and cars. Thousands of photographs were taken of vehicles in the streets, on highways, in parking lots, and at other places. The pictures were then sorted into two groups, those that contained trucks or parts of trucks and those that contained only cars. The pictures were shown in random order to the pigeons, but the same picture was never shown twice to the same pigeon. While the pictures were being shown, the pigeons could peck a key. Occasionally a peck would produce some food, but most of the time pecks had no effect. The critical point of the experiment was that for some pigeons pecks were reinforced only if the picture contained a truck or part of a truck. For other pigeons, pecks were reinforced only when the picture contained cars or parts of cars. In other words, for the first group of pigeons, trucks were S^D's and cars were S^Δ's; for the other group, conditions were reversed. As far as the experimenters could tell, there was no difference between the two groups of photographs other than the cars-versus-trucks distinction. The two groups of photographs were equally light, equally colorful, and equally complex. Yet, within a few weeks of daily exposure to the photographs, the pigeons came to peck rapidly when exposed to a picture containing a truck (if that was the S^D) or a car (if that was the S^D) and slowly or not at all when the picture contained the S^Δ vehicle.

It is important to remember that the same picture was never shown twice to the same pigeon. Furthermore, for the positive slides, only pecks prior to reinforcement were counted. Thus the pigeons could not have been learning anything about particular pictures — they must have learned the general (and abstract) concept of trucks or cars.

How was this discrimination made? Possibly each pigeon had its own strategy. Perhaps some counted the axles on the vehicles. Perhaps some recognized the distinctive hoods or fenders of trucks or simply discriminated the size of the vehicle. (Although, since some vehicles were close and some far away, this could not be a simple size discrimination. It would have had to be based on the relative size of the vehicle compared to its surroundings.) The complexity of the discrimination can be appreciated when we realize that with all our modern technology, we are only now on the threshold of building machines to make equivalent discriminations.

The important point here is that whatever the detailed strategy of the individual pigeons, there was an invariance in the molar properties of their behavior (pecking did occur in the presence of the S^D). Furthermore, whatever the strategy of the individual pigeons, their behavior is subject to manipulation in the same way by reinforcing pecks in the presence of the S^D. When differential reinforcement was discontinued, the discrimination deteriorated, and the pigeons responded equally during the two kinds of pictures. This covariance between properties of behavior (responding) and properties of the environment (cars or trucks) is the important part of the experiment. The strategy of a particular pigeon is a matter for speculation only insofar as it leads to future experiments. (For instance, if the pigeons counted axles, they would do badly in a "transfer" experiment requiring discrimination of cars from two-axled trucks.) When the particular strategy hypothesized does not lead to specific behavioral consequences, the behaviorist loses interest in it.

COGNITION: RULE-GOVERNED BEHAVIOR

The various procedures comprising instrumental conditioning may be aptly (if verbosely) described as control of behavior by contingencies of reinforcement and punishment. Learning, from the behaviorist viewpoint, is a continuous process of *tactical* readjustment to changes in reinforcement and punishment contingencies.

When we begin a new kind of activity, like a teenager on a first date, we often have to adjust to each new instance by trial and error — we expose ourselves to the contingencies of reinforcement (and punishment) each time, and each time we adjust. But as we gain experience within a general area, we establish *strategies* (which may be verbal or nonverbal, conscious or unconscious) by which we cope with the common aspects of various individual contingencies. ("Show an interest in the other person's concerns" or "Don't talk about previous girlfriends or boyfriends" perhaps.)

As such strategies develop, the behavior of animals (especially humans) adjusts faster and faster to each particular tactical situation until eventually adjustment appears suddenly. It will be convenient to call the more general contingency (the "metacontingency") by which behavior is adjusted across contingencies rather than within a given contingency a *rule*. Thus, discussion of such adjustments falls under the rubric *rule-governed behavior*.

A classic example of rule learning in animals is "learning to learn." If a monkey learns one instrumental discrimination problem (say, a circle is the S^D and a square the S^Δ) and is then switched to another problem (say, triangle versus hexagon), it tends to learn the second problem faster and a third problem still faster until, after many such problems, learning is complete on a single trial. Evidently the monkey has learned something more than a particular discrimination. It has learned how to solve the sort of problems posed by the experimenter—in other words, it has learned a rule.

One form of rule-governed behavior is behavior guided by language; language may serve as a discriminative stimulus for a rule. Some authors restrict the concept of rule only to this linguistic function. But as we shall see in the next chapter, language may have functions other than to serve as a discriminative stimulus for a rule. We therefore use the term *rule* here in its more general sense. Language is one sort of discriminative stimulus for a rule, but there may be other sorts of rules that may be obeyed (as contingencies may be obeyed) without any explicit discriminative stimulus.

Some rules appear naturally in behavior. Perhaps the most noticeable differences in the behavior of different species lie in the rules that each naturally obeys. Staddon and Simmelhag's "laws of variation" discussed in the previous chapter refer to such rules. Some rules, on the other hand (like teenagers' rules for dating), are acquired only after considerable experience with individual contingencies. Still other rules are conveyed by humans to each other by language. Let us take up each of these in turn.

WARNING

One question that may occur to the reader is: Where is the rule? Many behaviorists believe that rules are "in the animal" only in the sense that such molar characteristics as healthiness or unhealthiness are said to be in the animal. These behaviorists (for convenience let us call them "operant behaviorists") believe that, just as healthiness refers to a general bodily state, rules are just more or less general descriptions (formed by the theorist) of the animal's behavior—the behavior follows the rule. Once these behaviorists have discovered a consistent pattern in the overt behavior of an animal, they believe that they have discovered the rule. The rule, they say, is in the behavior as such. Other behaviorists (for convenience let us call them "cognitive behaviorists") believe that rules are in the animal in a more specific and discrete sense—they are encoded in the animal's nervous system. Cognitive behaviorists want to discover these internal rules.

To give you a better idea of the difference between the objectives of operant and cognitive behaviorists, imagine you are repeatedly playing chess with an invisible opponent. Assuming the reader (like the author) is far below a grandmaster-level chess player, there would be no way to tell whether you were playing with Deep Thought (a computer program that has beaten grandmasters) or an excellent human chess player. If you were knowledgeable in chess, you might attempt to formulate rules regarding your opponent's play (say, his or her tendency to use a certain opening or a certain defense in certain situations or a tendency to bring the queen out too soon), but these rules, however valid as a description of behavior, need not correspond to the rules encoded in the nervous system of a human opponent; they certainly do not correspond to the rules encoded in Deep Thought. Deep Thought functions by rapid exhaustive examination of the consequences of a large set of possible moves, while real grandmasters say they examine relatively few possible moves and consequences selected by (currently unspecifiable) personal criteria.

Obviously there are many conceivable rules in the behavior of a chess opponent, just as there are many conceivable rules in the nervous system (or the wiring diagram) of a chess opponent. It is the faith of all behaviorists that ultimately a relationship will be found between the two. Meanwhile operant behaviorists and cognitive behaviorists pursue their separate goals.

Operant behaviorists are usually to be found studying instrumental (i.e., operant) conditioning, while cognitive behaviorists are usually to be found studying classical conditioning (although this is far from a hard-and-fast rule). The author confesses to being of the school of operant behaviorists, and undoubtedly this bias is reflected in the book. Nevertheless, an attempt has been made (especially in this chapter and subsequent chapters) to present the views of both schools of thought fairly.

Natural Rules

A natural rule characteristic of the behavior of nearly all animals might be stated as follows: When things get bad, behavior varies a lot; when things get better, behavior varies less but never stops varying altogether. This is a modified form of what has been called a win – stay, lose – shift strategy.

One study dealing with variability in the spatial distribution of behavior is an experiment conducted by Richard Herrnstein with pigeons. In this experiment, pigeons' pecks at a strip of rubber were occasionally reinforced by access to grain (see Figure 5.5). Pecks were reinforced occasionally (according to a variable-interval schedule) regardless of where on the strip they were placed. Nevertheless, the pigeons did not peck equally along the strip. They mostly pecked the center with occasional forays to the side. After behavior had come to stability, reinforcement was discontinued (extinction). At that point the spatial variability of pecking suddenly increased; the distribution of pecks on the strip changed from peaked (low variability) to relatively flat (high variability).

This strategy of increasing variability during extinction (when things get worse) is pervasive in the behavior of almost all animals. Gamblers switch from unlucky roulette wheels or slot machines after a few strings of losses. But note that even when conditions were favorable, the pigeons in Herrnstein's experiment varied their behavior to some degree. Maintenance of a slight variability of behavior even under stable and generally favorable conditions is another general rule — a previously unlucky slot machine may suddenly get lucky.

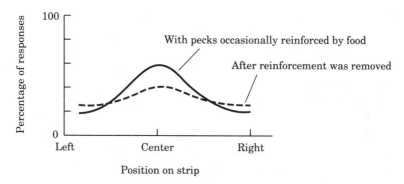

FIGURE 5.5 Example of spatial variation of responding. The long food hopper enabled the pigeon to move its beak from all points on the strip to the hopper with equal facility.

If you give pigeons repeated choices between two responses (two illuminated disks, pecks on one of which pay off at a higher rate), the pigeons will eventually settle *almost* exclusively on the better alternative (see Chapter 7). However, they will never completely abandon the worse one. If you change the payoff for pecking the worse one so that it pays back even better than the other, pigeons may take a while to catch on, but eventually they all will switch.

Considering only a particular pair of alternatives out of their context, it makes no sense (in terms of extracting reinforcement most efficiently from the environment) to *ever* waste a choice on the worse one. But considering the context—the way the world is and the way conditions are liable to change—it makes a great deal of sense to vary behavior even when things are going relatively well. Behavioral variability and its consequence—sensitivity to changing contingencies—is so pervasive among animals of all kinds that its occasional failure (such as with extinction of avoidance of electric shocks; see Chapter 3) is remarkable.

Note that just because a strategy is clever, that does not mean it is conscious (see the discussion of consciousness in the next chapter). What makes a strategy seem clever to us is its subtle adjustment to abstract features of the environment. If a feature is both abstract and common in the natural environment of an animal, it is likely to have had an effect on the animal's ancestors; thus the animal might be adapted to the rule genetically (by the same process that gives giraffes long necks). Genetic adaptation in turn might take one of three forms: (1) The animal might have been born with the rule, as most birds are born with the rules required to make nests in particular ways or (2) the animal might have been born with an enhanced ability to learn the rule or (3) the animal might be born with the ability to learn highly abstract rules in general. If, under natural observation or in an experiment, an animal demonstrates that it already possesses some subtle and clever behavioral adaptation to its natural environment, there is no way to tell which of these three possibilities apply.

The issue has been approached experimentally by trying to teach animals rules that are *not* common in their natural environments. We turn to these experiments next, after a cautionary note.

WARNING

Here is the nature/nurture controversy with all its attendant problems. If an experimenter can teach an animal an artificial rule (and the experiment is well designed), the animal must have been capable of learning that particular rule. But if the animal fails to learn the rule, there is no way to know whether some slight experimental variation might have succeeded. Even if the animal does learn the artificial rule, it is not clear what conclusions may be drawn. Although a rule itself may be artificial, the higher-level rule by which the rule is learned must be natural (in the sense that the animal must enter the experiment already having the ability to learn the artificial rule). But then all three of the above possibilities (that it is innate, that the animal was born with a tendency to learn it and previously learned it, that the animal was born with the ability to learn rules in general and previously learned this rule) apply with regard to the *higher-level rule*. Furthermore, the more abstract a rule is, the more difficult it becomes to create an artificial version (one that did not apply in the animal's preexperimental environment). The question that interests us is therefore not whether an animal's abilities are innate or previously acquired but what those abilities are and what are the aspects of the environment to which the animal's behavior is adapted?

Learning of Rules

At the beginning of this section we mentioned a very fundamental kind of rule learning — learning to learn — in which an animal comes to solve similar problems faster and faster as it is exposed to more and more problems.

A recent experiment by William Vaughan showed that pigeons could learn a more complex kind of rule. Vaughan assembled 40 slides, all containing pictures of trees. These slides were randomly divided into two groups of 20, a different division for each pigeon. Unlike the slides in the complex discrimination problems described above, where pigeons discriminated between pictures of trucks and pictures of cars, the two groups of slides contained nothing at all (discernible by Vaughan) by which they could be discriminated. Each slide was just a picture of a different scene with trees. For each pigeon one group of slides was then arbitrarily selected as the positive group (S^D), and the other as the negative group (S^Δ). Since the particular slides in the S^D and S^Δ groups were different for each pigeon, any perceptual difference (such as brightness or color or presence of some object by which one pigeon's slides might have been accidentally divided) could not apply to another pigeon's slides. The 40 slides were then projected in random order on a small screen on the front wall of the Skinner box. Each pigeon's pecks on a key were then reinforced in the presence of that pigeon's S^D slides and not in the presence of that pigeon's S^Δ

slides. Eventually all of the pigeons learned to peck (almost) exclusively when presented any of the S^D slides but not any of the S^Δ slides. This learning could only have been done individually for each slide because there was no abstract concept like "truck" tying them together.

Vaughan then switched the meaning of the S^D and S^Δ slides; all slides that were previously S^D's for a given pigeon were now S^Δ's, and all slides that were previously S^Δ's were now S^D's. Behavior rapidly reversed; every pigeon pecked where before it did not peck and vice versa. Then the meanings were switched again, and again, and again. Each time all of the pigeons learned to reverse their behavior.

Eventually the pigeons learned that when one of the slides in a (completely arbitrary) group had switched its meaning, all the other slides in that group would also have switched their meanings. The pigeons were able to discriminate at better than chance levels after about 15 reversals and continued to improve over more than 150 reversals. At that point, after a switch, the pigeons would make errors (peck in the presence of an S^Δ slide or fail to peck in the presence of an S^D slide) only on the very first slide they saw. After that, the pigeons made no errors with the other slides. They learned a *general* rule that may be stated as follows: Whatever *particular* rule applies to one slide in a group also applies to all the other slides in that group.

This sort of learning is a very primitive form of what is called (in logic) an *equivalence relation*. Its learning by pigeons is important because one characteristic of human language that makes it different from various forms of animal communication is its use of equivalence relations. For instance, you can meaningfully say "I bought an orange" or "I bought an apple" (replacing a noun by another noun), but you cannot meaningfully say "I apple an orange" (replacing a verb by a noun). Undoubtedly pigeons are far from able to learn any set of signals as complicated as human language, but it is significant that they are able to learn (albeit in a very primitive form) a fundamental grammatical rule.

Other complex rules have been taught to several different species of animals by means of a procedure called *matching to sample*. In the basic procedure, a sample stimulus, say an X, is presented to the animal. Then two comparison stimuli are presented. One is the X and the other is an O. The subject responds by manipulating one of the comparison stimuli. A correct response — a response to the comparison stimulus identical to the sample — is reinforced. An incorrect response is not reinforced. With pigeons, the X's and O's (the discriminative stimuli) are usually projected onto plastic disks (response keys), and pecks on the key that match the sample are reinforced. Let us now consider some of the rules that have been taught to pigeons with matching to sample.

An experiment by J. A. Nevin and K. Liebold (diagrammed in Figure 5.6) added a second degree of abstraction to the basic matching-to-sample procedure. The Skinner box contained three keys that could be illuminated with different colors of light. The center key is called the "sample key," and the two side keys are called "comparison keys." Pigeons discriminated by pecking one of the comparison keys. The sample key was either red or green; one comparison was red, the other green. In addition, there was a yellow light above the keys that was sometimes on and sometimes off. When the yellow light was on,

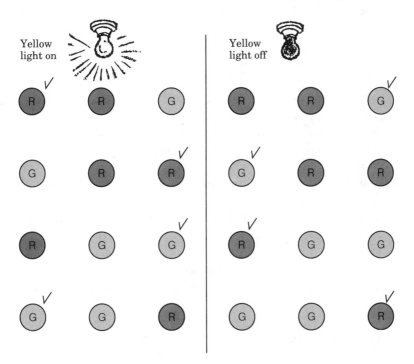

FIGURE 5.6   The Nevin–Liebold experiment. Each row of circles represents a possible configuration of colored keys. The correct key (pecks on which were reinforced) is indicated by a check. When the yellow light was on, pecks on the side key identical in color to the center key were reinforced. When the yellow light was off, pecks on the side key different in color from the center key were reinforced.

pecks on the comparison key that was the same color as the sample were reinforced. When the yellow light was off, pecks on the comparison key different from the sample were reinforced. The pigeons quickly came to perform this discrimination very accurately. The rule describing their behavior may be stated as follows: If the yellow light is on, peck the same color as the sample; if the light is off, peck the other color.

In the Nevin–Liebold experiment as in most matching-to-sample procedures, the discriminative stimuli were present in the environment when the choice response was made. We now turn to a group of experiments where the discriminative stimuli are absent when the choice is made.

Complex Behavior in the Absence of Contemporaneous Discriminative Stimuli

The standard matching-to-sample procedure may be modified as follows. The sample key is lit with a red or green light. The comparison keys are dark. When the pigeon pecks the sample key, it becomes dark, too. After a delay of so many seconds, the two comparison keys are lit, one red and the other green (randomly with respect to side). The sample key remains dark. Pecks on the comparison key matching the sample are reinforced. The typical finding with this procedure is that, as delay increases, the performance of pigeons (and all other animals tested with such procedures) deteriorates. The animals have to remember the sample when the comparison stimuli are presented and (universally) memory becomes worse with time.

Operant behaviorists and cognitive behaviorists have different ways of talking about this phenomenon. Cognitivists suppose that when the sample disappears it leaves an image, called an *internal representation*, somewhere in the animal's nervous system. As time goes on, this internal representation deteriorates. When the comparison stimuli come on, they are not compared to a sample that is no longer present but to an internal representation of the sample. The delay affects the representation and the representation affects the behavior. The object of the experiment, therefore, is to discover what has happened to the internal representation.

Operant behaviorists argue that, if the delay affects the internal representation and the representation affects discrimination, then you do not need the concept of internal representation at all. Why not just study the effect of delay on the discrimination? The cognitive way of speaking preserves temporal contiguity between cause and effect (delay affects internal representation which then affects discrimination) at the sacrifice of parsimony. The operant behaviorist's way of speaking parsimoniously eliminates the extraneous middle term in the relationship at the sacrifice of contiguity of cause and effect. For our purposes in this book it does not really matter which way of speaking one adopts. Operationally both come down to the same thing.

Charles Shimp conducted an experiment using pigeon subjects in which the discriminative stimuli were the pigeons' own former actions. As in the Nevin–Liebold experiment, there was a center key and two side keys. Unlike the Nevin–Liebold experiment, the center key was always the same color (white), and there was no yellow light. First Shimp trained the pigeons to peck the center key (the "sample" key) either fast or slow but not at moderate rates between these extremes.* Then pecks on one of the side keys ("comparison" keys) were reinforced only if the pigeon itself had just been pecking the sample key slowly. Pecks on the other side key were reinforced only if the pigeon had just been pecking the center key rapidly.

The pigeons in Shimp's experiment learned this discrimination quite easily. The rule governing the pigeons' choice between the side keys must refer to their own previous behavior. Such a rule might be stated as follows: After pecking fast, peck one side key (the red one, say); after pecking slow, peck the other.

The matching-to-sample procedure is only one of several methods of investigating complex behavior in the absence of contemporaneous discriminative stimuli. In a series of experiments by Olton and his colleagues, rats were placed in a maze containing a central chamber and a number of arms (usually eight) radiating outward. At the outer ends of the arms were goal boxes that might or might not have contained food. (The rats could not see the food from the central chamber.) In one experiment all of the goal boxes contained food. The rats in this experiment quickly learned to visit each arm just once, eat

---

*This was accomplished by selecting two distinct ranges of times (interresponse times; for example, 3–4 seconds and 9–12 seconds) between pairs of successive responses and presenting the comparison stimuli occasionally only after a pair of pecks within either one or the other range (the effective range being randomly determined with a probability of .5).

the food in the goal box, and then not visit that arm again. That is, the rats became very efficient about getting the food and not visiting empty arms.

It seems that the discriminative stimuli must have been the spatial cues present in the room (the maze was open so that rats could see the room with its fixed walls, windows, doors, and furniture) plus the rats' own past behavior (or a representation of that behavior) relative to those cues. However, there is another possibility. Perhaps the rats could smell the food or smell their own scent in the arms where they had already been. Or perhaps they learned to mark those arms in some way (say, with minute drops of urine). Then (like Hansel and Gretel dropping seeds) the rats could use those *current* markings as discriminative stimuli and would not need to be sensitive to their own past behavior (or to internal representations of past behavior).

To test this latter possibility, only three arms contained food and rats were trained to choose the arms in a specific order, as illustrated in Figure 5.7a. Then, after the rat had made its first visit (arrow 1), the maze was rotated between trials as shown in Figure 5.7b. If current cues within the maze were the discriminative stimuli, the rats should have rotated their visit (symbolized by dotted arrow 2). However, the visits of the rats remained in the same relation to the room (symbolized by a window, door, and lamp) rather than the maze. Thus the discriminative stimuli indicating which arm had just been visited must have been *previously* rather than *currently* present.

Still another series of experiments by H. S. Terrace and his colleagues, with pigeons again, shows that they can learn to peck a series of different-colored keys (say, red, green, blue and yellow) in a specific order regardless of the location of the keys. On one trial, going from left to right, the keys would be red, yellow, blue, and green; on the next trial, yellow, blue, red, and green, and so forth. But whatever the order in space, the pigeons always had to obey the rule: Peck the red key first, the green key second, the blue key third, and the yellow key last. There were no feedback stimuli to tell the pigeons how they were doing while they were pecking. Only correct completed sequences were reinforced. As in the Shimp and Olton experiments, the discriminative stimulus was the pigeon's own previous behavior relative to current environmental cues.

One interesting question is whether the discriminative stimulus was only the immediately preceding peck or some combination of previous pecks reaching further back in time. This was tested by

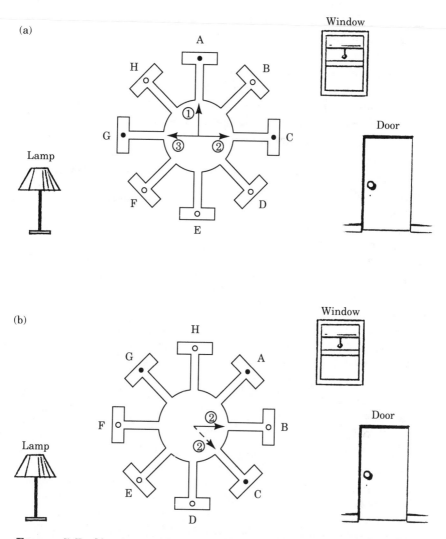

FIGURE 5.7 Olton's rotated-maze experiment. (a) Rat learns to visit arms with food (A, C, and G). After the first visit (1), arms are rotated. (b) Will rat now make second visit (2) to arm B (solid arrow) or arm C (dashed arrow)?

removing one of the intermediate colors (say green); pigeons then continued to peck the keys in the specified order (red, yellow, and blue). Thus, the rules followed must have been more abstract than: First peck red; if red was just pecked, peck green; if green was just pecked, peck blue; if blue was just pecked, peck yellow. Removal of green would upset the behavioral structure created by the set of simple rules. A more general (more abstract) set of rules must have been learned.

One way to guess at those rules is to devise a computer program that chooses colored keys in a sequence, skipping any absent colors. The rules that we would have to program into the computer constitute a guess at the pigeon's rules. (The student might try this as an exercise). Of course, there are many guesses of this kind possible, further experiments are necessary to decide between them.

The general nature of these experiments involves transfer tests of various kinds to determine what is learned. These experiments follow in the tradition of an early experiment reported in 1930 by Macfarlane, who taught rats to run through a maze for food and then flooded the maze; he found that the rats could now swim correctly through the maze. This showed that they must have learned something other than a series of chained movements; they learned something *general* (a general rule) about the maze.

Suggested Readings

The procedure upon which the discussion of testing for control by S^D and S^Δ is based was devised by H. M. Jenkins and reported in "Generalization gradients and the concept of inhibition" in *Stimulus Generalization*, D. I. Mostofsky, ed. (Stanford: Stanford University Press, 1965), pp. 55-62. Articles on stimulus control by Mark Rilling and N. J. Mackintosh in the Honig-Staddon *Handbook of Operant Behavior* (cited in the Bibliography at the end of Chapter 3) are useful summaries of early research on this topic. A good recent summary of research on complex discrimination may be found in the chapter by Peter Balsam entitled "Selection, representation, and equivalence of controlling stimuli" in R. C. Atkinson, R. J. Herrnstein, G. Lindzey, and R. D. Luce, eds. *Stevens' Handbook of Experimental Psychology, Vol. 2: Learning and Cognition*, 2nd ed. (New York: Wiley, 1988), pp. 112-165. An excellent collection of articles is *Animal Cognition*, H. L. Roitblat, T. G. Bever, and H. S. Terrace, eds. (Hillsdale, N.J.: Erlbaum, 1984).

Much of the material in this chapter on rule-governed behavior was taken from an article by Philip N. Hineline and Barbara A. Wanchisen entitled "Correlated hypothesizing and the distinction between contingency-shaped and rule-governed behavior," which appears in S. C. Hayes, ed. *Rule-Governed Behavior: Cognition, Contin-*

gencies, and Instructional Control (New York: Plenum Press, 1989), pp. 221–268. This collection contains many other articles relevant to the material of this chapter.

The following is a list of articles referred to in this chapter:

Herrnstein, R. J. Stereotypy and intermittent reinforcement. *Science*, 1961, **133**, 2067–2069.

Macfarlane, D. A. The role of kinesthesis in maze learning. *University of California Publications in Psychology*, 1930, **4**, 227–305.

Nevin, J. A., and Liebold, K. Stimulus control of matching and oddity in a pigeon. *Psychonomic Science*, 1966, **5**, 351–352.

Olton, D. S. Mazes, maps, and memory. *American Psychologist*, 1979, **34**, 583–596.

Shimp, C. P. The local organization of behavior: dissociations between a pigeon's behavior and self-reports of that behavior. *Journal of the Experimental Analysis of Behavior*, 1983, **3**, 61–68.

Terrace, H. S., Straub, R. O., Bever, T. G., and Seidenberg, M. S. Representation of a sequence by a pigeon. *Bulletin of the Psychonomic Society*, 1977, **10**, 26.

Vaughan, W. Formation of equivalence sets in pigeons. *Journal of Experimental Psychology: Animal Behavior Processes*, 1988, **14**, 36–42.

6

Language and Consciousness

Before Darwin it was generally thought that language and consciousness were particularly human traits not possessed in any form by
animals. Since Darwin it has been recognized that any trait of human
behavior must in some form, to some extent, exist in the behavior of
other animals who share our ancestors. In this chapter we discuss
efforts to analyze human language and consciousness behaviorally and
to discover similar behavior in other animals.

LANGUAGE

Consider the beaver laying one stick upon another. Whether the
beaver can be said to be playing with the sticks or building a dam
depends *not* on what it is doing at this very moment (a still photograph
or a two-second film clip would not settle the issue) but on what it has
done previously and what it is going to do. Similarly, a pianist plays a
note in an arpeggio as one single act, but if he is skilled, the act not
only occupies the fraction of a second of its technical boundaries but

bears an intimate relation to the pianist's actions during the rest of the arpeggio and the rest of the piece. He leads up to it and down from it. The coherent nature of the act can be appreciated if we consider the feelings of the pianist and his audience if he were to be suddenly interrupted.

As psychologists we are concerned with discovering (or devising) rules that govern such behavior. These rules may be logical rules or grammatical rules or formal rules, like those of chess or baseball. All are rules governing behavior, and all take on meaning only when they are considered in a broad (molar) context. As the philosopher Ludwig Wittgenstein says, "It is not possible that there should have been only one occasion on which someone obeyed a rule. It is not possible that there should have been only one occasion on which a report was made, an order given or understood; and so on. To obey a rule, to make a report, to give an order, to play a game of chess, are *customs* (uses, institutions). . . . To understand a sentence means to understand a language. To understand a language means to be master of a technique."

Wittgenstein is saying that language is on a continuum with other kinds of behavior (with that of the beaver and the pianist). We cannot tell whether a person is speaking a language (in the sense that he is guided by the rules of the language) or merely parroting it until we see how effective his use of language is.

There are many ways in which language can be used effectively. Consider the following list (from Wittgenstein):

Giving orders and obeying them
Describing the appearance of an object or giving its measurements
Constructing an object from a description (making a drawing)
Reporting an event
Speculating about an event
Forming and testing a hypothesis
Presenting the results of an experiment in tables or diagrams
Making up a story and reading it
Play acting
Singing round songs
Guessing riddles
Making a joke and telling it
Solving a problem in practical arithmetic
Translating from one language to another
Asking, thanking, cursing, greeting, praying

All these are ways of using language. Each way has something in common with some of the others, but they *all* do not have any one thing in common.

The psycholinguist Roman Jakobson has listed five ways language is used:

1. *Emotive.* Used primarily to express emotion, as during arguments or during lovemaking.
2. *Phatic.* Used merely as a means of contact between two organisms, as between a mother and baby, where the sounds of each (especially those of the mother) serve mainly to establish their presence.
3. *Metalinguistic.* Used about language itself, as when speech is being taught or a child's pronounciation is corrected. The child will say a sentence incorrectly ("I gone to school"), and the mother will repeat the sentence correctly ("I went to school"). Such a correction is a metalinguistic use of language.
4. *Poetic.* Used when the structure of language is emphasized for its own sake as in a poem ("red red rose," "luscious lady," etc.).
5. *Conative.* Used with behavior of some kind as its object ("Get out of here," "Pass the salt," etc.).

Jakobson's five classes are interesting, but they are inadequate. For example, when we try to put Wittgenstein's list of the uses of language into Jakobson's categories, we see that not all of them fit. Language has long been described by psychologists in this piecemeal way, no doubt because it is such an elusive concept.

Meaning as Association

The associationistic philosophers discussed in Chapter 1 speculated that every environmental stimulus calls up images to the mind that are both a faint copy of the stimulus itself and a faint copy of other stimuli that have previously accompanied (been associated with) the stimulus in question. If the stimulus is a word, the meaning of the word would be the images that are associated with its sound (see Figure 1.4). For instance, if every time a mother hands her child a cookie she says "cookie," the child will associate the sound of the word with the image of the cookie itself. Then, when the mother says "cookie" without handing the child anything, the image (the internal representation) of a cookie will rise spontaneously in the child's mind. According to the associationists, the meaning of a word consists of the images it evokes.

Psychologists have not been able to get inside a person's head to study meaning by examining the images evoked by words, but they have asked people to give them indirect reports. In an experiment by Clyde Noble, subjects were given a word, say *kitchen*, and then asked to write down all the other words that the original word reminded them of. For instance, they might write *knife, fork, apron,* and so on. Noble reasoned that the words the subject wrote down might stand for ideas generated by the original stimulus word. The more of these words suggested by the original word, the more meaning that stimulus word was said to have.

Nobel determined for each stimulus word an "*m*-score." This was the average number of response words that his subjects could write down in one minute. *Kitchen* turned out to have a high *m*-score. More abstract concepts such as *justice* had a lower *m*-score. By itself, the *m*-score of a word is a rather useless piece of information, but Noble found that *m*-score was a reliable predictor of how well words were remembered and how quickly associations between them and other words could be taught.

James Deese made a more refined approach to the study of responses to words. He examined not the *number* of associations to a word but the *kind* of associations. He reasoned that two words were alike in meaning when the responses to those two words overlapped. For instance, *kitchen* might produce *knife, fork, table,* and *window*; and *porch* might produce *swing, air, front,* and *table.* The word *table,* common to both response groups, makes the words somewhat similar in meaning according to Deese. The more such common responses are found, the more similar the words are in meaning.

A further analysis of associations reveals two general types, called *syntigmatic* and *paradigmatic.* Syntigmatic associations are those that refer to sequence. For instance *table* and *cloth, yankee* and *doodle,* and *red* and *rider* would be syntigmatic because they normally occur in sequence. Another thing to note about such associations is that they are not usually reversible. Many people will respond *cloth* to the stimulus *table*; few people will respond *table* to the stimulus *cloth.*

Paradigmatic associations, on the other hand, represent associations not of sequence but of kind. For instance, *table* and *chair, Yankee* and *Southerner,* and *red* and *green* are paradigmatic. Unlike syntigmatic associations, these are generally reversible. It has been found that children tend to give more syntigmatic associations, changing to paradigmatic associations as they get older.

This general approach, treating language as association between individual words, has illuminated only a small corner of the immense area of linguistic behavior. It fails to consider at least two important complexities:

1. It does not consider linguistic behavior as extended in time. Instead, it considers immediate responses to immediate stimulation and thus misses those aspects of language (such as following grammatical rules) that can only be understood over a period of time.

2. It does not consider the functional properties of language. It ignores the question of the *uses* of language. From the above studies, the mind of the person associating words appears as a passive receptacle of stimuli. But we know that a person plays an active role in what he learns.

The following sections tackle some of this complexity in a more direct fashion. In these sections we will lose a little of the elegant simplicity of associationism and its quantitative precision. We hope, in return for these sacrifices, to gain a better approximation to the world as it actually is.

Language and Thought

One line of speculation about the relation between language and thought stems from the early behaviorists, whose concern was to explain behavior — including thought — in terms of simple mechanistic principles. Through the ages thought has been considered to be part of the spiritual nature of man. The early behaviorists denied man any spiritual nature, hoping to explain all behavior in terms of stimulus–response connections. Yet, they could not deny that a human thinks (this seemed as fundamental a fact to them as it did to Descartes — "I think, therefore I am.").

They resolved their quandary by regarding thought as a kind of action — but action of so small a magnitude that it could not be seen. For instance, when a man was asked to think of hitting a nail with a hammer, he was said to actually move the muscles in his hand slightly. This movement, no more and no less, was supposed to comprise his thought. When sensitive measurements were taken, it was found that such movements often occurred without the awareness of the man making them. That is, the man said he thought of hitting the nail with the hammer, but he didn't realize he was making any movements. Although concrete actions such as hitting a nail with a hammer could be represented by small movements of the arms, most thoughts, especially of the more abstract kind (thoughts of justice, for instance) would be represented by unspoken language — that is, unnoticed movements of the tongue and larynx. Sensitive instruments indeed do pick up such movements occasionally.

The problem with notions such as these is that they are inherently untestable. When movements corresponding to certain thoughts are not found, one can always imagine that they still occur but at a level too minute for the instruments used to detect.

A more subtle relationship between language and thought was postulated by the Russian psychologist L. S. Vigotsky. According to Vigotsky, thought and speech are two separate processes that develop independently for a while and then come together. Thought without speech would be exemplified by the kind of intelligent behavior exhibited by Köhler's chimpanzee Sultan when Sultan moved a box underneath a banana hanging out of reach and then jumped up from the box to get the banana (see p. 49 in Chapter 1). This kind of behavior seems complex enough to us (the observers of it) that we are tempted to say it was thoughtful.* Vigotsky would agree with our judgment, but he would say that it lacks a component of most adult human thought, namely combination with inner speech. Vigotsky claims that most "intelligent" acts of children below about three years of age are of this

---

*But what is thought itself? Vigotsky, a follower of Pavlov and a precursor of cognitive behaviorism, would have identified thought with brain activity. Vigotsky viewed the overt behavior he studied as a clue to brain physiology — nominally the main focus of interest of all Russian psychologists after Sechenov and Pavlov. Other behaviorists would claim that an animal's "thoughtfulness" may lie wholly in its behavior. We are concerned here primarily with the still-interesting behavioral observations of both Köhler and Vigotsky and not with their inferences about the brain, inferences that are considered by modern physiologists to be simplistic at best and probably false.

kind—perhaps the acts have a complex nature, but they are not accompanied by either overt or covert language. This, according to Vigotsky, is thought without speech. Similarly, he contends, there can be speech without thought. Jakobson's categories of emotive and phatic uses of language are examples, as well as affective expression and the babbling of infants in their cribs.

According to Vigotsky, thought and speech join in humans when they are about three years old. At first a word is treated as a property of an object rather than a symbol of that object. For instance, the sound "chair" is something that a chair *has*, like color and shape. A child treats each object as if there were something (like a record) inside the object constantly saying the object's name. Thus a cookie is not only round and small and good-tasting, but it also has the sound "cookie" built into it. Later, the sound of the word is separated from things like shape, size, and color and comes to be a symbol for the object.

While this is going on, the child develops a kind of speech that has often been noticed but seldom studied. Vigotsky calls it egocentric speech. It goes on practically all the time with little children but can be noticed particularly when they are put to bed at night and are alone in their crib. They start talking, repeating words they heard that day—stringing phrases together. To an outsider, what the child says makes little sense. Sometimes the child's egocentric speech is social—referring to other things and designed, however poorly, to tell somebody else something. But often the speech is directed to himself.

A two-year-old, Tommy, will say, "Tommy bad boy" or "Tommy go home." This speech serves as a sort of feedback tending to organize behavior better. Tommy can perform intelligent acts (as Köhler's chimpanzees can) without speech, but he can do them better when he gives himself an order first. Tommy may go into the kitchen when he is hungry, but he will go faster if he first tells himself to go into the kitchen. Thus, much of the actual vocalization of young children is self-directed. Anyone who has observed a three-year-old child has noticed it. After a child's fourth or fifth birthday, however, egocentric speech becomes less noticeable in childrens' vocalization and finally drops out altogether. From then on, audible speech becomes a social act.

Vigotsky's theory is that egocentric speech becomes *more* egocentric as time goes on, finally becoming inner speech. The child, in other words, keeps on with egocentric speech, in fact more than ever, but now no one hears it because the child says it to herself. Egocentric speech loses all communication function and becomes a complex stimulus for one's own behavior. Some evidence for this is that just before egocentric speech disappears, it becomes even more frequent and less intelligible to others. In other words, it becomes more egocentric. By this time it has lost all function as a communication device and becomes purely a mechanism for self-direction. What remains in the external vocalization is social speech. Thus, according to Vigotsky, adults have essentially two languages, a private one that guides their actions and structures their thoughts, and a public one that serves for communication.

An interesting study in this area was done in Russia with a pair of twins who were raised together and who were both retarded in speech. It seemed to the experimenters that the twins had been so close to one another that they could understand each other's egocentric speech and never had to develop social speech with others. In effect, their egocentric speech had never become internalized. The experimenters reasoned that, if the twins were separated, they would have to develop social speech. Indeed, within three months of their separation the children spoke and understood normally. One twin was given systematic training in social speech. Although both twins improved, the one with systematic training improved more rapidly.

Russian psychologists have been very interested in how speech serves to organize behavior. Following Pavlov as well as Vigotsky, they call language the "second-signal system." What do they mean by this? In Pavlov's early experiments with dogs, the sound of the bell is a signal for food. But the word "bell" would be a signal for the sound of the bell; it would be a second signal whose function is to direct attention to the bell. Environmental signals themselves direct *action*. Language is said to direct *attention* — much as the yellow light in the Nevin and Liebold experiment (see Figure 5.6) directed the pigeon's attention to similarities or differences in the colors of the keys. The function of language would be to put the organism in a position, prior to the signal itself, so that it could act promptly when the primary signal came; hence, the name "second-signal system." Linguistic second signals can come from the outside or may, like Vigotsky's inner speech, be generated by people to themselves.

How the second-signal system guides behavior is shown in an experiment by the Russian S. A. Luria. He had children squeeze a rubber bulb when a light came on. Then he introduced a discrimination: When the light was green, the child was to squeeze; when the light was red, the child was not to squeeze. Children younger than three years of age find this task very difficult. They just keep squeezing constantly. However, Luria trained the children to say "squeeze" when they saw the green light and "don't squeeze" when they saw the red light. Then Luria trained the children to actually squeeze the bulb when they said "squeeze" but not to squeeze when they said "don't squeeze." Thus Luria succeeded in teaching children to perform a task correctly with the mediation of language that they could not perform without.

Like the early behaviorists in America, Pavlov's followers in Russia believe that inner speech is accompanied by small muscular movements. They differ from the early behaviorists in that they do not identify such movements with thought. Rather, they see these movements as an aid or guide to thought. When thought runs smoothly, it is likely to be unaccompanied by inner speech, but when difficulties arise, thought needs guidance from inner speech. Hence, with difficult problems, such small movements are more likely to arise.

An experiment by the Russian psychologist, Sokolov, illustrates the point. He asked his subjects to read a passage silently while he measured small movements at various points on their bodies — including the neck and face, where usually undetectable speech movements would be likely to occur. Later, to insure that they had understood the passage, he asked them to write a summary. The subjects had three kinds of passage to read: standard Russian (their native language), easy English, and difficult English. Sokolov found, in general, that the subjects made many minute movements at the start and few at the end of all passages and that there was a sudden increase of such movements at paragraph breaks. In particular, he found that the number of minute movements was higher when the material to be read was more difficult. In other words, the more difficult it was to think, the more the aid of inner speech was necessary.

Another experiment on the second-signal system was done by Luria. To appreciate this experiment, we must recall that the second-signal system does not regulate an immediate response but serves as a discriminative stimulus for subsequent events. In other words, the second-signal system regulates, not responding itself, but attention to signals that, in turn, regulate responding. The response to language is not action per se but attention or orientation. Thus the response for which language is a stimulus is called an "orienting response," and the linguistic stimulus plus the response are together called an "orienting reflex." Now, it seems that when people are attending to something, the blood volume in their extremities (such as a finger) decreases while the blood volume in the head increases. Thus a sudden increase in the difference between the head and finger blood volumes, measured by a plethysmograph, could be labeled as an orienting response. Luria and his colleagues found that when they presented a new stimulus to a subject, the orienting response increased; the response then decreased with repeated presentations. In other words, the orienting response decreased with familiarity, as one would expect attention to decrease.

Luria and his colleagues read a list of words to their subjects and kept repeating the list. After the initial orienting responses died down, they told the subjects to watch for a particular word (word X) from the original list and press a button after that word was presented. They noticed then a resurgence of the orienting response after word X — but not generally after the other words. When they presented the subjects with other words from the list similar in sound to word X, they found that the subjects did not make orienting responses. However, when they presented the subjects with other words from the list similar in *meaning* to word X, they did sometimes get orienting responses. This indicates that subjects translate the sound of the word into its meaning at a very early level of processing in the nervous system — even before the nervous system decides whether or not to pay attention to the word.

Although thought and speech certainly bear an intimate relation to each other, we should be careful before we identify the two. Subjectively, we can all remember having thoughts with no apparent visual or verbal content. Further reasons for caution come from pathology. An aphasic (someone with a severe language impairment) may be able to act intelligently in all other respects.

An even stronger line of evidence against the thought-equals-language argument is the presence of ambiguous sentences in the language. Consider the sentence "It is drinking water," which could have at least two meanings depending on context. In one context these words would accompany one thought; in another context, another thought.

So, although the proposition that thought and language are one has not been fruitful in explaining either thought or language, it is nevertheless clear that language and thought are closely interwoven processes. Recently American psychologists have taken a fresh look at language and have investigated some of its structural characteristics. We will turn to these studies next.

Chomsky and Skinner: How and Why

In 1957 the behaviorist B. F. Skinner published a book, *Verbal Behavior*, which was critically reviewed by the linguist Noam Chomsky. Skinner had analyzed language using the principles of conditioning much as they have been presented in previous chapters. Chomsky claimed that a behavioristic analysis would never get at the heart of language because what a person learns about a particular language in the course of a lifetime is less important than the rules (the grammar) of the language, which, Chomsky claimed, are the same in all languages at the most general level.

The details of the Chomsky–Skinner dispute are beyond the scope of this book, but many subsequent discussions of the debate have concluded that the two sides of the argument did not come to grips with one another. Skinner's *functional* analysis of language was an attempt to answer the question, *Why* do people say the things they do? Chomsky's *structural* analysis was an attempt to answer the question, *How* do people say the things they do? As Evelyn Segal pointed out in a scholarly discussion of the dispute (see Suggested Readings), the answer to one of these questions, no matter how complete, does not automatically answer the other. Regardless of the apparently obvious need for both structural and functional analyses of language, psycholinguistic research over the last 20 years has focused almost exclusively on Chomsky's structural questions. Current research asks *how* language is organized (physiologically and cognitively) and *how* this organization is manifested in actual production and comprehension. The questions of *why* language is organized that way and *why* people say the things they do have been compartively neglected.

As an example, consider a topic of much current interest — that of *indirect* verbal production such as irony (saying, for instance, "Very smart" when you mean just the opposite) or metaphor (saying, for instance, "Your room is like a swamp.") A metaphor may be analyzed into its *topic* (the thing it's about — your room) and its *vehicle* (the thing the topic is being compared to — a swamp). The topic and the vehicle may each in turn be located in a different *word - space structure* (a hypothetical space in the nervous system containing organized representations of words). The positions of the elements in their respective structures are assumed to correspond (the correspondence is what the metaphor points out), while the structures themselves may differ more or less widely.

In the sentence "Your room is like a swamp," a cognitive structural space of the arrangement of furniture and clothing in rooms may be supposed—perhaps along the two dimensions quantity and symmetry (or orderliness). A cognitive structural space of the arrangement of natural objects (vegetation, water, and mud) in large areas may be supposed—also perhaps along the two dimensions quantity and symmetry. The metaphor points out that your room and swamps occupy corresponding points in their respective spaces (high on quantity and low on symmetry).

Empirical research may then be directed at the degree of judged goodness of the metaphor (independent of its truth) as a function of the relation of the topic and vehicle each to its own structure and of structures to one another.

Irony has been classified (by the psychologists Sperber and Wilson) as an instance of a *mention* as distinguished from a *use*. "Go home," for instance, is used by itself to tell a person to go home. But as part of the sentence "He said, 'Go home,'" the phrase has meaning only in relation to its context. By itself "Go home" is *used*. As part of "He said, 'Go home,'" it is *mentioned*. Similarly, in the context of my driving the car into a tree and denting the fender, my wife's remark, "Very smart!", is technically a *mention* (however scathing its effect may be).

Given this sort of analysis, experimental research has focused on the relation between the hearer's understanding of the meaning of the statement by itself and its relation to its context. For instance, do people have to understand the statement literally *before* they can understand its ironic meaning? Research (using reaction time measures) indicates that as long as the context is clear, people can understand the *intended* meaning of irony (and other indirect verbal productions) without first understanding their *literal* meaning.

But still, why should my wife have said "Very smart!" when she meant "Very dumb!"? Modern psycholinguistic research has not generally addressed this type of question (although there are exceptions).

One conceivable step towards answering the *why* question (only an example, not to be taken too seriously) might be to note that a *mention* functions something like a CS + in that it refers to language itself (as a CS refers to another stimulus, the US), while a *use* functions something like an S^D in that it signifies a relation between actions and consequences. Then one might note that Sechenov and Pavlov both observed that when a CS + is overused, an inhibitory force develops in opposition to it. Given enough overuse, the only way to elicit the response is not to present the CS + at all but to present the CS − (Pavlov referred to this as "paradoxical disinhibition.") Modern behaviorists have been very interested in this sort of effect, which they call an "opponent process" (see Suggested Readings). If after the car crash my wife wants to get my attention, she should not use the much overworked phrase "Very dumb!"; in the context, the relatively novel remark (from her to me) "Very smart!" will have its intended effect.

One might then notice similar uses of irony elsewhere. In many cultures, the phrase "How cute!" has through overuse completely lost its meaning as applied to babies. My grandmother, when confronted with a baby, would gush in Yiddish "Meiskeit!", which literally means "ugliness." Everyone knew what she meant. My grandmother's listeners (the baby's parents) had, according to Pavlov, developed strong internal inhibitions to "How cute!" (or its Yiddish equivalent). Once these inhibitions build up strongly enough, nothing will gratify the baby's parents but the typical CS − for that reaction — "Meiskeit!"

Of course, this sort of functionally based analysis directed at *why* a person should use indirect speech says nothing about *how* it is generated. We will never understand language without both sorts of analysis. But functionally based analyses have not been common in modern psycholinguistic research. We turn now to a discussion of a small part of the modern work on language — both structural and functional.

Grammar (Words in a Sentence)

Grammar comprises a system of rules regarding the use of language. To get these grammatical rules into proper perspective, let us consider two other systems of rules. First, consider the rules of chess. Virtually everyone who learns to play chess learns the rules and can discuss them. You can ask the chess player about the rules that limit the movements of her pieces and she will tell you what they are. Then, if you watch her play, you will notice that the actual movement of the pieces generally conforms to the rules she has articulated.

On the other hand, consider Newton's laws of motion. Almost everything in the universe obeys this set of rules: a stone, a human body, an apple, a molecule, a mountain. Yet, despite the fact that Newton's laws of motion are obeyed by a stone, only a visitor from another universe could conceivably expect the stone to articulate the rules. The rules of grammar lie somewhere between the rules of chess and Newton's laws of motion. The rules of grammar are like the rules of chess in the sense that they are social, their use is acquired over time (that is, their use must be learned even if in some form they are innately encoded in our brains), and they are frequently disobeyed. On the other hand, the rules of grammar are like Newton's laws in the sense that most of us cannot articulate them and even those of us who can articulate them are not conscious of obeying them while speaking. Although no one could play chess until the rules had been established, it is certain that people were speaking grammatically before anyone thought to codify the rules of grammar. Chomsky and his followers tend to think of the rules of grammar as things ("modules" or "organs") existing in the heads of people who speak grammatically. Followers of Skinner see grammar as a convenient description of how people organize and comprehend sentences.

Most modern psycholinguists, following Chomsky, distinguish between competence and performance. Competence is "having the rule." Performance is using it. Behaviorists, on the other hand, would see grammatical rules as molar descriptions of behavior from which there may be molecular deviations in the form of "ungrammatical expressions." According to this view, "competence" would be a molar description of behavior (over periods of time long enough to include several instances of comprehension and production to be sure that the person said to be competent is not just accidentally stringing words together grammatically), and "performance" would be a molecular description of immediate behavior.

The problems posed by the facts of grammatical speech were spotlighted by Karl Lashley in a paper written in 1951 called "The problem of serial order in behavior." Lashley argued that much behavior, of which grammatical speech is merely one example, exhibits properties that cannot be attributed to a chain of reflexes in which each behavioral link is determined only by a preceding link; rather, the entire sequence must be planned in advance. To support this view,

Lashley argued that languages are translated by thoughts, not by individual words. For instance, when translating from German to English, Lashley found that he read the German text and then translated an entire thought to English (which has a different word order) without remembering a single word of the German text. The ease and speed with which translators (at the United Nations, for instance) transpose the word order of two languages shows that word-for-word translation is not what they do. According to Lashley, serial order in behavior results from an interaction of spatial and temporal systems. The order of a sentence, for instance, is predetermined according to grammatical rules and somehow represented completely in the nervous system even before the sentence is begun. Then, when the sentence is about to be uttered, this representation is scanned and the elements flow sequentially to the vocal cords.

Consider the following sentence, cited by Lashley: "Rapidly righting with his uninjured hand, he saved from loss the contents of the canoe." When you hear someone read the sentence you understand "righting," not "writing," but only after you hear the word "canoe." Thus, there must be an integrating mechanism for the sentence as a whole. The sentence must be planned in advance before it is uttered because its meaning is ambiguous until the entire sentence is out. One cannot imagine a speaker starting the sentence without already having determined how it is to end. The planning of a sentence in a language is done according to grammatical rules. But the problem of serial order is more general than just sentences. There are hierarchies of order: the order of vocal movements in pronouncing a word, the order of words in a sentence, sentences in a paragraph, and paragraphs in a discourse. Within each, three sets of events need to be accounted for: The activation of the elements (words) without regard to order, the events to which the elements refer (meaning), and the order itself (grammar).

It has been suggested that a sentence is stored in memory as a kernel with variations. That is, the sentence "John was not hit by Mary" would be stored as "Mary hits John" plus the fact that the sentence is passive, negative, and in the past tense. Many psychologists feel that the principles of this sort of grammar are the same principles by which people understand and produce sentences. But this is likely to seem true for any grammar that concisely describes the sentences people actually do produce.

Remember, we said that grammar may be thought of as a molar description of the use of language, and that ungrammatical expressions may be thought of as molecular deviations from that molar description. Another kind of variation in grammar was studied by Jacques Mehler. He gave subjects lists of sentences and asked them to recall the sentences later. He was interested in the errors made in recall. He found two major kinds of errors: (1) omissions of words and (2) changes of grammatical structure (syntactic errors). As the time between initial learning and testing increased, the omission errors went down but the syntactic errors went up. Subjects tended to remember sentences in a simpler form than that in which they were presented. In other words, subjects would say they heard "Mary hit John" when they really heard "John was hit by Mary."

An experiment to separate the effect of grammar from the effect of other properties of sentences was done by William Epstein. He found that a grammatically structured series of nonsense words was easier to learn than unstructured nonsense. There were four categories of things to learn:

1. Structured nonsense, for example: "The frumous grably frabled a plinky trucket in his glimp."
2. Unstructured nonsense, for example: "Frabled glimp trucket grably plinky frumous."
3. Structured but meaningless sentences, for example: "Colorless green ideas sleep furiously."
4. Unstructured meaningless sentences, for example: "Ideas furiously green sleep colorless."

Epstein first showed subjects each complete string of words on a card. He found that structured meaningless sentences were learned best and unstructured nonsense was learned least well. The structured nonsense was learned better than the unstructured nonsense. Why? The material was equally familiar (or unfamiliar), equally meaningful, and, since none of the nonsense had presumably occurred before in the subjects' experience, the sequential probabilities of one word following another were the same. The only explanation for the ease in learning the structured nonsense is the structure (or syntax) itself even though there were more words ("the," "and," and "of" included) in the structured material.

After showing some subjects the entire sentences on cards, Epstein took other subjects and showed them the sentences one word at a time. This kind of presentation deemphasized the structure, so that the sentences were not perceived as units, and all four categories were learned equally slowly. Epstein reasoned that the ability of subjects to learn sentences depended on their ability to organize those sentences into a small number of units. The unstructured material was difficult to organize, but the structured material already came in with an organization (that of grammar) and thus was easy to organize — there was less to remember.

So, what have we learned about grammar? First, that it is a set of rules, to some extent arbitrary (like the rules of chess) and to some extent natural (like Newton's laws). Our speech generally obeys these rules but sometimes does not. When we make mistakes, they are often in the direction of simpler grammatical forms. In order to speak a sentence, we have to plan it in advance because the grammatical rules we follow sometimes force us to make adjustments in the beginning of sentences to prepare for what we are going to say at the end. The fact that we can do this shows that we do indeed have some sort of outline (or molar appreciation) of what we are about to say — similarly, the outfielder does not run to where the ball is but to where the ball is going to be. In understanding sentences the rules of grammar help us organize the input and thus remember them better. Even nonsense, when it is syntactically consistent (like "Jabberwocky"), can be organized in this way.

Now let us consider the work of John Bransford and Jeffrey Franks on how sentences are put together in discourse. Bransford and Franks concentrated on how listeners understand groups of sentences by presenting groups of sentences like the following:

1. The rock rolled down the mountain.
2. The rock crushed the hut.
3. The hut was tiny.
4. The hut was at the edge of the woods.

Note that the ideas in these four sentences can be expressed in a single sentence:

5. The rock, which rolled down the mountain, crushed the tiny hut at the edge of the woods.

Now, the subjects in this experiment were *never* presented with sentence 5. They only saw 1 through 4, mixed with several other groups of sentences like sentences 1 through 4 but expressing other ideas. Some were long sentences and some were short. Later the subjects were given long lists of sentences and asked, first, whether the new sentences were on the old list, and second, how confident they were that they recognized the sentences. Bransford and Franks found that most of their subjects thought they had seen the composite sentence 5, and were, in fact, more confident that they had seen 5 than that they had seen the original sentences 1 through 4. This study shows that incoming material does not directly affect behavior. Behavior differs from input by: (1) being more efficiently organized (having fewer units of information than the input) and (2) being more consistent with other (previously emitted) patterns of behavior.

Reinforcement and Language

It is clear that reinforcement plays a role in the use of language. There are several lines of evidence, but our own common sense tells us the answer. We say "Please pass the salt" as long as the salt is passed. When it is not passed, we will stop saying "Please pass the salt" and start saying something else. An experiment by the psychologist Greenspoon indicates that linguistic behavior can be modified sometimes without the subject being aware. Greenspoon in an interview, the real purpose of which was disguised from the subject, would occasionally nod his head and say "mmm-hmm" in a tone indicating he understood what the subject was saying. He said this each time the subject uttered a plural noun and recorded the frequency of plural nouns. He found that "rewarding" subjects with "mmm-hmm" increased the frequency of their plural nouns and withdrawal of "mmm-hmm" decreased the frequency again. Afterwards the subjects said that they were not aware that their utterance of plural nouns had changed during the experiment. There is some dispute about whether all subjects were *really* unaware of what was going on, but this is irrelevant to our purposes. The point is that their behavior changed according to the contingencies.

   A more difficult question is, Can language be taught in the same way that a rat's pressing a lever can be taught, by reinforcing correct behavior and punishing or extinguishing incorrect behavior? First of all, it is necessary to define the area of the problem. Many of Wittgenstein's categories undoubtedly can be taught. The critical ability we seek to find out about is the ability to form sentences that one has never heard or used before (with familiar elements that have been used before). Can this be acquired by traditional reinforcement techniques?

There is little question but that reinforcement plays a part in the learning of words. Each child learns her parents' language. The child babbles and certain sounds are reinforced. There is evidence that as babies get older, their babbling takes on more of the character of the speech of their parents. When a child duplicates the sounds of her parents, she gets rewarded by her parents; also, the very sounds she makes remind her of her parents (from whom primary reward comes) and take on a secondarily reinforcing quality.

According to Jakobson, understanding speech proceeds by successive discriminations. First consonants are distinguished from vowels, then aspirated consonants (for example, p, t, and h) from nonaspirated consonants (for example, f, m, and r).

The problem, though, is not with understanding sounds; it is with using grammar. How does one acquire grammatical rules? Some linguists (Noam Chomsky is the best known) have found certain grammatical universals that seem to characterize languages. (Warning: Here comes the nature/nurture controversy again.) Are these universals inborn — part of our evolutionary heritage — or are they the way various cultures react to similar environmental forces (for instance, one could discover farming techniques such as sowing and reaping that cross cultural lines, but is this because these farming actions are innate or because one must do the same sorts of things everywhere to produce crops)?

One way in which this question has been approached is to try to teach nonhuman animals (particularly chimpanzees) to talk. The reasoning goes like this: As far as we know, only humans have a grammatical language. Perhaps this is because only humans are born with the special mechanism necessary for grammatical language. If nonhumans can be taught to speak grammatically, we could speculate that the language behavior of humans is merely a highly developed form of other behavior and not a special characteristic of humans alone. Complete evidence in this area is still to come, but it is instructive to look at some of what has been done so far.

First, we know that animals communicate with each other in complex ways. For instance, Emil Menzel found that if one chimpanzee has seen where food is hidden and then a group of chimpanzees (including the one who saw the food) is released into the area where the food was hidden, the other chimpanzees run straight to the food and often reach it before the one who saw it being hidden. Something about the behavior of that chimp must have told the others not only that food was hidden somewhere but also where it was.

In a more structured setting, Duane Rumbaugh and Sue Savage-Rumbaugh trained one chimpanzee to use various tools to open boxes containing food. Then they placed that chimp in a cage next to a second chimpanzee. The chimps were visible to each other, and there was a slot between the cages through which various items could be passed. The second chimpanzee was then trained to pass tools through the slot in response to "requests" from the first. (A tool could be requested by exchange of a token that stood for the tool.) When all of the tools were given to the second chimpanzee, the following sequence of events occurred:

1. The first chimpanzee requested the tool that would open the box with the food.
2. The second chimpanzee passed the correct tool through the slot.
3. The first chimpanzee opened the box with the tool and removed the food.
4. The first chimpanzee gave some of the food to the second.

The significant part of the exchange was of course step 4, where one chimpanzee actually reinforced the behavior of another. Evidently chimpanzees can communicate with each other. The question we ask now is, Can a nonhuman be trained to use language for communication?

There is the case of Vicky, a chimpanzee that was raised from infancy by a husband–wife team of psychologists along with their own child. At first, Vicky outperformed the human baby in nearly every respect, but slowly and surely the human baby caught up. Vicky could (finally) understand some human speech, but she never learned to speak beyond uttering a few rudimentary words like "milk," "mama," and so forth. As soon as the human baby learned to speak, she quickly outdistanced the chimp.

In a more successful experiment, the chimp Washoe was raised by two psychologists and "spoken to" only in American sign language (Ameslan). The reasoning behind this was that Vicky's problem might not have been with grammar as such but with the mechanics of speaking. Although chimps seem to have a reasonable approximation of the human vocal apparatus, they may not have enough of the subtle nerve–muscle connections to coordinate lips, tongue, diaphragm, and jaw in the way that humans do. However, chimps do have remarkable coordination in their fingers. When Washoe was addressed in sign language and rewarded by approval for appropriate gestures of its own the chimp soon learned to communicate with humans. (Following similar techniques, a gorilla, Koko, was also trained to communicate with humans using sign language.)

Another attempt to teach chimps to use language is the more formal approach of David Premack. Premack constructed a special language for chimps. Premack reasoned that a simple language might contain a few nouns, like *honey, bread,* and *Sarah* (the name of the chimp); a few verbs like *take, give* and *insert*; and a few functional words and signs like *yes, no,* and a question mark. Each word in Premack's language was represented by a plastic marker. These differed in color and shape.

Premack first taught Sarah to identify the colored markers by having the chimp put available markers on a board when it wanted something like a banana. Then it learned the difference between "give banana" and "take banana." Then Premack reinforced the correct answering of questions with "yes" or "no" markers, and by gradual stages he got the chimp to use markers to form sentences such as "Sarah insert banana (in) pail" or "Sarah insert apple (in) dish." Premack found that Sarah could not only correctly use the specific sentences she was taught but could also use the sentence structure correctly with new words. That is, she could identify and use the sentence "Sarah insert milk (in) pail" even though she had only learned the sentence with apples and bananas.

Furthermore, Premack found an even more sophisticated operation could be taught to Sarah. She could actually discuss the words (plastic markers) themselves. She could correctly understand and produce the marker for "apple," then another marker standing for "is the name of," then an apple itself. This is one of the most rigid criteria for having a language—being able to discuss the language itself.

Vicky, Washoe, and Sarah teach us that although humans certainly possess something that makes it easier for them to learn languages, it is by no means impossible to teach animals to exhibit elements of language use.

At this point you may be tempted to conclude that human language is just a more complex and detailed version of nonhuman communication. But then there is the case of H. S. Terrace and the chimp

Nim (full name: Nim Chimpsky). Terrace taught Nim to speak in sign language just like Washoe and Koko were taught. However, after a detailed analysis of Nim's behavior (and a retrospective analysis of films of Washoe and Koko), Terrace concluded that none of the animals actually produced original sentences. Washoe, Koko, Nim, and even Sarah, according to Terrace, were very good indeed at getting food and praise from their adoring human trainers and enjoyed playing with humans in this way. But none of them ever created and used an original sentence in a consistent and coherent way — as almost all human children do at a very early age.

There is much current debate about the degree to which nonhuman communication can approach human language. One interesting speculation has been made recently by Sperber and Wilson, who suggest that nonhumans may have very complex representational systems that help them get from place to place in their environments (as rats do in mazes) and very complex communication systems by which they engage in elaborate social interactions (like Menzel's and the Rumbaughs' chimpanzees), but only in human language do representation and communication act in harmony with each other. Sperber and Wilson speculate further that the interaction between representation and communication as expressed in human language may parallel an overlap between corresponding mechanisms in the human brain acquired in the course of evolution.

Language as a Guide to Behavior

As Wittgenstein's list (p. 209) indicates, language has many uses. Let us now consider a category into which several of those specific uses fit: language as a guide to behavior (one's own or someone else's).

The most direct way in which language guides behavior is when person A describes a set of contingencies to person B. A car-driving instructor might say, "The harder you press the accelerator [points to accelerator], the faster the car goes; the harder you press the brake [points to brake], the faster it stops." For this to make any sense to the neophyte driver, she has had to have pressed various things in the past and to have traveled in an accelerating or decelerating vehicle. The instruction ties the two concepts together. It specifies a contingency by connecting a behavior (emitted in the past) with the feedback contingent upon that behavior. To understand the instruction, the student must already be familiar with (1) the behavior in other contexts, (2) the feedback in other contexts, and (3) the if–then relationship conveyed by the structural properties (the grammar) of the sentence. Behavior conforming to the far more general rule "Do what the instructor says" is reinforced along with obedience to the specific instructions when the student performs the behavior and experiences the predicted feedback. As the student advances, feedback might be left out of the instructions ("Press the brake when you come to a red light"), or the behavior might be left out of the instructions ("Stop when you come to a red light"). In these cases the student is supposed to have already learned the press–stop rule; the instructions are part of a higher rule ("Stop at red lights").

A more subtle sort of instruction specifies no contingency at all but superimposes a description of a higher-order discriminative stimulus (like the yellow light in the Nevin–Liebold experiment illustrated in Figure 5.6) on some particular situation. Suppose humans were trained to perform correctly in the Nevin–Liebold procedure (pushing lit buttons). Then without the yellow light the experimenter said, "Imagine that the yellow light were present." After these instructions people might well behave as if the yellow light were indeed present.

Let us now consider two experiments that illustrate these two ways in which language is used to guide behavior. Both experiments are concerned with language as exemplified in instructions from experimenter to subject. In the first case, an experiment by Steven Hayes, A. J. Brownstein, A. J. Haar, and D. E. Greenway, instructions are used to present contingencies directly. In the second case, an experiment by Walter Mischel and N. Baker, instructions refer to higher-order stimuli.

In the experiment by Hayes and colleagues, adult human subjects were given the task of pressing a button to move a marker from one corner to another of a displayed grid. A light (much like the light in the Nevin–Liebold experiments) signaled whether the button would be more effective if pressed fast (light on) or slowly (light off). One group of subjects was told in advance about the signaling function of the light (accurate instructions); a second group was just told to press fast (inaccurate instructions); a third group was just told to press slow (also inaccurate instructions). Despite the inaccurate instructions, several subjects in the second and third groups eventually came to respond appropriately as signaled by the light.

Then, without telling the subjects, the button was made ineffective for all groups — the marker would no longer move at all regardless of what the subjects did. The experimenters observed which subjects stopped pressing soonest (responded quickest to the change of contingency). The results were that the subjects in the first group (accurate instructions) continued to press fast and slow depending on the light for a long time. Their behavior, the experimenters reasoned, must have been based on the rule conveyed by the original instructions (which had not changed). On the other hand, those subjects in the second and third groups, who had originally come to press fast and slow depending on the light (despite inaccurate instructions), stopped pressing much quicker when the contingencies were changed (when the marker failed to move). Their behavior, the experimenters reasoned, must have been based on the contingencies as they were and not on the rule conveyed by the instructions.

The experiment demonstrates that while two people may behave identically, what controls their behavior may be quite different — ranging from global rules to local contingencies. The properties of global and local means of control are different. Rule-governed behavior persists despite changes in specific contingencies because it takes a long time to convincingly disconfirm (or confirm) a general rule. (As Aristotle said concerning this very issue, "One swallow does not make a summer."). Contingency-governed behavior, on the other hand, changes quickly as local contingencies change. In this experiment the more flexible contingency-governed behavior proved to be the better adaptation, but in real life the reverse is often the case. People who save for a rainy day in obedience to a rule learned early in life from parents and teachers are often (but not always) better off then those who spend and save in response to local contingencies.

In the above experiment by Hayes and colleagues, the instructions served as discriminative stimuli for contingencies in the sense that they directly described contingencies (accurately or inaccurately). Let us now consider the other experiment by Walter Mischel and N. Baker (entitled "Cognitive transformations of reward objects through instructions"), where instructions do not directly describe contingencies but describe superordinate stimuli in the presence of which various contingencies have applied in the past.

The subjects in Mischel and Baker's experiment were four-year-old children exposed to the *delay-of-gratification* procedure developed by Mischel. The delay-of-gratification procedure is illustrated in Figure 6.1. It works as follows: The experimenter puts a less-preferred reward (say, a pretzel) on a table in front of the child (the pretzel either remains exposed or is covered). Then the experimenter tells the child that she will be leaving the room and will return with a more preferred reward (say, a marshmallow), which the child may obtain provided he does not signal the experimenter to come back into the room (by ringing a bell) before the experimenter does so by herself. If the child makes the signal, he gets the small reward (the pretzel) and forfeits the large one (the marshmallow). If the child refrains from signaling until the experimenter comes back, he gets the large reward. The experimenters observed how long each child would wait before signaling.

This game between the experimenter and child subject is a version of the standard self-control paradigm, about which we shall have a lot more to say in Chapter 8. The critical issue in this case was not the self-control paradigm itself but the effect on self-control (on how long the child would wait) of what the child saw while the experimenter was out of the room and what the experimenter said before she left.

Normally children wait much longer if the pretzel is covered and out of sight than if the pretzel is visible. However, if the pretzel is covered and the experimenter instructs them to think of the pretzel in "hot" consummatory ways as crunchy or salty, the children with the pretzel covered wait no longer than they would with the pretzel exposed. And if the experimenter instructs them to think of the pretzel in "cool" ways, say as a tiny stick or a log, the children with the pretzel exposed wait just as long as they would with the pretzel covered.

The experimenter's instructions regarding how to think of the pretzel essentially supervened as a discriminative stimulus over the presence or absence of the pretzel itself. Again let us go back to our hypothetical human equivalent of the Nevin–Liebold experiment. After training a person with the basic procedure (Figure 5.6), the experimenter might say, while the yellow light is on, "Imagine the light is off," or, with the light off, "Imagine the yellow light is on." These instructions essentially say to the subject "Behave as you would behave if the yellow light were on [if it were in fact off] or off [if it were in fact on]." Similarly, the "hot" and "cool" instructions in the

FIGURE 6.1 Effect of instructions on a child's ability to delay gratification.

Mischel–Baker experiment say to the subject "Behave as you would behave if the pretzel were covered [if it were in fact uncovered] or uncovered [if it were in fact covered]." Here is a case where verbal instructions serve as a higher-order discriminative stimulus for one sort of behavior while the actual (nonverbal) physical stimulus is a discriminative stimulus for the opposite behavior. In this conflict, the behavior of four-year-old children conformed to the language of the adult experimenter (following the still-higher rule "Do as you are told") rather than to the visual presence or absence of a pretzel.

We have described both the experiments by Hayes and colleagues and by Mischel and Baker with the behavioral terms *contingency, discriminative stimulus,* and *reinforcement.* But we could talk about both experiments in terms of internal representations. In the former experiment, accurately instructed subjects behaved in accordance with an internal representation of a rule, while inaccurately instructed subjects were forced to deal with the contingencies as they found them. The representation or lack of it then caused the behavior.

Similarly, we could talk about the latter experiment in terms of internal representations: "Hot" instructions gave rise to an internal representation of a pretzel as vivid as a real pretzel. "Cool" instructions changed the internal representation of the real pretzel to that of a stick. The internal image of a pretzel or lack of it then caused the behavior. To the extent that the workings of internal representations were understood, there would be no harm (and possibly a great deal of benefit) in talking this way. Unfortunately, neither cognitive psychology nor behavioral psychology has yet provided a satisfactory understanding of the operation of internal representations.

Language and Self-Control

Behavior conforms better to changing contingencies when those contingencies are accompanied by explicit discriminative stimuli than when the changed relationship between behavior and reinforcement is itself the only sign of the changed conditions. For instance, if, when a schedule of positive reinforcement is changed to extinction, a light is turned on, extinction proceeds more rapidly. As we said before, a contingency itself takes time to occur (and therefore adjustment must take time). But a signal of a contingency can appear suddenly and adjustment may be rapid.

The more vivid is the stimulus, the better is the discrimination. When discriminative stimuli are indistinct or complex, subjects may themselves increase discriminability by adding a verbal response. Recall Luria's experiment (p. 215–216) in which children helped themselves discriminate by saying "squeeze" and "don't squeeze." This is an example of language as self-control.

Another example is a more recent experiment by Charles Catania, B. A. Matthews, and E. Shimoff in which people were exposed to complex and changing schedules of reinforcement. One group of subjects was explicitly (and accurately) instructed about the nature of the contingencies. Another group was asked to guess what the contingencies were, and correct guesses were reinforced. The group that guessed (provided their own discriminative stimulus) adjusted faster and more consistently to the changing contingencies. In this experiment the self-generated language served a double function: It described the contingency (the relation between behavior and feedback), and it organized behavior with respect to that contingency.

CONSCIOUSNESS

One (very narrow) definition of consciousness is the use of language as in the previous section to describe contingencies and organize behavior. Since this is communication to oneself (oneself at time A to oneself at other times — a relationship we will discuss further in Chapter 8), the words may be uttered to oneself (like a shopping list repeated on the way to the store). But in this section we will discuss a much more common and wider definition — consciousness as a state of mind, as the repository of inner mental life that includes knowledge, hopes, wishes, dreams, and so forth.

Since Darwin made it clear that the human mind is a product of evolution, biologists, psychologists, and philosophers have been concerned with animal consciousness. Because this wider sort of consciousness is a sense of personal or private awareness of one's own inner life, each animal can only be aware of its own consciousness. However, precisely *because* the consciousness of other people (let alone nonhuman animals) is unobservable to anyone else, animal consciousness cannot be studied except through its behavioral manifestations.

Through the years biologists, psychologists, and philosophers have attempted to draw a line to separate by one or another behavioral criterion those animals that have consciousness from those that do not. It will be instructive to trace out some of those attempts.

One of the earliest was the famous Pfluger–Lotze controversy, which took place in Germany in the early nineteenth century. The agreed criterion for consciousness was the ability of an animal to exhibit "purposive behavior." Pfluger (a biologist) and Lotze (a philosopher) agreed further that frogs (by virtue of an ability to learn to withdraw their legs to avoid painful stimulation) were capable of purposive behavior, hence consciousness. The point at issue was whether, after a frog's head was cut off, any consciousness remained in the frog (presumably in its spinal cord). Pfluger showed that avoidance learned by a whole frog was retained (for a while) after the frog had been decapitated. He claimed that a headless frog must therefore be conscious. Lotze argued, on the other hand, that the behavioral criterion of consciousness was not *performance* of avoidance but *learning* of avoidance. Because a headless frog could not learn to avoid, it must not be conscious, argued Lotze. The argument between Pfluger and Lotze was rendered moot by Pavlov, who explained such learning in terms of conditional reflexes.

Another attempt to specify the behavioral criterion for consciousness was a series of experiments on "insight" (see Chapter 1) by the Gestalt psychologist Köhler. The criterion there was the smooth and rapid appearance of a response in a new situation with no apparent trial and error. Chimpanzees are conscious, Köhler argued, because they can acquire responses in this rapid way (as exemplified by Sultan's "insightful" behavior with the banana and the box). Since that time, however, it has been found that any animal will show "insight" (as demonstrated by rapid behavioral adjustment) if it has had enough experience in similar situations (so that it would have learned a higher-order discrimination). The question then became, How similar was the problem Köhler studied to others in Sultan's own past experience (so that Sultan himself could have learned the higher-order contingency) or how similar was the problem to others in the past of chimpanzees in general (so that Sultan's ancestors would not have survived had they not been born with the tendency to solve such problems)? As the reader might suspect, the more similarity of either kind, the more insight is shown. But this is true for all animals, not just chimpanzees. Hence, the mere demonstration of insight in a particular situation is not a good behavioral criterion for consciousness.

Some recent experiments by Gordon Gallup have suggested another criterion. A mirror is placed in a young chimpanzee's cage. At first the chimp behaves toward its own reflection as if it were another chimp and makes threatening motions towards it. Eventually, however, the chimp comes to see the image in the mirror as a reflection of itself, as shown by use of the mirror in grooming. That the chimp sees itself (rather than another chimp) in the mirror can be tested by anesthetizing the chimp and placing a red mark on its forehead. When the chimp wakes up and looks in the mirror, it immediately and spontaneously reaches to its own forehead to touch the mark. When corresponding tests are performed with other animals, including almost all primates other than humans and chimpanzees, they reach toward the *mirror* rather than toward themselves. Although other animals can be explicitly taught to use mirrors as tools for grooming, they do not seem to do so naturally as do chimpanzees and human beings.

Gallup's experiments do seem to reveal an innate ability of chimpanzees and human beings regarding the use of transposed images of themselves as discriminative stimuli. But must psychologists (including Gallup) are unwilling to speculate what this ability may have to do with consciousness.

The philosopher Daniel Dennett has argued that consciousness may exist in animals to various degrees. The first degree of consciousness may be observed as purposive behavior. But Dennett admits there is no way to be sure that such behavior is not just some simpler process (such as classical or instrumental conditioning) with more or less complicated discriminative stimuli. The second degree of consciousness, however, is deomonstrated, according to Dennett, when one animal behaves as if it believed another animal were conscious. If one animal attributes consciousness to another, it can only be, Dennett argues, by analogy to its own consciousness. Therefore it is conscious. This sort of behavior, Dennett claims, is unmistakable.

Consider monkey A, a submissive monkey, and monkey B, a dominant monkey. Whenever A gets food in the presence of B, A runs away or hides the food; otherwise B takes it away. Now A is given a pair of blackout goggles to play with that completely block out the light. A is seen to try the goggles on and take them off several times. The goggles are taken away, A is given some food, and finally B is let into the area wearing the selfsame goggles. After an initial shock, A calmly eats the food; A *knows* that B *does not know* that A has the food. In general, spontaneous acts of deception between one animal and another have been cited as evidence for this kind of consciousness. Still higher levels would be that A knows that B knows that A knows, and so forth.

Dennett's concept of levels of consciousness holds promise of eventually providing some behavioral index of inner events, but until the cognitive mechanism underlying consciousness is known, this sort of behavioral analysis remains vague. If we say that monkey A's behavior demonstrates consciousness, we do not necessarily imply that monkey A's cognitive state is the same as that of a person doing the same thing. As we have seen (in the experiment by Hayes and colleagues), identical actions may be governed by local contingencies or by global rules. As yet psychologists have not been able to determine how the mechanism of consciousness works, let alone to distinguish between monkey and human consciousness.

A more troubling aspect of much of the research on consciousness is its anecdotal, nonsystematic nature. If an animal's behavior is observed for only a brief period, the observer has to guess at its context; such guesses are notoriously subject to error.

On this topic I would like to share with the reader a brief (hence anecdotal and untrustworthy) observation of my own. I recently attended a seminar at which a well-known philosopher was presenting his theories on animal consciousness. The philosopher (much like Lotze) was trying to draw a distinction between conscious and nonconscious animal species. In the audience was a famous biologist (much like Pfluger), an expert on the behavior of bats (rather than frogs). The philosopher claimed that bats fall below the line of consciousness because of various deficiencies (relative to human beings) in their behavioral repertoire. The biologist immediately raised his voice in protest. Such a conclusion, the biologist claimed, just showed that the philosopher did not know bats. Anyone who spent his life studying bats, the biologist said, would see extreme subtleties in their behavior (including acts of deception) that satisfy any behavioral criterion that might be raised.

The biologist's argument, I suspect, could be made about any species no matter how lowly (and indeed has been made by highly respected biologists even about the very lowly amoeba). If you have spent your life studying a species as biologists have or if you have engaged in an intense relationship with a particular member of a species as pet owners have, you are bound to know those animals extremely well and to resent their "demotion" relative to other species. We therefore ought to assume that the behavior of all animals is highly complex. We are interested here in the particular nature of that complexity and how it differs from the complexity of the behavior of other species.

It has been claimed that the study of consciousness in animals is important because our ethical conduct toward conscious animals must differ from our ethical conduct toward nonconscious animals. But our treatment of any animal should, it seems, be based on understanding and thereby preserving as far as possible the animal's normal relationship to its environment. As pet owners, farmers, or scientists, we put ourselves into a social relationship with an animal. Essentially we have taken the place of some other animal or object in the animal's normal environment (or that of its ancestors). To do this with the least possible disturbance requires knowledge of the animal's normal relationship to its environment rather than speculation about events inside the animal based on superficial anatomical or behavioral resemblances to humans.

Suggested Readings

Ludwig Wittgenstein's *Philosophical Investigations*, translated by G. E. M. Anscombe (New York: Macmillan, 1958) is notoriously difficult but is nevertheless enjoyable to read and repays the effort spent in trying to understand it. The Pfluger – Lotze controversy is discussed in E. G. Boring, *A History of Experimental Psychology*, 2nd ed. (New York: Appleton-Century-Crofts, 1950), p. 29.

George Miller's *Language and Communication* (New York: McGraw-Hill, 1951) contains discussions of the early work on language by Chomsky, Jakobson, and Lashley.

Recent work on language is discussed in Miller and Glucksberg's "Psycholinguistic aspects of pragmatics and semantics" in R. C. Atkinson, R. J. Herrnstein, G. Lindzey, and R. D. Luce, eds., *Stevens' Handbook of Experimental Psychology*, Vol. 2: *Learning and Cognition*, 2nd ed. (New York: Wiley, 1988), pp. 417–472.

A book of articles by Daniel Dennett called *Brainstorms: Philosophical Essays on Mind and Psychology* (Montgomery, VT.: Bradford Books, 1978) discusses language and consciousness from a cognitive viewpoint. Discussions of animal language appear in the Roitblat, Bever, and Terrace book *Animal Cognition* and in the Hayes book *Rule-Governed Behavior*, both cited in the Suggested Readings at the end of Chapter 5. The entirely speculative analysis of indirect speech presented here is based very loosely on opponent process theory that is presented in R. L. Soloman and J. D. Corbett, "An opponent process theory of motivation: I. Temporal dynamics of affect," *Psychological Review*, 1974, **81**, 119–145.

Articles by Premack and by Rumbaugh and Savage-Rumbaugh on the higher cognitive abilities of animals appear in *Behavioral and Brain Sciences*, 1978, **1**(4), 515–657. The experiment by Hayes and colleagues, and the Mischel–Baker experiment are discussed with a slightly different slant in a recent book by the present author, H. Rachlin, *Judgment, Decision, and Choice* (New York: W. H. Freeman, 1989). Recent work of Mischel and his colleagues appears in W. Mischel, Y. Shode, and M. Rodriguez, "Delay of gratification in children," *Science*, 1989, **244**, 933–938.

The following is a list of articles referred to in this chapter:

Bransford, J., and Franks, J. The abstraction of linguistic ideas. *Cognitive Psychology,* 1971, **2**, 331–350.

Catania, C., Matthews, B. A., and Shimoff, E. Instructed versus shaped human verbal behavior: interactions with nonverbal responding. *Journal of the Experimental Analysis of Behavior,* 1982, **38**, 233–248.

Deese, J. *The Structure of Associations in Language and Thought.* Baltimore: The Johns Hopkins University Press, 1965.

Epstein, R., Lanza, R. P., and Skinner, B. F. Symbolic communication between two pigeons (*Columba livia domestica*). *Science,* 1980, **207**, 543–545.

Epstein, W. Recall of word lists following learning of sentences and of anomalous and random strings. *Journal of Verbal Learning and Verbal Behavior,* 1969, **8**, 20–25.

Gallup, G. G. Chimpanzees: self-recognition. *Science,* 1970, **167**, 86–87.

Greenspoon, J. The reinforcing effect of two spoken sounds on the frequency of two responses. *American Journal of Psychology,* 1955, **68**, 409–416.

Hayes, S. C., Brownstein, A. J., Haar, J. R., and Greenway, D. E. Instructions, multiple schedules, and extinction: distinguishing rule-governed from schedule-induced behavior. *Journal of the Experimental Analysis of Behavior,* 1986, **46**, 137–148.

Lashley, K. S. The problem of serial order in behavior. In C. A. Jeffreys, ed. *Cerebral Mechanisms in Behavior.* New York: Wiley, 1951.

Mehler, J. and Miller, G. A. Retroactive interference in the recall of simple sentences. *British Journal of Psychology,* 1964, **55**, 295–301.

Menzel, E. W. Group behavior in young chimpanzees: responsiveness to cumulative novel changes in a large outdoor enclosure. *Journal of Comparative and Physiological Psychology,* 1971, **74,** 46–51.

Mischel, W., and Baker, N. Cognitive transformations of reward objects through instructions. *Journal of Personality and Social Psychology,* 1975, **31,** 254–261.

Segal, E. Toward a coherent psychology of language. In W. K. Honig and J. E. R. Staddon, *Handbook of Operant Behavior.* Englewood Cliffs, N.J.: Prentice-Hall, 1977.

Sperber, D., and Wilson, D. *Relevance: Communication and Cognition.* Oxford: Blackwell, 1986.

Terrace, H. S. *Nim.* New York: Knopf, 1979.

7

Context in Classical and Instrumental Conditioning

What most distinguishes modern behaviorism from the earlier behaviorism of Pavlov, Watson, and Thorndike is its account of context. The earlier behaviorists were concerned with the conditioning of individual reflexes or responses. For them, the strength of a reflex or a response was independent of the condition of other reflexes or responses. But just as the brightness of the headlights of an oncoming car is different depending on its context — whether it is day or night — we know that the strength of a response depends on its context, the frame, within which it occurs.

In classical conditioning the power of a conditional stimulus to elicit a response depends on the occurrence of the unconditional stimulus in the *presence* of the conditional stimulus as well as the nonoccurrence of the unconditional stimulus in the *absence* of the conditional stimulus. In instrumental conditioning the strength of a given response depends on the reinforcement of alternative responses as well as on the reinforcement of the response itself.

Because the role of context in classical and instrumental conditioning is a very active current area of research and there are many competing theories about how context works, it is not possible here to trace all of those theories or to give credit to their proponents. The classical conditioning section incorporates work by Peter Balsam, John Gibbon, Herbert Jenkins, Robert Rescorla, Allan Wagner, and others. The instrumental conditioning section incorporates work by William Baum, Charles Catania, Michael Davison, Edmund Fantino, Leonard Green, Richard Herrnstein, Alexandra Logue, James Mazur, J. A. Nevin, Diane McCarthy, William Vaughan, Jr., and others. The bibliographical section at the end of this chapter provides references to appropriate works by the authors.

CONTEXT IN CLASSICAL CONDITIONING

Classical conditioning is essentially the establishment of a signal (the CS) for a significant event (the US). Some psychologists believe that the conditional response (salivation to the bell, for instance) is the same as the unconditional response (salivation to food); others believe that the conditional response is ultimately a way of preparing for the oncoming unconditional stimulus. However, psychologists on both sides of this argument agree that the better the CS signals the US, the faster the conditional response is learned.

One way in which the CS can be a good signal is by its *salience*, or vividness. An alarm bell needs to be loud, the louder the better. The more salient the CS is, the faster the conditional response appears. What makes a signal salient, however, is not its absolute intensity but its intensity relative to the background. A fire alarm that serves adequately in a quiet office building might be totally inadequate in a boiler factory. In the Shenger-Krestovnikova experiment (Figure 2.6) the original discrimination depended on the difference between the ellipse and the circle, not on the shape of either figure alone.

But simply making the CS stand out from its background in intensity or shape is not sufficient to rapidly establish conditional responses. The most important characteristic of a CS, as of any signal, is its timing relative to the signaled event (the US in this case).

Timing

Figure 7.1 illustrates the temporal relation of a CS, a US, and their context. The dark rectangle represents the frame in which conditioning takes place. We assume a period (a "trial") lasting T seconds. In

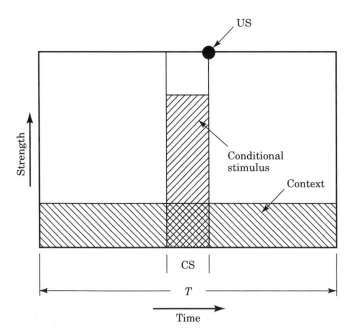

FIGURE 7.1 Strength of a conditional stimulus relative to strength of its context. The single US raises the strength of both the CS and its background, but CS strength is raised more because the CS is brief relative to background.

the simplified example shown in Figure 7.1, a single conditional stimulus lasting CS seconds occurs in the middle of the trial. The solid dot at the top of the frame at the end of the CS represents the occurrence of a brief unconditional stimulus (US). The strength of conditioning after a certain number of trials is represented by the height of the bar representing the CS relative to the height of the bar spanning T, which represents the strength of background conditioning.

With salivary conditioning of dogs, a tone might be sounded for CS seconds, at the end of which food powder is injected into the dog's mouth. The relative height of the CS over its background represents the strength of the dog's tendency to salivate during the tone (as measured by rate of salivation relative to baseline salivation). With emotional-response conditioning of rats, a tone might be sounded for CS seconds followed by a brief electric shock. The relative height of the CS over its background would represent the degree of the rat's fear or anxiety during the CS (as measured by suppression of an instrumental response). With autoshaping of pigeons, a plastic disk (a key) might be illuminated for *CS* seconds after which a pellet of food is delivered to a hopper beneath the key. The relative height of the CS over its background would represent the strength of responding during the light (as measured by the rate at which the pigeon pecks the lit key).

The important point about Figure 7.1 is that a trial does not begin with the onset of the CS and end with the offset of the US. The trial includes not only the conditional stimulus but also the background or context against which the conditional stimulus is presented. The strength of the context during *T* represents a baseline level of response strength upon which the conditional stimulus is superimposed. For instance, Staddon and Simmelhag (see p. 169–173) found that a pigeon periodically fed in a Skinner box *without* a lit key has a certain tendency to peck (at the air, the floor, or the walls of the box). For Staddon and Simmelhag's pigeons, this box represented the background upon which the lit key was superimposed. *The measured conditional response does not just depend on its absolute strength during the CS but on its relation to the background strength.* The reader might think of the strength of the context (during *T*) as a sort of ocean, and the strength of the conditional stimulus (during *CS*) as an island. Conditioning then depends on the degree to which the island rises out of the ocean.

Let us consider two ways in which the strength of the CS may be reduced relative to its background: by adding USs in the background and by increasing the duration of the CS relative to its background. Figure 7.2 illustrates these two ways individually. One way to decrease the apparent strength of conditioning, shown in Figure 7.2a, is by adding USs to the background. Starting with a brief CS as a strong signal for the US, more USs are added until, at the end, the CS tells you no more about the oncoming US than does its absence. The rate of the US throughout the trial is constant whether the CS is present or not. Thus the initially high signaling power of the CS is drowned by the rising strength of the background.

Another way to decrease the strength of conditioning is shown in the bottom row of Figure 7.2. There is only one US throughout this sequence, but the signaling power of the CS is reduced by making it occupy more and more of the time. As the CS gets bigger and bigger relative to the background, its power as a signal sinks further and further until finally the CS sinks completely into the background.

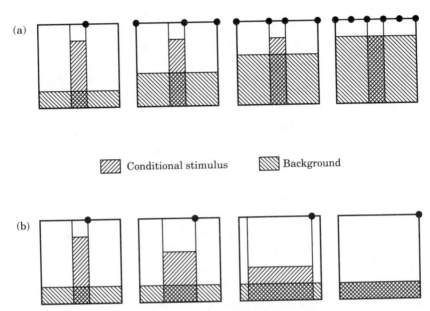

FIGURE 7.2 Two ways of decreasing CS strength relative to background: (a) Adding USs raises the strength of the background; (b) increasing duration of the CS lowers its strength.

The USs added to the background in Figure 7.2a are unsignaled by the CS. Imagine a country where it rained every day without fail. An occasional weather report predicting rain that day would be totally useless as a signal for rain. The increasing duration of the CS in the bottom row of Figure 7.2 also weakens it as a signal. A prediction of rain some time today might be useful. A prediction of rain sometime this month (in a place where it is sure to rain at least once a month anyway) is useless. To return to the island analogy, adding USs is like raising the ocean level. Increasing duration of the CS is like flattening the island.

WARNING

It was not possible to explain the complex concepts of this chapter without taking some sort of stance on theoretical issues that are actually matters of considerable debate. For example, we assume for the moment that the "level of the ocean" depends on the frequency of *all* USs, not just those presented in the absence of the CS. There is actually a lively dispute at present on this very issue. A second simplifying assumption is that level of conditioning strength is constant *within* the CS and *within* the background. If the duration of the CS is fixed or the duration between USs is fixed, considerable inhibitory forces develop at the beginning of these signals, causing large swings of conditioning strength within the CS and between the USs. Constant levels of conditioning strength, more in keeping with Figures 7.1 and 7.2, would be obtained if the CS and the between-US durations were variable. The reader should therefore think of the fixed intervals in the diagram as averages of actually variable durations. But even with this caveat, there is considerable debate about how context works in classical conditioning, which for the sake of simplicity we ignore here.

In the simplified model of classical conditioning represented in Figures 7.1 and 7.2, what counts most are two fractions: First, the number of USs signaled by a given kind of CS divided by the duration of the CS (the higher this fraction, the higher the height of the island); second, the total number of USs divided by the total time T (the higher this fraction, the higher the height of the ocean). Note that the second fraction includes signaled as well as unsignaled USs in its numerator, and the part of T during which the CS is present as well as the part during which the CS is absent in its denominator; after all, the CS is *superimposed* on the background (as indicated by the intersection of the crosshatching in the diagrams).

In an experiment by Herbert Jenkins, new USs were added by signaling each one with a new CS (Figure 7.3a). As a result, the background still gained in strength ("raising the ocean level"), reducing the resultant conditional response during each CS. When new CSs are added alone (Figure 7.3b) the effect is the same as increasing the duration of a single CS — reducing conditional response strength. Thus, two subjects, the first exposed to the conditions in the right frame of Figure 7.3a and the second exposed to the conditions in the right frame of Figure 7.3b, might both acquire the conditional response equally slowly. For the first subject, however, slowness of acquisition would be attributed to the high strength of the background; for the second, to weakness of the CS itself. The difference might be tested by

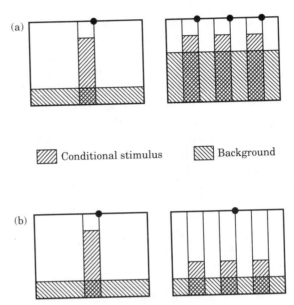

FIGURE 7.3   Jenkins's experiment in which the strength of a CS was reduced relative to its background: (a) By adding USs, each with a CS; (b) by adding CSs without USs.

superimposing the old CS on a new background. The first subject should then show a much stronger conditional response than the second.

Restructuring

The concept in Figures 7.1 through 7.3 that the animal is sensitive to the *relation* of a CS to its background over a trial represents a molar restructuring of the basic classical conditioning procedure. Note that each of these diagrams may be seen as the alternation of two separate conditions: the background alone and the CS superimposed on its background. All of the effects we have discussed may be explained in more molecular terms as the conditioning and extinction of each separate instance of one or the other condition. Thus the right diagram of Figure 7.3b may be seen as seven separate trials. Representing the background by "T" and the lack of a US by "EXT," we can describe these seven trials as (1) T + EXT, (2) T + CS + EXT, (3) T + EXT, (4) T + CS + US, (5) T + EXT, (6) T + CS + EXT, and

(7) T + EXT. A model of classical conditioning by Allan Wagner and Robert Rescorla (not discussed here) attempts to break down classical conditioning in this way. Current research and analysis proceeds on both levels.

CONTEXT IN INSTRUMENTAL CONDITIONING

The first difference between instrumental and classical conditioning is that while in classical conditioning the CS is superimposed on its background (you can have the CS and the background at the same time), instrumental activities crowd each other out. If you decide to pick berries, you cannot milk a cow at the same time. Usually you have to give up one instrumental activity to take up another. Thus, *the study of instrumental behavior is the study of choice.* Even a pigeon pecking a key or a rat pressing a lever is choosing between the consequences of responding (obtaining food) and the consequences of other activities. Whereas in classical conditioning we considered the CS on the one hand and the background (including the CS) on the other, in instrumental conditioning we begin with responding and its consequences versus all *other* activities and their consequences.

A second difference between instrumental and classical conditioning has to do with boundaries. In classical conditioning, the durations of the CS and its background are fixed in advance of conditioning. In instrumental conditioning, the durations of the response and its background depend on the effects of conditioning. Each situation affects responding, which in turn alters the situation, which in turn affects responding, and so forth. This is nothing but the action of the feedback loop in the basic instrumental conditioning procedure (Figure 2.11). As a consequence, the effects of conditioning are measured not by acquisition of responding in a fixed situation but by a point of stability at which responding and the situation created by responding have come into balance.

Restructuring

Just as context in classical conditioning can be explained easiest with a molar restructuring, so can instrumental conditioning (keeping in mind the importance of eventual molecular analysis). Figure 7.4 shows

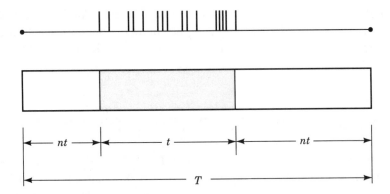

Figure 7.4 Restructuring of a burst of discrete responses into a period of responding (t) and pausing (nt).

how this restructuring works. The upper line represents pecks by a pigeon (or lever-presses by a rat, or button-presses by a person, or any cluster of discrete responses) as pips on a horizontal line. The long rectangular box indicates somewhat arbitrarily the point at which the pigeon started to peck and stopped pecking by shading (the interval t). Now we can speak of the intervals t and T just as we spoke of CS and T in classical conditioning. An advantage of this temporal restructuring is that more complex sorts of behavior like taking a walk, eating, and sleeping are much more easily analyzed as temporal periods than as discrete pips on a line. Furthermore, there is much evidence that even such responses as pigeons pecking and rats pressing levers are easily grouped into "bursts" (during which responses occur at a high rate) and "pauses" (during which they respond at a low rate or not at all).

Choice

To see how instrumental reinforcement results in a balance, let us consider a practical example — picking berries from a cluster of bushes. Berry picking is a perfect example of a virtually universal law of economics and psychology — the law of diminishing marginal returns. (Let us temporarily call this law "diminishing reinforcement rate.") When you begin, ripe berries are easy to find, but as you keep picking, they become scarcer and scarcer until finally you have to look almost forever to find that last ripe berry. Suppose t represents the time picking berries and nt represents all other activities in which one might engage on a summer's day (T). You start to pick berries at noon (t begins). At first the picking is easy, but as the afternoon wears on you get fewer and fewer berries and more and more tired; eventually other activities (for instance, a nap in a hammock) begin to look pretty good. You stop picking berries and do other things (t stops and nt begins). As with berry picking, any other particular activity is also subject to a diminishing reinforcement rate. You get bored napping after a while and begin to do something else (for convenience, we lump all non-berry-picking activities together as nt). The important question for instrumental conditioning is: What is the rule that an animal uses to stop doing one activity and begin the next?

We will consider two simple rules: melioration and local maximization. Either rule explains much of the behavior observed in the laboratory and some behaviors observed in real life, but neither in its simple form accounts for highly complex human and nonhuman behavior. The next chapter, on self-control, will indicate how these simple principles may be broadened so as to illuminate the ultimate question of human interest: How should people live their lives?

The Melioration Rule and Matching Behavior

Because of the nature of diminishing reinforcement rate, the longer you spend at an activity, the less that activity is worth. In our discussion of classical conditioning, we assumed that the value of a conditional stimulus spreads out evenly across that stimulus. Figure 7.5 illustrates a corresponding assumption in instrumental conditioning —that the value of reinforcement spreads out evenly across a situation. As the reinforcers (the dots) are separated by longer and longer intervals, the average number of reinforcers per unit time (which we here call the "melioration level") sinks further and further. It is as if the reinforcers, coming at a *decreasing* rate, served to pour water into a tank that kept getting bigger and bigger at a *constant* rate so that, instead of rising, the level of water in the tank kept falling. The melioration rule says that an activity will cease when its value sinks to

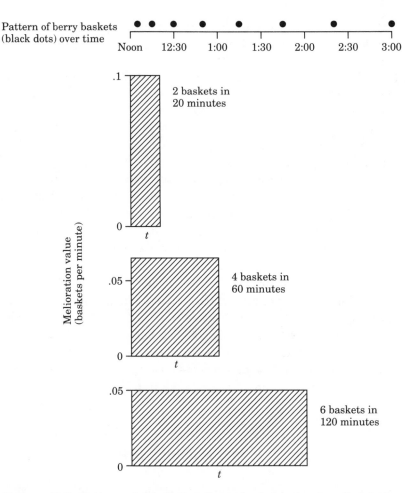

FIGURE 7.5 Pattern of reinforcers (berry baskets) showing diminishing marginal rate with time.

the level (actually, just below the level) of the background.* Figure 7.6 illustrates how melioration accounts for the adjustment between one activity and its background.

To meliorate means "to improve or make better." When the value of an activity sinks just below that of an alternative, conditions will be improved or made better by switching to the alternative.

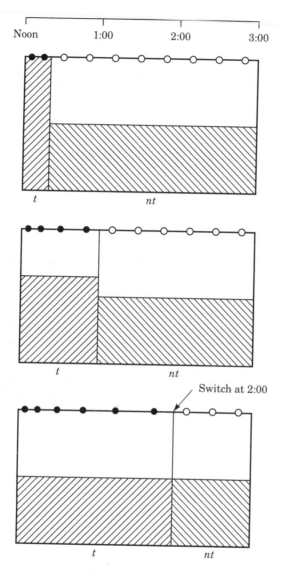

FIGURE 7.6   When the melioration level of one activity (berry picking, indicated by filled circles) falls to the level of other activities (such as napping, indicated by open circles), the melioration rule dictates switching from the first activity to another. For simplicity, the melioration level of other activities is assumed to be constant.

Although the reinforcement rate of almost any individual activity diminishes with time, let us assume that by switching at will among all other available activities, the background rate of reinforcement (the background melioration level) is kept constant regardless of the duration of the nt period. This constant level is indicated by the even spacing of the open circles in nt. In the example of picking berries on a summer afternoon, the value of taking a nap, taking a walk, going swimming, and so forth together provide, we assume, a constant flow of satisfaction (a constant melioration level symbolized by the even-spaced open circles), while picking berries provides a diminishing flow of satisfaction (a diminishing melioration level symbolized by the closed circles). The melioration rule says that the subject switches from a given activity (t) to a background activity when the rate of reinforcement during t reaches the level of the background. When the situation reaches that of the bottom diagram of Figure 7.6, a balance is achieved between t and nt, the adjustment process of instrumental conditioning is complete, and we observe what fraction of T is spent at t.

The height of the t and nt boxes of Figure 7.6 represents the local rate of reinforcement during t and nt. The melioration rule says, therefore, that an animal adjusts its behavior until the local rate of reinforcement during t equals the local rate of reinforcement during nt. Let rf equal the number of reinforcers during t (the number of solid dots in Figure 7.6 or the boxes of berries in our example) and let ro equal the number of reinforcers for doing something other than t (each, in our example, equivalent to a box of berries). Then, in symbols:

$$\frac{rf}{t} = \frac{ro}{nt} \tag{1}$$

A mathematically equivalent expression (using the fact that $t + nt = T$) is:

$$\frac{t}{T} = \frac{rf}{rf + ro} \tag{2}$$

Equation 2 is what is meant by "matching behavior." It says that the fraction of time an animal spends at a given activity (t/T) equals the fraction of total reinforcement $(rf/(rf + ro))$ received from that activity.

Matching behavior has been observed in hundreds of experiments with thousands of individual animals of many species, including human beings.* It occurs not only in the case described here, where the context of an activity is considered to be the sum of all other activities, but also with choice between two activities, where each is considered to be the context of the other. For two activities t_1 and t_2, we have:

$$\frac{t_1}{t_2} = \frac{rf_1}{rf_2} \tag{3}$$

and (mathematically equivalent):

$$\frac{t_1}{t_1 + t_2} = \frac{rf_1}{rf_1 + rf_2} \tag{4}$$

In an early experimental observation of matching, Richard Herrnstein studied pigeons pecking at two keys in a Skinner box. Pecks at each key were reinforced by a variable-interval (VI) schedule, a schedule that embodies the diminishing reinforcement rule characteristic of many sources of reinforcement in real life. Like a berry bush, the longer you stay away from a variable-interval schedule, the sooner you are likely to be rewarded when you return; also like a berry bush, the longer you stay with a variable-interval schedule, the longer you are likely to have to wait for the next reward (up to a point). Herrnstein varied the average interreinforcement intervals on each key. (In our analogy, Herrnstein's procedure is like a choice between two berry bushes, one with lots of berries initially and one with few berries initially.) He observed the distribution of the pecking between keys. Figure 7.7 shows his results. The solid line is the locus of points

---

*With some modification. A more general form is:

$$\frac{t}{nt} = \left(\frac{rf}{ro}\right)^b$$

where the exponent b may vary from situation to situation. Behavior when $b < 1$ is called *undermatching;* behavior when $b > 1$ is called *overmatching.*

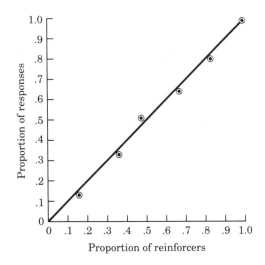

FIGURE 7.7 The relative frequency of responding to one alternative in a two-choice procedure as a function of the relative frequency of reinforcement for that choice. Variable-interval schedules governed reinforcers for both alternatives. The diagonal line shows matching between the relative frequencies. [From Herrnstein, R. J. On the law of effect. *J. Exp. Anal. Beh.*, 1970, **13**, 243–266. Copyright 1970 by the Society for the Experimental Analysis of Behavior, Inc.]

obeying equation 4. Note how closely the data (the points) conform to matching.

Figure 7.8 shows a different sort of choice, one where the law of diminishing reinforcement applies neither during t_1 nor during t_2. This would be exemplified not by two berry bushes but by two wells supplying water or two slot machines. If one well were more productive than the other or one slot machine paid off at a higher rate, a person would (subject to the still higher law of varying behavior occasionally no matter what) just use the better well or just play the better-paying slot machine. Similarly, when a pigeon chooses between pecking a key that pays off with a food reward on 25% of its pecks (variable-ratio 4, or VR-4) and one that pays off on 5% of its pecks (VR-20), the pigeon pecks (almost) exclusively on the former key. As Figure 7.8 shows, the pigeon's exclusivity is predicted by the melioration rule. Since rate of reinforcement does not diminish as the pigeon spends more time pecking on the better-paying key, the local rate of reinforcement (the melioration level) remains constant. Stability (and matching) occurs

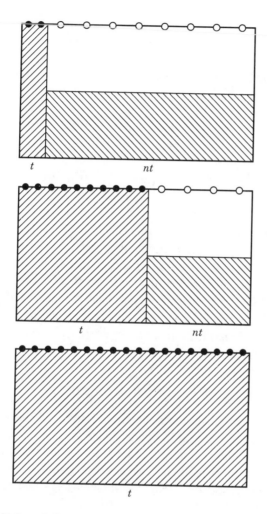

FIGURE 7.8 If the reinforcement rate of one activity were constantly higher than that of a second activity, its melioration level would remain constantly higher. Therefore the melioration rule would never dictate a switch to the second activity.

only after pecking on one key (drawing water from only one well, playing only one slot machine) takes over completely.

Why then don't people, pigeons, and all other animals settle down to a single high-frequency activity (such as eating or sleeping) and just do that activity for the rest of their lives? The answer is that while some activities are not subject to the law of diminishing reinforcement *rate*, all activities are subject to the law of diminishing reinforcement *value*. Variable-interval schedules (and berry bushes) exemplify within a single commodity (berries) a law that applies universally between one commodity and another. Although water may come out of a well at a constant rate, the value of water for an individual person or pigeon (relative to anything else) does indeed diminish as more and more of it is obtained. When you have no water, water is exceedingly valuable (worth more than its weight in gold), but as you get more and more water (or any other single commodity), its value diminishes until at last it may actually become negative (as the Sorcerer's Apprentice discovered).

Thus the instability illustrated by Figure 7.8, where one activity takes over completely, applies only to choices between two nondiminishing sources of the same commodity (well A versus well B or slot machine A versus slot machine B) and not generally to choice between one commodity and another (between drawing water from a well and eating breakfast or between playing a slot machine and going to the movies). When applied to such choices, the melioration rule works with the law of diminishing *value* rather than the law of diminishing *reinforcement rate*.

Maximization and Further Restructuring

At this point we must break the simplifying rule that we have been following and look at conditions *within* a situation. Figure 7.5 calculates reinforcement value by taking the unevenly spread reinforcers and averaging them as if they were spread evenly across a situation. Thus in Figure 7.6 value during *t* is shown as a horizontal line sinking lower and lower from the top to the bottom diagram. But this sort of restructuring is not the best way of extracting reinforcement efficiently from the environment; it has two problems that we will now discuss in detail.

The first problem can be seen in the bottom diagram of Figure 7.6. Note that at the point of switching from *t* to *nt* the spaces between the solid dots are wider than those between the open dots. This means that the *current* value of activity *t* is already less than the current value of its background. To get the most reinforcement (in our example, the most pleasure out of a sunny day in the country), the switch from *t* (picking berries) to *nt* (taking a nap) should occur when these current values are equal and not at the point where the *average* value of *t* sinks to the *average* value of some other activity. After all, what is past is past. Those initially rapidly coming reinforcers are gone. What should count when considering switching from one activity to the next is how fast reinforcers *will* be coming if you switch or do not switch (the consequences of your choice), not how fast they used to come.

To take another example, holding on to the stock of a company that makes buggy whips because it used to make a big profit (and its average return over the last 100 years is still higher than that of a computer company) is not the way to make a lot of money in the stock market. In general, what ought to count for a person deciding to sell or not to sell a stock are conditions at the point the decision is actually being made. In economics this point is called the *margin* (the edge). To get the best out of a summer's day, therefore, you should switch from berry picking to taking a nap at the point where the satisfaction you are currently getting from berry picking falls to the level of satisfaction you *will* get from taking a nap. You should balance not the average value but the marginal value. In Figure 7.6, the best point to switch between *t* and *nt* is the point where the space between (the interval between) the filled-in dots equals the space between the empty dots.

Figure 7.9 shows the restructuring that together with the melioration rule balances marginal rates of reinforcement rather than average rates of reinforcement. In Figure 7.9, instead of spreading reinforcement rate across the entire period of a signal (as in classical conditioning) or an entire burst of responding (as in instrumental conditioning), reinforcement is assumed to be spread only within a narrow "window" that travels with time and therefore always remains centered at the margin. This window is shown in Figure 7.9 by dashed lines. The melioration rule is now applied within the window. At the point where the within-window values during *t* and *nt* are equal, the animal (according to the melioration rule) should switch from *t* to *nt* (in our example, from picking berries to taking a nap).

Note how much faster value sinks with the marginal restructuring of Figure 7.9 than with the average restructuring of Figure 7.6, and consequently how much sooner the animal switches between *t* and *nt*. The difference—the extra time spent during *t* with average restructuring—is a time of low reinforcement rate; elimination of low-reinforcement-rate periods serves to maximize the reinforcement attainable under the circumstances we have postulated; this method of adjustment is therefore called *maximization*.

How do animals actually structure choice situations—as in Figure 7.6 or in Figure 7.9? Because the processes illustrated in Figures

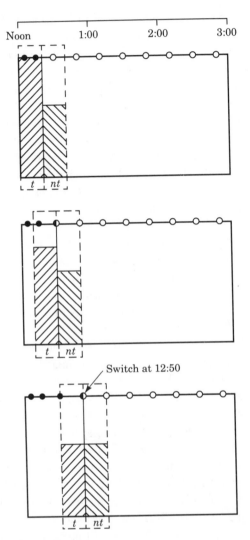

Figure 7.9 Switching when marginal reinforcement rates are equal occurs much sooner than switching when average reinforcement rates are equal.

7.6 and 7.9 are both fundamentally meliorative, both imply that matching behavior (equation 4) will be observed. The question to ask is therefore not whether matching occurs (it would occur in either case) but how animals structure their environments, that is, how they define t and nt in specific situations. The evidence shows that *both* structures are oversimplifications of the real life of humans and of other animals.

We now turn to a more complex kind of restructuring—one that takes *patterning* of reinforcement into account. We have assumed so far that the point where an animal switches from t to nt depends only on the immediate conditions in t and nt. In fact, switching from t to nt may be governed not only by t and nt but also by events far in the future. The narrow structure illustrated in Fugure 7.9 has the benefit of getting rid of the past, which may be irrelevant to current decisions, but it also has the disadvantage of getting rid of the future, which may be vitally relevant. In going from the structure of Figure 7.6 to that of Figure 7.9, we have in a sense thrown the baby out with the bathwater.

To see how the future may affect current behavior, consider an experiment with pigeons exposed to what is called a "progressive ratio schedule of reinforcement" (PR) concurrently with a normal fixed ratio (FR) schedule. The pigeon is put into a Skinner box with two keys, one the PR key and the other the FR key. Initially 10 pecks on the PR key are required for reinforcement, while 50 pecks on the FR key are required. Of course all pigeons strongly prefer the PR key. However, after each PR reinforcement, the ratio increases by 10 pecks, while the FR ratio remains at 50. So, with each reinforcement, the ratio changes, from $10:50$ to $20:50$ to $30:50$ to $40:50$ to $50:50$ to $60:50$ and so forth.

At some point all pigeons switch over and begin to peck the FR-50 key. At this point the critical feature of the experiment is imposed. *After the pigeon switches over to the FR-50 key and receives a food reward for 50 pecks, the requirement for reward on the PR key is reset to 10 pecks.* A pigeon obeying the melioration rule with the marginal structure illustrated in Figure 7.9 would ignore the resetting of the PR schedule—it has nothing to do with the conditions at the margin— and simply switch from the PR key to the FR key when marginal conditions were equal (at $50:50$).*

---

*A pigeon obeying the melioration rule with the averaging structure illustrated in Figure 7.6 would also ignore the resetting of the PR schedule but would wait still longer than with the marginal structure of Figure 7.9. To see why, assume that the local reinforcement rate is inversely proportional to the ratio requirement (as is approximately the case). Then as the PR ratio increases, the average local reinforcement rate for the PR key sinks from $1/10$ to $2/(10 + 20)$ to $3/(10 + 20 + 30)$ to $4/(10 + 20 + 30 + 40)$ and so forth until it finally reaches $9/(10 + 20 + 30 + 40 + 50 + 60 + 70 + 80 + 90)$. At this point the average local reinforcement rate for the PR key equals the average local reinforcement rate for the FR key ($1/50$), and the pigeon would finally switch. This would be a very bad rule in terms of getting the most possible reward in the shortest possible time, and indeed pigeons do not follow it.

With concurrent PR and FR schedules, pigeons in fact switch from the PR to the FR key before the conditions even reach 50:50. To see why this is a good strategy, let us create an analogous set of contingencies in everyday life. Say there are two grocers selling some commodity (apples) and only one buyer (you). Grocer Frank Reynolds (FR) keeps the price per apple constant at 50¢. Grocer Paul Richards (PR), in order to attract your business, sells you the first apple at 10¢, the second at 20¢, the third at 30¢, and so forth.

Disregarding any loyalties you might feel to FR, you would obviously begin buying apples from PR. When should you switch to FR in order to pay the least for apples in general? On one hand, you might wait until grocer PR's price reaches 50¢ per apple. But your decision would depend on what grocer PR did once you switched. If PR lowered his price to 10¢ after you switched to FR, it would pay you to switch much sooner. Although a switch to grocer FR raises the price of your very next apple, it also serves the function of lowering the price of apples in the future, when you go back to grocer PR.

Consider the following sequence of prices for six apples for a person obeying the strict marginal melioration rule of Figure 7.9 (grocer indicated in parentheses): 10¢ (PR), 20¢ (PR), 30¢ (PR), 40¢ (PR), 50¢ (PR) and 50¢ (FR) for a total of $2.00 for six apples. Now consider the sequence of prices for a person switching sooner: 10¢ (PR), 20¢ (PR), 50¢ (FR), 10¢ (PR), 20¢ (PR), and 50¢ (FR) for a total of $1.60 for the six apples.*

The fact that pigeons switch sooner than the narrow marginal considerations of Figure 7.9 dictate does not mean that pigeons are capable of conscious calculation of the benefits of various strategies. It does mean, however, that the current behavior of even so (metaphorically) lowly a creature as the pigeon can be affected by events in the future. The next chapter takes up the question of how the marginal melioration rule (maximizing) takes future events into account.

---

*The price of a sequence of six purchases could be lowered still further by staying with PR at the end, paying 30¢ (PR) rather than 50¢ (FR) for the sixth apple. But again this ignores the future. The cheap seventh and eighth apples, costing 10¢ (PR) and 20¢ (PR) consequent on switching, would more than make up for the loss on the sixth. We will discuss this issue further in the next chapter.

Suggested Readings

A volume entitled *Autoshaping and Conditioning Theory*, edited by C. M. Locurto, H. S. Terrace, and J. G. Gibbon (New York: Academic Press, 1981) contains several articles relevant to this chapter. The article by Gibbon and P. D. Balsam entitled "The spread of association in time" (pp. 219–253) is particularly relevant to the material on classical conditioning presented here. Wagner and Rescorla's molecular account of context in classical conditioning is presented in detail in R. Rescorla and A. R. Wagner, "A theory of Pavlovian conditioning: variations in the effectiveness of reinforcement and nonreinforcement," in *Classical Conditioning II*, edited by A. H. Black and W. F. Prokasy (New York: Appleton-Century-Crofts, 1972), pp. 64–69. The Wagner–Rescorla theory is described for undergraduates by the present author in H. Rachlin, *Behavior and Learning* (San Francisco: W. H. Freeman, 1976), which also presents an account of context in instrumental conditioning.

Another point of view of melioration, maximizing, and matching is taken in the present author's *Judgment, Decision, and Choice* (cited in the Suggested Readings at the end of Chapter 6). More advanced summaries appear in an article by Ben Williams entitled "Reinforcement, choice and response strength" (pp. 167–244) in *Stevens' Handbook of Experimental Psychology* (cited in the Suggested Readings at the end of Chapter 5) and the book by Michael C. Davison and Diane McCarthy, *The Matching Law: A Research Review* (Hillsdale, N.J.: Elrbaum, 1987).

8

Self-Control

Self-control is actually a misnomer for self-induced change, for although some patterns of behavior may come from within ourselves in the sense that they were acquired before birth or soon thereafter, whatever causes a behavior to appear at a given time must come from interaction with the environment. Thus *self*-control really refers to the control of behavior by certain aspects of the environment.

The kinds of behavior that we shall place under the rubric of self-control are most easily defined by listing some examples. A person can exert self-control by biting his tongue, clapping her hand over her mouth to keep from laughing, putting a box of candy out of sight to keep from eating, or putting an alarm clock out of easy reach. All these are overt performances of one sort of behavior in order to change the probability of later engaging in another sort of behavior. Less overt strategies of self-control are observed when an overweight person refrains from dessert or when someone refuses a cocktail at a party because he is driving home later. A close look at the contingencies in each of these examples reveals a common issue: *immediacy* versus *delay* of reinforcement or punishment.

Take the temporal issue away and the issue of self-control goes away as well. If it were suddenly discovered that cottage cheese was just as fattening (and therefore had the same ultimate consequences for me) as a roast beef sandwich, and if I still ate the cottage cheese, I would have to admit that I simply liked the cottage cheese better. The decision would become, like one between blue and brown suits, simply one of taste.

Psychologists have long noticed the now-versus-later character of self-control. Self-control comes into play not only when people prefer larger rewards in the future to smaller rewards in the present but also when they avoid greater pain in the future in return for lesser pain in the present. In the latter context, visiting the dentist shows self-control and not visiting him shows a lack of self-control. The reason for indecision between two alternatives — one clearly better than the other — is that the better alternative is only better in the long run. The worse alternative offers immediate benefit. The difference between someone who is controlling himself and someone who is not is thus not in where the control is located (inside his skin or outside his skin); the difference is in whether or not his present behavior is taking future contingencies into account.

If we want to know how self-control is learned, the question to ask is, How do we shift the temporal locus of control from immediate to distant consequences?

Figure 8.1 diagrams a choice between the immediate pain of visiting the dentist and the more distant but greater pain of not visiting him. As in the diagrams of Chapter 7, alternatives are indicated by solid and open circles. In Figure 8.1 the fact that both alternatives are aversive is indicated by circles below the zero line. In the last chapter we considered only the rate of such events. Here we consider intensity. A large reward would be indicated by a circle high above the zero line; a large punisher would be indicated by a circle far below the zero line. As rewards and punishers diminish in intensity, they come closer and closer to the zero line.

Figure 8.1 expresses a typical human self-control problem in diagrammatic form but the analysis remains qualitative. To achieve our goals of prediction and control it is necessary to provide a quantitative framework for self-control and to relate that framework to the one established in the previous chapter for choice in general.

Human behavior is more complicated than rat behavior. But this is not because human behavior is controlled from the inside and rat behavior from the outside, but because the environmental events controlling human behavior generally occur over a much longer interval

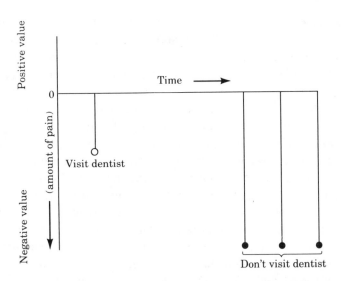

FIGURE 8.1 Mild pain (open circle) expected soon upon visiting dentist versus more severe and frequent pain (filled circles) expected later if the dentist is not visited.

than those that control the behavior of the rat. According to this view, when we refuse the third martini at a party (if we do refuse it), it is not because an internal force directs our behavior, but because we are responding to a set of contingencies spread out widely in time after we are offered the drink. The wider contingencies include potential events on the way home and the next morning; the narrower contingencies include only events at the party itself. Why should humans act in accordance with the wider contingencies rather than with the narrower ones? The answer depends on the degree to which people *discount* future consequences.

DISCOUNTING

The last chapter illustrated the problems people have when they ignore future consequences of a choice. Obviously people do not always ignore future consequences. Students study exactly because they do not ignore the future. Even a rat has to press a bar before it obtains a food reward. Future rewards therefore are not ignored, but they usually are *discounted*. A discount is a way of directly comparing future and present rewards. A "discount function" brings future events (events outside of the narrow time frame illustrated in Figure 7.9) into the frame.

Figure 8.2 illustrates three different discount functions. In Figure 8.2 an animal is faced with a choice between an immediate reward of moderate value, symbolized by the filled circle, and a much larger reward some time in the future symbolized by the open circle on the right. The three heavy arrows in parts (a), (b), and (c) are discount functions. The height of the gray circle at the point of the discount-function arrow represents how much the delayed reward (open circle) has been diminished in value by being delayed. The topmost arrow represents no discounting; the larger reward is worth as much in the present (at the margin) as it is in the future. Thus, the larger reward would be chosen as indicated by the relative heights of the bars.

The middle arrow represents a moderate rate of discounting; as the bars indicate, the animal would be indifferent at this point between the smaller immediate reward and the larger delayed reward. The lower arrow represents a steep rate of discounting; with such a steep discount function, the immediate smaller reward is preferred.

As Figure 8.2 shows, if the shape of the discount function is known, it may be used to predict whether an immediate or a delayed reward will be chosen. Behavioral researchers have performed experiments to discover the shape of human and nonhuman discount functions. Current research indicates that the discount functions usually take the form of a hyperbola. In mathematical terms:

$$\text{Discounted value of reward} = \left[\frac{1}{1 + kd}\right] \times \text{Undiscounted value of reward} \qquad (1)$$

where d is the delay of reward and k is a constant representing the degree of discounting. In words, equation 1 says that to calculate the discounted value of a reward, multiply the undiscounted value by the fraction in brackets. For no discounting (Figure 8.2a), $k = 0$. As k grows bigger and bigger, discounting becomes steeper and steeper (Figures 8.2b and 8.2c).

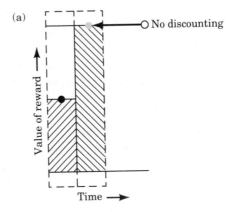

(a)

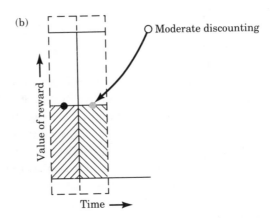

(b)

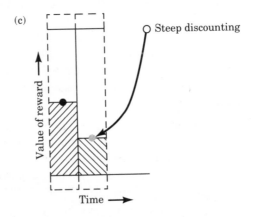

(c)

Regardless of the value of k, when reward is immediate ($d = 0$) the fraction in brackets equals 1.0 and there is no discounting. As delay (d) increases, the fraction becomes smaller and smaller and the reward is worth less and less. If delay to a reward is long to begin with and the reward is fixed in time, as time passes the delay grows less and less and the value grows greater and greater.

For instance, if you had a written promise (a "bond") from a reliable source (such as a bank) to pay the bearer $1000 on a fixed day 10 years from today, you could sell that bond today for some amount less than $1000. As time passed, the amount you could sell that bond for would grow until on the very day it became due, 10 years from today, it would be worth exactly $1000.

Figure 8.3 illustrates what happens as you move closer and closer to a large reward (open circle) fixed in time with a moderate degree of discount. The discounted reward (gray circle) is compared with a reward of fixed value (filled circle). At first, when d is large, the delayed reward is much less valued than the immediate reward. At this point (Figure 8.3a) the smaller immediate reward would be chosen. But as time passes (Figures 8.3b and 8.3c) the delayed reward value equals and then exceeds the value of the immediate reward.

To illustrate the effect of delayed reward in self-control problems, let us return to the concurrent progressive- and fixed-ratio schedules discussed in the previous chapter (p. 261). Recall that the progressive-ratio (PR) alternative increases response requirements, reinforcing the 10th response, then the 20th, then the 30th, and so forth; the fixed-ratio (FR) alternative keeps the requirement constant at 50 responses. Recall also that the PR alternative is reset to 10 responses whenever the subject chooses the FR alternative.

Let us suppose now that each response costs the subject a constant amount of *time*; it takes t seconds to make 10 responses, $2t$ seconds to make 20 responses, and so on. As before, it is clearly better, in terms of getting the most reward, to begin with the low-requirement PR schedule. The question we ask now is, When is it best to switch to the FR? Suppose the subject has initially chosen the PR alternative and has just completed the 10-response and 20-response requirements.

FIGURE 8.2 Three different degrees of discounting yielding (a) choice of large delayed reward, (b) indifference, and (c) choice of small immediate reward.

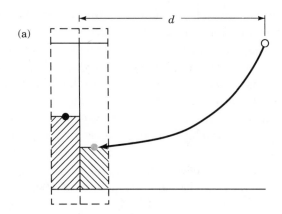

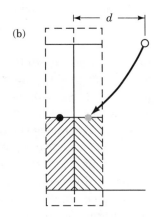

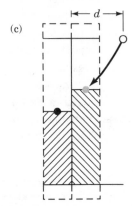

The current choice is between staying with the PR alternative — now a 30-response requirement — or switching to the FR alternative — a 50-response requirement. Considering the 30-response and the 50-response requirements alone, the correct choice is obvious. Figure 8.4a illustrates that the current value of a reward delayed by the time taken to make 30 responses is higher than that of a reward delayed by the time taken to make 50 responses. However, a switch to the FR has a consequence in addition to the 50-response requirement — it resets the PR requirement to 10 responses. A switch to the FR followed by a switch back to the PR entails a string of rewards whose total value may well exceed that of staying with the PR schedule.

Figure 8.4b illustrates the consequences of staying and switching extended over three rewards instead of just one. Staying with the PR is initially better than switching to the FR, but things get worse and worse. By switching and then switching back, the delays to the second and third rewards are considerably reduced. Whether the value gained by reducing the delay to the second and third rewards compensates for the value lost by increasing the delay to the initial reward depends on the shape of the discount functions. For very steep discount functions, future rewards are worth little and it might be better to stay. However, for the discount functions drawn in Figure 8.4, it would be better (in terms of total value of the three rewards) to switch than to stay, as demonstrated at the right of Figure 8.4b, where the present (marginal) values of the three rewards consequent on each alternative (grey circles) are added and compared.

As the previous chapter indicated, pigeons exposed to concurrent PR and FR schedules do indeed switch to the FR well before the two requirements become equal. How do the pigeons know about the contingencies? How do they come to expect what is going to happen? Given that they know what to expect, how do they exert self-control and refrain from the more immediate reward? There is one answer to all three questions — direct and repeated exposure to the contingencies. The pigeons in these experiments are exposed to the consequences of each alternative thousands and thousands of times. When

FIGURE 8.3 A small immediate reward (filled circle) versus a large delayed reward (open circle) as time passes and the delayed reward comes closer and closer.

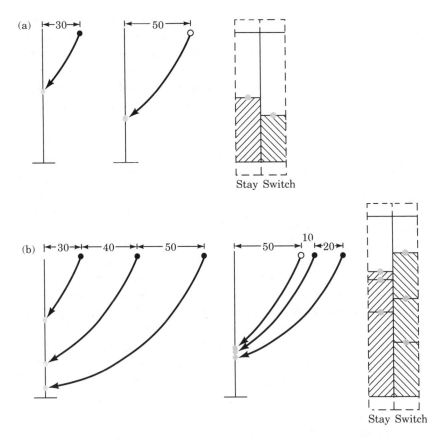

FIGURE 8.4 (a) Choice between a reward coming sooner (filled circle) and one coming later (open circle). (b) Addition of subsequent rewards to each alternative. To the right, the current values of the reward (grey circle) are added and their sums compared.

their behavior finally stabilizes, it stabilizes at the point that we identify as self-controlled. This means only that the pigeon's behavior varies (or is forced to vary) sufficiently so that over those thousands of instances many patterns are sampled; the behavioral pattern that proves best in the long run (that is most consistently reinforced) prevails despite the fact that other patterns may be better in the short run.

We humans are often faced with choices that would go one way based on the next reward and the other way based on subsequent rewards. If a student decides to go to the movies rather than study, the next reward will certainly come sooner. Yet the rewards of studying will eventually be so much more frequent (for example, the student might get a better job and thus be able to go to the movies more frequently) that, despite the initial delay of reward, students occasionally do study.

The order of magnitude of the delays in pigeon experiments is vastly different from that involved in a student's studying. Pigeons can wait for seconds, while humans (some of us) can wait for years. This difference may be described in terms of differences in human and pigeon discount functions (differences in the constant k of equation 1). But still the reader might wonder why there are such large differences. Sometimes people can be very impatient — when waiting for elevators, for instance (or in New York City when the traffic light changes to green and you wait more than a second before moving). What is it that makes discount functions so shallow at some times or for some animals and so steep at other times or for other animals?

As we said in Chapter 7, one important difference between pigeons and people lies in language. What does language do for us? It must substitute in some way for the pigeon's experience with the consequences of the various alternatives so that after instructions, the very first time we are faced with the contingencies, we behave (sometimes) with even more self-control than a pigeon does after thousands and thousands of instances. According to the behaviorist, language is a complex discriminative stimulus that classifies the present situation along with (superficially different) contingencies that we have indeed experienced thousands and thousands of times. What the experimenter says to the subject (and what the subject says to herself) provide a common frame between the experiment and certain situations the subject has in fact experienced many times in the past. If the instructions are accurate, the pattern of behavior that was reinforced in those situations will also be reinforced in this experiment. When the experimenter says, "Imagine this pretzel [the lower-valued reward] is a toy log," the child behaves as he would if the pretzel were indeed a toy log — the child does not eat the pretzel. The child's imaginative behavior is then reinforced by the higher-valued reward.

INDIVIDUAL DIFFERENCES IN
HUMAN SELF-CONTROL

The above example comes from a series of experiments by Walter Mischel and his colleagues discussed earlier (pp. 231–234). In those experiments children chose between a less-valued reward available immediately and a more-valued reward available later. The experiment took the form of a game between the experimenter and the child. The experimenter left the room; the child had to wait. If the child waited until the experimenter came back on her own, the child would get the more-valued reward. However, the child could summon the experimenter back at any time by ringing a bell. Then the experimenter would come right back, but the child would get the smaller reward. The critical question was, How long would the child wait before ringing the bell?

We have previously discussed the strong effect of language (what the experimenter says to the subject) on how long children wait in these situations. Now let us consider individual differences among children in how long they wait when they have the rewards in front of them. Children wait longer who are older, richer, smarter, more socially responsible, more ambitious — just what you might expect. Furthermore, children who wait longer (in this 15-minute experiment) tend to get higher SAT scores and to be judged by their parents to be more competent when they grow up.

What is going on here? Why does the difference in the steepness between two 4-year-old children's delay discount functions as measured in a brief game with the experimenter reflect itself years later in parents' judgments and in academic competence?

All of the children whose childhood and adolescent behavior was related had the rewards in front of them while waiting and were not told by the experimenter how to think about them. *Thus the children who waited for long periods had to behave in the presence of the rewards as though they weren't there.* Some of the children closed their eyes, some actually went to sleep, some sang or talked to themselves. An animal that behaves in the presence of one stimulus as it normally does in the presence of a different stimulus is performing a complex act of imagination. Thus the ability demonstrated by the 4-year-old children (who waited) was the *ability to imagine*.

It is this ability of imagining that must have been reflected in later tests of academic performance and parental approval. It is tempting to speculate beyond the data and conclude that those educational theories that emphasize the development of a child's imagination in early years are more valid than those that emphasize practical skills. However, such a distinction would have to be drawn very carefully; from a behavioral viewpoint imagination *is*, after all, a practical skill.

COMMITMENT

On the morning of the day before a big exam a student deposits a fairly large sum of money with a friend. He instructs the friend to check every half-hour during the evening to see that he is studying. If the friend does not find him studying, the friend is instructed to send the money to a political party whose views are exactly contrary to those of the student. In other words, the student has committed himself to study that evening.

The effectiveness of commitment as a method of self-control depends on discount functions that cross as time goes by. Figure 8.5a diagrams crossing discount functions of two rewards each fixed at some time in the future. The open dot symbolizes a larger but more delayed reward, while the solid dot symbolizes a smaller, more immediate reward. As long as both rewards are in the distant future, the present value of the larger reward is higher than that of the smaller one. However, because of the crossing discount functions, as time passes, the smaller reward eventually becomes available immediately and comes to be worth more (Figure 8.5b). The immediate availability of the smaller reward constitutes a temptation. If the larger and smaller rewards are mutually exclusive (if choice of one precludes choice of the other) and if the smaller reward is available at the point when its value rises above that of the larger reward, the smaller reward will eventually be obtained and the larger one forfeited.

If, however, something is done either to prevent the subsequent availability of the smaller reward or to substantially reduce its value while the larger reward is still preferred, the larger reward will eventually be obtained. This something that is done is called a *commitment*

(a)

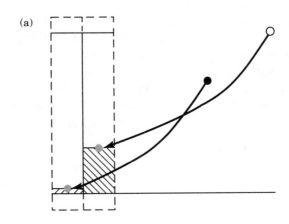

(b)

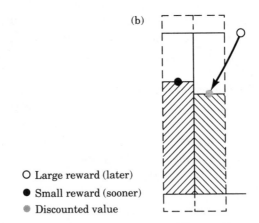

○ Large reward (later)
● Small reward (sooner)
● Discounted value

FIGURE 8.5 Why crossing discount functions imply preference reversal as time passes.

response. In the example of the student who deposits money with his friend to get himself to study, Figure 8.5a diagrams the earlier conditions (in the morning) and Figure 8.5b, the later conditions (that evening). Early in the day, when contemplating studying or going to the movies that night, the distant rewards contingent on studying (symbolized by the open dot) are valued more than those contingent on not studying (going to the movies, symbolized by the solid dot). But that evening (Figure 8.5b) these values will reverse. However, if the student had previously committed himself by depositing money with a friend (not illustrated in Figure 8.5), the net value of the movies would have been reduced sufficiently so that when evening came it would have been effectively removed as an option.

Figure 8.6 is a diagram of the commitment decision process. There are two decisions in question. Decision X, between studying and not studying, takes place in the evening when the student is supposed to study. At the time decision X is made, the short-term consequences of not studying are very likely to determine the student's choice. Thus, not studying is the probable result. Decision Y takes place the morning before. Decision Y is between making the commitment and not making it. Assuming the commitment is effective (that the student absolutely will not tolerate the sending of his money to an opposing political party), making the commitment is equivalent to choosing the lower branch of Figure 8.6, to studying, and to experiencing the consequences of studying. At the time decision Y is made, the value of

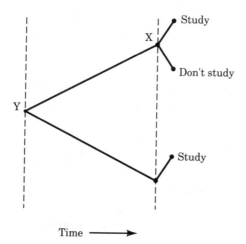

Time ⟶

FIGURE 8.6 Flow diagram of commitment to study. Choice at X is between studying immediately and not studying. It is assumed that a student would not study at X. Choice at Y is between having a choice later (top arm) and being forced to study later (bottom arm). Students who would not study at X might nevertheless commit themselves to study by choosing the lower arm at Y.

studying is likely to be higher than that of not studying and the student will probably agree to the commitment.

Once decision Y is available, and if we assume that the contingencies are effective, commitment behavior should follow *automatically*. To make the point that this exercise of commitment is not dependent on ego strength, internalization, resistance to frustration, or other sophisticated cognitive or motivational phenomena, Leonard Green and the author showed that relatively naive animals, pigeons, would exhibit commitment.

The experiment Green and I did closely follows the schema of Figure 8.6. The pigeons were placed in a Skinner box with two translucent plastic disks side by side on one wall. Below the disks and equidistant from each was a hopper where food could be presented. Choice X for the pigeons was indicated by illuminating one of the two disks with red light and the other with green (as illustrated in Figure 8.7). If the pigeon pecked the red disk, the hopper opened immediately and gave the pigeon access to food for 2 seconds. If the pigeon pecked the green disk, the lights in the chamber went out for 4 more seconds and then the hopper opened for 4 seconds. Thus, a peck at the green disk produced a reward twice as large but delayed by 4 seconds. Choice Y for the pigeons was indicated by illuminating both disks with white light. If the pigeon pecked the left-hand disk 15 times, the lights turned off for a 10-second blackout followed by choice X (illumination of the disks with red and green light). If the pigeon pecked the right-hand disk 15 times, the lights turned off for a 10-second blackout followed by illumination of one of the keys only with green light. A peck at the green key then produced the delayed large reward. The other key was dark and there was no way (once the right-hand disk had been pecked 15 times) to obtain the small immediate reward. Thus, pecking the right-hand disk (when it was white) *committed* the pigeon to accepting the larger, delayed reward. Pecking the left-hand disk (when it was white) allowed a choice later between the large delayed reward and the small immediate reward.*

In order to draw a parallel between the behavior of pigeons in this experiment and the kind of commitment exhibited by the student, we

---

*After the 4-second delayed reward, the disks turned white again and a new trial began. However, after the 2-second immediate reward, a further blackout of 6 seconds preceded the next trial. This equalized total trial duration for the two alternatives of choice X.

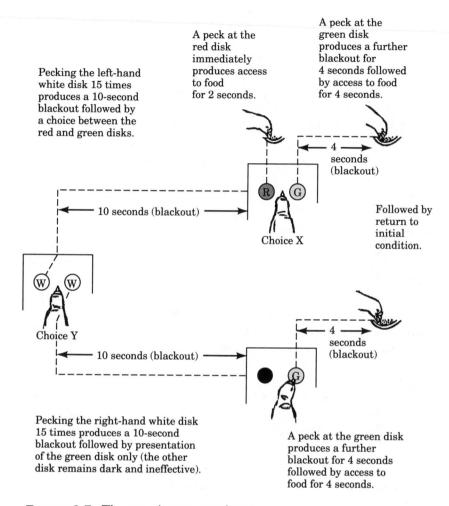

Pecking the left-hand white disk 15 times produces a 10-second blackout followed by a choice between the red and green disks.

A peck at the red disk immediately produces access to food for 2 seconds.

A peck at the green disk produces a further blackout for 4 seconds followed by access to food for 4 seconds.

4 seconds (blackout)

10 seconds (blackout)

Choice X

Followed by return to initial condition.

Choice Y

10 seconds (blackout)

4 seconds (blackout)

Pecking the right-hand white disk 15 times produces a 10-second blackout followed by presentation of the green disk only (the other disk remains dark and ineffective).

A peck at the green disk produces a further blackout for 4 seconds followed by access to food for 4 seconds.

FIGURE 8.7 The commitment experiment.

have to show (1) that the pigeons were indeed tempted by the immediate small reward—that when offered the green and red disks together (choice X), they would peck the red disk and obtain an immediate reward; and (2) that the pigeons would commit themselves at choice Y to obtaining the larger delayed reward by pecking the right-hand disk more than the left-hand disk.

The results on the first point were unequivocal. After two weeks of daily sessions of about an hour each in the apparatus, when the red and green disks were presented together to any of the five pigeons in this experiment, the red disk was pecked more than 95 percent of the time. This was not due to a preference for one side of the chamber to the other, because the red and green lights were randomly switched from side to side. It was not a color preference, because the pigeons switched within a session to pecking the green disk when the consequences of pecking the two colors were reversed. Thus preference for the red disk can be ascribed only to a preference for the small immediate reward over the large delayed reward.

The results on the second point were less striking. When both disks were white (choice Y), three of the five pigeons pecked the right-hand disk (thus committing themselves to the large reward) more than they pecked the left-hand disk. But because two of the birds pecked the left-hand disk more, it was possible that the preference we measured was simply the result of chance, that the pigeons were randomly pecking on the two white disks and ignoring the contingencies of the experiment. To test this, we varied the time of the blackout after the 15 pecks of choice Y. Blackout time was 10 seconds in the original experiment. We now varied it between 1 and 16 seconds. If the pigeon's distribution of pecks on the two white keys was random in the first experiment, it might be expected to remain so as the blackout was varied. On the other hand, if the pigeons were exhibiting commitment, they might change their behavior systematically as the time between the commitment response (choice Y) and the temptation (choice X) was varied. Reasoning by analogy to human behavior, the closer the temptation, the more difficult it should be to make the commitment.

In fact, this effect of time on commitment is exactly what we found. When we reduced the blackout interval to 1 second, four of the five pigeons pecked more on the left-hand disk (no commitment). When we increased the interval to 16 seconds, four of the five pigeons pecked more on the right-hand disk (commitment). All of the pigeons shifted their preference in the expected direction as the duration of the blackout was varied. Figure 8.8 shows the average percentage of commitment responses at various values of blackout duration. We took this as evidence that animals other than humans could exhibit self-control, or at least the kind of self-control required for commitment.

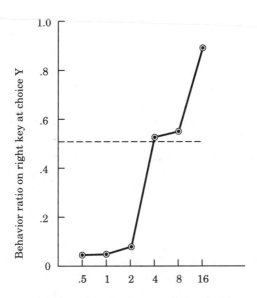

Blackout duration (in seconds, log scale)

FIGURE 8.8 Average behavior ratio on the right-hand white disk for the experiment illustrated in Figure 8.7. The abscissa represents variation of the blackout time between 0.5 and 16 seconds (instead of the 10 seconds indicated in Figure 8.7).

Since other current theories of self-control require a degree of sophistication on the part of the subject that a pigeon is not supposed to possess, they cannot account for the pigeons' behavior in our experiments.

This behavior can be accounted for, however, by viewing commitment in terms of contingencies. Suppose, instead of assuming conflicting forces within the pigeon, we assume that the pigeon actually prefers what it chooses — the immediate small reward in choice X and the large delayed reward in choice Y. As it happens, virtually all quantitative models of choice behavior predict this reversal of preference. The critical factor is the shape of the discount function. One form of discount function (the exponential form exemplified by the compound interest paid by banks for savings accounts) does not cross. All others, including the hyperbolic form of equation 1, do cross.

In everyday life we sometimes impose rigid commitment devices on ourselves. People may be willing to pay to go to a "fat farm" where they will be deprived of food. Many academics (including the author) choose to have their fixed salary (starting in September) spread over 12 months instead of 9. With the 9-month option, it would be possible to privately pay ourselves each month ¹⁄₁₂th of our total yearly salary and deposit the difference in an interest-earning savings account, thereby obtaining extra money (the interest) during June, July, and August. However, the temptation that might arise to spend our basic summer salary between September and May is evidently great enough so that the complete avoidance of this temptation balances (for most of us) the interest given up.

The resolutions we make to each other and to ourselves are also forms of commitment. Breaking a resolution or a promise made to others brings on a certain degree of social condemnation and subsequent mistrust. Breaking a resolution, even one made to yourself, carries the price of cheapening future resolutions. Resolutions do not entirely avoid temptation; rather like the example of the student donating to an opposing political party if he fails to study, commitment in the form of a resolution only decreases the net value of succumbing to temptation. The effectiveness of resolutions (and promises) for an individual person depends not on the intensity or immediate emotional feeling with which they are made but on the degree to which they have remained unbroken in the past. Thus, much like a person who borrows money solely in order to establish credit at the bank, people ought to practice making and keeping resolutions and promises. Otherwise they may have to resort to still stronger commitment devices — ones from which they cannot escape should conditions change. Such extreme commitment is common in everyday life, so common that its overemployment has been suspected as at least one factor underlying behavioral and physical dysfunction. Being alcoholic or overweight, for instance, may serve (in part) as a commitment to avoid sexual temptation.

Like other behavioral patterns, commitment need not be expressed in words to be effective. In fact, when its net effect is negative, commitment may be more powerful precisely because it is not verbal. Behavior therapy often begins with an attempt to put into words possibly harmful behavioral contingencies (such as overcommitment) so as to bring them under better stimulus control.

SELF-CONTROL AND SOCIAL CONSCIENCE

In Chapter 6 we briefly discussed cognitive conceptions of consciousness and self-consciousness. Let us now consider the following behavioral conception: A person's "self" may be seen as a set of values persisting over time. Much of this book has been devoted to an attempt to define *value* in behavioral terms. As indicated previously, modern behaviorism substitutes the conception of value for the conception of reinforcement in older behaviorism. The predictive power of behaviorism (its status as a science) depends on the identification of values as they interact with behavior–environment contingencies. The intact animal whose behavior is predicted is the behavioral "self."

It is therefore when values come into conflict, as we have been discussing in this chapter, that self-control becomes meaningful. As an example of this conflict, let us return to the progressive-ratio schedule (Figure 8.4). Figure 8.4a diagrams a certain set of values within a narrow time span. Figure 8.4b diagrams another set of values within a wider time span. Obviously these sets of values are in conflict. The narrow values dictate staying with the PR schedule; the wide values dictate switching to the FR schedule. Self-control is defined as dominance of the wide values over the narrow ones; the temporally wider self controls the temporally narrow self—for its own good, because ultimately the temporally narrow self will suffer if it gets its way. To put it slightly differently, the narrow self moves blindly from time A to time B, to time C, to time D. The wider self embraces times A through D.

The analogy between an individual narrow self as it moves through time and an individual person in a social community has been noted in philosophies from Plato to the present day. A group of people, each acting for his or her own selfish good, may individually be better off in the long run if they cooperated for the social good. To take a mundane example, each person might be better off in the short run by littering (the convenience outweighs the insignificant addition of dirt to the street), but the community is benefited in the long run when no one litters. In ants and other social insects, individual acts of self-sacrifice are innate. In humans social conscience, a more general disposition to behave for the good of the community, seems to be innate. In the human case, altruism is an extrapolation from self-control. The conflict between a person at a single time and that same person at many times is analogous to the conflict between a single person and many people. Whatever causes a person to sacrifice present pleasures for his or her own good at future times may also cause a person to sacrifice individual good for social good. The idea underlying the analogy is that cooperating with others *generally* results in greater long-term good for the individual (although it may not do so all the time).

Without such cooperation we could not trade with each other. If John has all the food and Mary has all the water, both will benefit by trading.*

THE SOCIAL DILEMMA

There is a problem regarding cooperation that appears both between individual people and between individual, narrow sets of values for a single person. Although cooperation is clearly better than noncooperation for all individuals concerned, a still greater benefit may be achieved for an individual if that individual does not cooperate when all others do. An individual person benefits on the whole if everyone cooperates but him; a family benefits if all its members work hard and suffers if none of them works; but (assuming, contrary to fact, that work is wholly negative) an individual benefits most if he just stays home and relaxes while everyone else in the family works. An individual benefits both by having (almost) perfectly clean streets and by the convenience of littering whenever she wants if she is the only one who litters. A similar phenomenon exists for the same person over time: A person controlling his weight benefits most if he eats an ice cream sundae once a month but not at other times. An alcoholic would be happier if she could have one drink a week rather than abstaining completely.

In the social sphere the dilemma is solved by a more complex reorganization of behavior wherein we take turns acting selfishly. Each member of the family gets a vacation once in a while and then

---

*Economic demand theory is essentially a psychological theory of how people benefit by trading with each other or how an individual benefits by trading with the group as a whole (as in paying taxes). In a more advanced text, *Judgment, Decision, and Choice* (see Suggested Readings in Chapter 6), the present author describes the concordance between behavioral choice theory and economic demand theory.

goes back to work. Complex social rules together with vivid discriminative stimuli typically enforce each person's permitted defection from cooperative behavior. As George Ainslie has pointed out, we also establish complex rules for defections from our own individual self-control: The dieter has his ice cream sundae only on his birthday; the alcoholic drinks only during cocktail hour. Once the author tried to control his cigarette habit by smoking only on those infrequent occasions when he had an alcoholic drink. As the reader (who remembers Premack's principle) might suspect, this technique failed miserably. While my smoking did decrease slightly, my drinking increased substantially (I was reinforcing drinking as well as punishing smoking).

One place where defections from cooperation may be most common is at the end of a situation with fixed temporal boundaries. The last few days of a job or an enlistment are notorious for defections from cooperative behavior. The same phenomenon occurs in self-control: People in our culture generally want to be thin but often, just after marriage, tend to gain weight—an important goal has been reached and our narrow self defects.

We may get the most out of an event of limited duration by saving something plasant for last. In eating a meal, children often consume all of what they like best first, then all of the next best item, and so on. As adults we plan what we eat so that our pleasure over the whole meal is greater—the meal forms a pleasing pattern appreciated over a longer period than a single bite.

One thinks also of the structure of a work of art. A serious novel or a symphony is appreciated on the highest level for its larger structure, appealing to wider values—wider selves. But many novelists and composers begin their works with more accessible material to bring the reader or listener into the work. Also, at the end, as our narrower selves begin to demand their due, the sympathetic novelist or composer will offer something pleasurable on that level, just as the sympathetic chef will offer dessert.

Suggested Readings

A review of recent research on self-control is A. W. Logue's "Research on self control: an integrating framework," *Behavioral and Brain Sciences*, 1988, **11**, 665–710. Mazur's experiments on discount functions are reported in an article entitled "An adjusting procedure for studying delayed reinforcement" in a volume edited by M. L. Commons, J. E. Mazur, J. A. Nevin, and H. Rachlin entitled *Quantitative Analysis of Behavior, Vol. V The Effect of Delay and of Intervening Events on Reinforcement Value* (Hillsdale, N.J.: Erlbaum, 1987). This volume also contains several other articles by various authors on discount functions. Two early experiments with the commitment paradigm using pigeon subjects are G. W. Ainslie, "Impulse control in pigeons," *Journal of the Experimental Analysis of Behavior*, 1974, **21**, 485–489; and H. Rachlin and L. Green, "Commitment, choice, and self-control," *Journal of the Experimental Analysis of Behavior*, 1972, **17**, 15–22. Mischel's experiments are reported in the article by Mischel, Shode, and Rodriguez cited in the Suggested Readings at the end of Chapter 6.

Glossary

ASSOCIATION. The connection of two or more sensations, ideas, images, or other mental phenomena. Laws of association are laws formulated to account for the establishment of such connections.

BEHAVIOR. Ranging from specific to general usage: (1) Any action of an animal. (2) The actions of an animal. (3) Actions of animals. This book refers only to animal behavior, but of course plants and even inanimate objects are said to behave in systematic ways.

BEHAVIORAL ANALYSIS. A branch of experimental psychology, the object of which is to discover laws describing the behavior of animals.

BEHAVIORAL THERAPIST. A psychologist who is concerned with helping people to better adapt their behavior to their environment.

BEHAVIORISM. The belief that the primary object of psychological study is the overt behavior of animals. In this book we distinguish between *operant* behaviorism, where overt behavior is not only the primary object of study but also the ultimate object of interest, and *cognitive* behaviorism, where overt behavior is used to infer the existence and operation of cognitive or physiological mechanisms.

BELONGINGNESS. A term coined by E. L. Thorndike to indicate that certain associations are more easily formed than others because in some sense the components belong together.

CHOICE. The possibility of more than one response. Essentially every situation in which behavior may vary is a choice situation. Even with one alley or one manipulandum (a lever, a disk, or the like), an animal may choose to run or not to run, to press a lever or not to press it. Choice can be measured most easily, however, when two similar alternatives are available, as in a T-maze or multilever Skinner box.

CLASSICAL CONDITIONING. as an operation, the pairing in fixed temporal relation of a neutral stimulus with a stimulus correlated with a response (a reflex). (For example, a bell — a neutral stimulus — may be paired with food powder, which is originally correlated with salivation — a reflex. An animal exposed to such repeated pairings often comes to respond to the originally neutral stimulus as it did to the other stimulus. In this example, the animal would come to salivate upon presentation of the bell.)

CONDITIONAL REINFORCEMENT. A positive correlation of a response, not with a reinforcer, but with a conditional stimulus (CS +) or a discriminative stimulus (S^D).

CONDITIONAL RESPONSE. The response elicited by the conditional stimulus alone (after the process of classical conditioning has taken place). In some cases this is only quantitatively different from the response originally elicited by the unconditional stimulus (the unconditional response). In other cases there may be qualitative differences between the conditional and unconditional responses.

CONDITIONAL STIMULUS (CS). A stimulus that does not ordinarily elicit a certain response but that comes to elicit that response by virtue of its pairings in a **classical conditioning** procedure with another stimulus, an unconditional stimulus, that does ordinarily elicit the response.

CONSCIOUSNESS. That part of one's **mind** that one knows. A conscious mental process would be a process that one knows about, like doing mental arithmetic; an unconscious mental process would be a process about which one has no knowledge. John Stuart Mill's concept of **mental chemistry**, in which sensations get combined into ideas, would be described as an unconscious mental process, since we seem to have many ideas without being aware of component sensations.

CONTINGENCY. A set of conditional probabilities relating the occurrence and nonoccurrence of events. In **classical conditioning**, the critical contingencies are between the conditional and unconditional stimuli. In **instrumental conditioning**, the critical contingencies are between responding and reinforcement. The word *contingency* has also been used in a more general sense, as in *Contingencies of Reinforcement*, a book by B. F. Skinner. Here *contingency* refers to the general relationships between **behavior** and the environment (without reference to any specific set of correlations or probabilities).

CORRELATION. In general, any relation between two variables. If the knowledge of the value of one variable helps predict the value of the other, then the variables are correlated. In a positive correlation, increases in one variable correspond to increases in the other, as in the correlation between rising atmospheric temperature and trips to the beach. In a negative correlation, increases in one variable correspond to decreases in the other, as in the correlation between rising atmospheric temperature and skiing.

CRITICAL PERIOD. A period during the early life of an animal when it can most easily acquire certain behaviors. The behaviors may be exhibited at a later time, but their nature is determined by events during the critical period. For instance, the object that a duckling learns to follow during a critical period may become a focus for sexual behavior months later. (See **imprinting**.)

CUE. Another term for a **discriminative stimulus**.

DISCRIMINATION. Reliable differences in behavior in the presence of two or more stimuli.

DISCRIMINATIVE STIMULUS. (S^D and S^Δ). An S^D ("ess dee") is a stimulus during which there is a nonzero correlation between responding and reinforcement. An S^Δ ("ess delta") is a stimulus during which there is no correlation between responding and reinforcement. Somewhat confusingly, both S^D's and S^Δ's are called "discriminative stimuli."

DISINHIBITION. Removal of an inhibitory force resulting in the action of the excitatory force formerly inhibited. (For instance, experimental extinction of classically conditioned salivation was thought by Pavlov to consist of the development of an inhibitory force opposing salivation. If, during **extinction**, a loud noise or other strong stimulus is presented, salivation suddenly increases. This is thought to be due to the disinhibitory effect of the noise.)

DUALISM. In the history of Western philosophy, the nature of man understood according to two principles, matter (the body) and spirit (the mind), which are not derivable from each other.

ELICITED RESPONSE. A certain response or set of responses that reliably follows a stimulus. The notion of elicitation rests on an observed correlation between a stimulus and a subsequent response.

EMITTED RESPONSE. A response not found to be correlated with any prior stimulus. An emitted response may be brought into correlation with a subsequent stimulus by the environment, in which case the subsequent stimulus could reinforce or punish the response.

EMPIRICISM. (See **nativism**.)

ESCAPE CONDITIONING. A form of instrumental conditioning in which responding is negatively correlated with aversive stimulation. Also called **negative reinforcement**.

EVOLUTION. Gradual development. According to Darwin's theory of evolution of the structure of species, the mechanism of evolution works by survival (and reproduction) of those organisms best fitted to the environment. An analogous mechanism seems to govern functional changes of behavior in the repertoire of individual organisms. Behavior fitted to the environment is repeated, while behavior not fitted to the environment is not repeated.

EXCITATION. Any increase in rate or amplitude of responding. Some psychologists refer to an "excitatory force," which is said to underlie the increases in responding actually measured.

EXPERIMENTAL PSYCHOLOGY. A branch of psychology in which behavioral observations are made in artificial and restricted environments, in which conditions can be controlled and behavior observed more easily than in natural settings.

EXTINCTION. In **classical conditioning**, a zero correlation between the unconditional stimulus and **conditional stimulus**. In **instrumental conditioning**, a zero correlation between **response** and reinforcer. In most cases, a zero correlation is imposed simply by eliminating the unconditional stimulus or the reinforcer. However, it may also be imposed by continued presentations of unconditional stimulus or reward temporally independent of conditional stimuli or responses.

FEEDBACK. Any system in which a process is governed by its results. Most behavior involves feedback of some kind. (The act of picking up a pencil is governed to an extent by the position of the hand relative to the pencil. Thus the position of the hand is "fed back" by the visual system to govern further movements of the hand.)

FIXED-ACTION PATTERN. A complex unconditional response.

FUNCTIONALISM. According to the Darwinian notion of evolution, the theory that the structure of species is determined by its function. Functional (that is, useful) traits remain after dysfunctional (nonuseful) traits disappear as organisms evolve over generations. The original "functional psychologists" believed that the mind evolved along with the body. Because evolution "selects according to function," the mind is best understood through its uses, or functional qualities. According to Thorndike's law of effect, functional behavior is strengthened and repeated while nonfunctional behavior dies out within the lifetime of a single animal. Present-day functionalists attempt to understand behavior through its function as the animal interacts with the environment.

GENERALIZATION. In conditioning (whether classical or instrumental), an animal learns to behave in a certain way with the presentation of or in the presence of a certain stimulus or "stimulus situation." If this learned behavior also comes to be made in the presence of stimuli other than those used in conditioning, the animal is said to be generalizing from the training stimulus to the new stimulus. The closer the behavior in the presence of the new stimulus is to the behavior in the presence of the training stimulus, the greater the generalization. The most generalization is to be found with stimuli similar to the training stimuli. Often generalization is ascribed to a failure to discriminate or pay attention to differences between stimuli.

GRADIENT. A function that relates a measure of responding to stimuli arranged along a continuum. (See also **generalization**.)

GRAMMAR. A set of rules for speech and writing.

GSR. (galvanic skin response). A change in resistance on the palms of the hands. The GSR is part of the unconditional response to electric shock and other painful stimuli. The GSR may come to be emitted after an originally neutral stimulus, such as a bell or light, by classical conditioning procedures. The GSR is sometimes said to reflect a "central anxiety state" of the animal.

HABIT. Any systematically repeated behavior.

IMAGINATION. An act of discrimination in the absence of its habitual object.

IMPRINTING. During a **critical period** in the life of an animal, certain responses may be elicited by a great variety of stimuli. Once a particular stimulus has served to elicit the response, however, it is imprinted; that is, it is better able to elicit the response than other potential stimuli. For instance, a duckling will follow any of a great variety of objects, but once it follows a given object it continues to follow that object thereafter, ignoring or avoiding others. (See **critical period**.)

INHIBITION. Any decrease in rate or amplitude of responding. Some psychologists refer to an "inhibitory force," which is said to underlie the decreases in responding actually measured. According to Pavlov, all decreases in responding result from an active inhibitory force opposing the force of **excitation**. This implies that there is a distinction between decreases in responding due to loss of excitation and decreases in responding due to the active inhibitory force.

INNATE IDEAS. "Mental contents" or "mental structures" that appear at birth or develop with maturation independently of experience.

INSTINCT. Any innate habit or any habit acquired by all normal members of a species through the process of maturation.

INSTINCTIVE DRIFT. The tendency of the form of learned behavior to change spontaneously to the form of instinctive behavior.

INSTRUMENTAL CONDITIONING. Instrumental conditioning involves establishment of a habit by a correlation between some aspect of behavior and reinforcement or punishment.

INTROSPECTION. A technique for observing mental events in which the mind is said to reflect on its own operations or contents.

ISOMORPHISM. Having the same form. The Gestalt psychologists believe that consciousness has the same form as its representation in the nervous system. Thus, if a figure is seen as distorted, the distortion must take place somewhere in the nervous system.

LANGUAGE. A pattern of behavior by which communication is ordinarily achieved.

LEARNING. Any consistent change in behavior (any habit) not brought about solely by maturation.

MEANING. The relevant context of an object. The *behavioral* context of an object is a pattern of words and acts. The *cognitive* context is an internal mechanism. The more extensive and elaborate the context, the deeper the meaning. A context is relevant to the extent that it affects understanding or production of the object.

MENTAL CHEMISTRY. John Stuart Mill's term for the association of simple sensations to form an idea. The idea's properties may differ from those of its components just as the chemical properties of a compound (e.g., water) differ from those of its components (hydrogen and oxygen). (For example, the idea of visual depth may be composed of forms, textures, and shading, yet visual depth may have conscious properties other than those of form, texture, and shading.)

MIND. The repository of consciousness, sensation, thought, feeling, and so forth. According to Descartes, man could be divided into two parts: mind and body. The mind, unlike the body, is not machinelike and does not obey physical laws, but it may obey laws of its own. Originally the task of psychology was to discover mental laws by the technique of **introspection**. More recent attempts to discover mental laws have relied on observations of behavior.

MOLARISM. A broad classification of environment or behavior; the belief that stimuli or responses broadly classified may be lawfully described without reference to smaller units. (See also **stimulus, response**.)

MOLECULARISM. A narrow classification of environment or behavior; the belief that complex processes, whether mental or behavioral, may be explained in terms of small units and rules for their combination.

NATIVISM. In the mental sphere, the belief that people's most basic or important ideas come to them without experience by virtue of their humanity. (The idea is in contrast to *empiricism*, the belief that people's most basic or important ideas come to them through experience.) In the behavioral sphere, the belief that basic behavior patterns are inborn and only modified slightly by experience or that the capacity to acquire certain behaviors is unique to certain species. (For example, while the particular language a person speaks is governed by his or her experience, a nativist would argue that humans are born with a special mechanism that enables them to learn language and, furthermore, that certain rules common to all languages are determined by the nature of this inborn mechanism. An empiricist would argue that the structure of language is determined by its function manifested only through experience.) The nativist/empiricist controversy is one of emphasis. There is general agreement that all behavior has innate and acquired components. The nativist stresses inborn patterns, while the empiricist stresses the methods by which they can be modified.

NEGATIVE PUNISHMENT. A negative correlation between responding and reward. (Also called *omission*.)

NEGATIVE REINFORCEMENT. A negative correlation between responding and aversive stimulation.

NONSENSE SYLLABLE. A three-letter trigram (e.g., BAV, RUX, JIC, CIB) used by Ebbinghaus and others to study association. The principal advantage of nonsense syllables, according to Ebbinghaus, is that they have few previous associations; thus, any associations between them formed during an experiment can be studied independently of past experience.

OMISSION CONDITIONING. (See **negative punishment.**)

OPERANT. All responses having a single common effect. Each instance of any response differs in some way, however small, from any other instance. Under what conditions can we say a response is repeated? One way to classify responses is by their common effect on the environment. All responses having a single common effect belong to the same operant class. For instance, all behavior that results in a bar-press could be considered a single operant. The definition of an operant is up to the observer of behavior (often the experimenter). The observer may base the delivery or removal of a reinforcer or punisher upon the occurrence of the operant.

PARAMETER. A constant in an equation. A parametric experiment is one that tests a relationship with various parametric values. For instance, "days of deprivation" would affect the function relating "number of responses in extinction" to "number of prior reinforcers." An experiment that related responses in extinction to number of prior reinforcers at various deprivation levels would be a parametric experiment.

PERCEPTION. An act of discrimination of abstract (and functional) properties of the environment in the context of habitual discriminations of the same object.

PHENOMENOLOGY. A type of introspection that attempts to view immediate experience as a whole, naively, without analysis. According to the Gestalt psychologists, phenomenological observation is the preferred method of collecting psychological data.

PHYSIOLOGY. The study of the body, usually in terms of its parts (e.g., the nervous system) as opposed to study of the behavior of the animal as a whole.

PSEUDOCONDITIONING. Any conditioning obtained with a pairing that is shown to have been unnecessary to establish the response is pseudoconditioning (not genuine conditioning). The essential element in **classical conditioning** is the pairing or correlation between the unconditional and conditional stimuli. The essential element in **instrumental conditioning** is the pairing or correlation of response and reinforcer. If a certain response can be made to appear without that pairing, then any experiment using pairing to establish that response is suspect; the pairing may not have been necessary.

PSYCHOLOGY. Originally a branch of philosophy devoted to the study of the mind. More recently, a science whose subject is the behavior of animals. The observations of behavior (verbal behavior included) may or may not be used to infer mental processes.

PSYCHOPHYSICS. The study of sensation as a function of the physical properties of stimulation.

PUNISHMENT. A positive correlation between responding and aversive stimulation

REFLEX. Originally *reflex* referred to stimuli and responses related by specific nervous connections within the animal. Recently the concept of reflex has been broadened to include any relationship between a stimulus and a response. The stimulus may be any event in the environment, and the response may be any behavior of the animal.

REINFORCEMENT. In **classical conditioning**, the presentation of the unconditional stimulus. In **instrumental conditioning**, the presentation of a reward (positive reinforcement) or the removal of an aversive stimulus (**negative reinforcement**).

RESPONSE. Another word for a **behavior**. Usually a response is defined as a rather discrete form of behavior, such as a knee jerk, the pressing of a bar, or the pressing of a key. However, responses can also be broadly defined, such as "standing on one side of a chamber" or "not pressing a key."

SELF. A set of values persisting in time that accounts for the behavior of an individual animal.

SENSATION. An act of discrimination of color, sound, touch, smell, or taste in the context of habitual discriminations of the same object.

SOUL. The soul is said to be the spiritual and immortal part of man. Psychologists have tended to ignore the religious questions of the soul's immortality, its possible moral implications, and its role as the "essence of being." Stripped of religious implications, the concept of the soul approaches the concept of the **mind**. The two concepts have generally been treated similarly by psychologists.

STIMULUS. Any environmental event. Stimuli may be classified broadly (for instance, any picture of a horse) or narrowly (e.g., a tone of a particular frequency and amplitude). With respect to behavior, stimuli may be relatively neutral, having no discernible effect on the animal, or they may elicit violent behavior. Stimuli may be positively reinforcing or punishing, depending on whether they increase or decrease the strength of the behavior they follow. A neutral stimulus in one situation may be nonneutral in others.

STIMULUS CONTROL. Another word for the effects of **discrimination** and **generalization** in instrumental conditioning.

TEMPORAL CONTIGUITY. The state of events happening at the same time.

VOLUNTARY BEHAVIOR. Behavior, the original cause of which is said to lie within the mind. The class of behavior labeled *operant* is virtually congruent with the class labeled *voluntary*.

Index